Barriers to Sustainable Transport

Transport, Development and Sustainability

Series editor: David Banister, Professor of Transport Planning, University College London

edited by Piet Rietveld and Roger R. Stough

Barriers to Sustainable Transport
Institutions, regulation and sustainability

Routledge
Taylor & Francis Group

LONDON AND NEW YORK

First published 2005 by Spon Press

Published 2014 by Routledge
2 Park Square, Milton Park, Abingdon, Oxfordshire OX14 4RN
Simultaneously published in the USA and Canada
711 Third Avenue, New York, NY 10017

Routledge is an imprint of the Taylor & Francis Group, an informa business

Typeset in Sabon and Imago by PNR Design, Oxfordshire

British Library Cataloguing in Publication Data
A catalogue card of this book is available from the British Library

Library of Congress Cataloging-in-Publication Data
Barriers to sustainable transport : institutions, regulation and sustainability / edited by Piet Rietveld and Roger Stough.
    p. cm.–(Transport, development and sustainability)
    Includes bibliographical references and index.
    ISBN 978-0-415-32362-8 (hbk)
    ISBN 978-0-415-64604-8 (pbk)
        1. Transportation–Environmental aspects. 2. Transportation–Social aspects. 3. Transportation and state. 4. Sustainable development.   I. Rietveld, Piet. II. Stough, Roger. III. Series.

Contents

Part Three International Transport

Part Four Freight Transport

This book is the outcome from the STELLA-STAR initiative. STELLA (Sustainable Transport in Europe and Links and Liaisons with America) is a Thematic Network project of the European Commission's 5th Framework Programme for Research and Development. STAR is the North American sister thematic network (Sustainable Transportation Analysis and Research), which is supported by the National Science Foundation and Transport Canada. Initiated in January 2002, STELLA-STAR network centres around common issues in transatlantic transport research. It aims to generate value-added knowledge, research exchange, and the development of a common research approach from both sides of the Atlantic. This network will benefit the international research community, and be of interest to policy-making bodies and industrial organizations.

The STELLA-STAR network addresses five major focus areas which have been identified as critical fields of interest for a transatlantic thematic network in the transportation field. These are:

1 Globalization, e-economy and trade;
2 ICT, innovation and the transport system;
3 Society, behaviour and private/public transport;
4 Environment, safety, health, land use and congestion;
5 Institutions, regulations and markets in transportation.

Obviously, the transatlantic setting offers the STELLA-STAR initiative good opportunities for an analysis of the role of institutions in transport. Therefore, in its first meeting, which took place in Brussels in 2002, Focus Group 5 decided to focus on institutional barriers to sustainable transport. The present book grew out of this meeting.

There are several people that we want to thank for their assistance and contributions to this book. These include Hadewijch van Delft for her support in the organization of the Brussels meeting and the correspondence with contributors, Christine Pommerening and Daisy Botros for making editing changes and formatting of the texts. We also gratefully acknowledge the advice of Keith Keen, Ann Rudkin and David Banister on the substance of the book.

Piet Rietveld and Roger R. Stough
July 2004

Contributors

William P. Anderson is Professor of Geography and member of the Center for Transportation Studies at Boston University. He is an economic geographer with research interests in economic and environmental impacts of transport policy choices; urban transportation modelling; transportation markets; multiregional economic modelling; and international trade.

David Banister is Professor of Transport Planning at University College London. He has also been Research Fellow at the Warren Centre in the University of Sydney (2001–2002) and was Visiting VSB Professor at the Tinbergen Institute in Amsterdam (1994–1997). He has an international reputation in linking transport analysis to the wider issues of urban development and sustainability. He is editor of the international journal *Transport Reviews* and joint editor of the journal *Built Environment*, and the author and editor of 17 research books.

Kenneth J. Button is a Fellow of the Chartered Institute of Logistics and Transport and a Fellow of the Institution of Highways and Transportation. Dr. Button is Professor of Public Policy in the School of Public Policy, George Mason University. His research interest includes transport economics, transport planning, environmental analysis and industrial organization.

Edward Calthrop completed his PhD in transport economics at the University of Leuven, Belgium in 2001. This chapter was written during a period of post-doctoral study at Jesus College, Oxford. His research interests include the theory of taxation and investment in transport markets and the political economy of transport policy. He has recently taken up a position within the rail industry in Brussels.

Marcus Enoch is a lecturer in Transport Studies at Loughborough University in the UK. He has research interests in a number of areas concerned with how to manage car use. Specifically, he has studied how mobility management measures (for example, parking, road user charging, travel plans) have been implemented and how they might be transferred elsewhere; road-based public transport systems, and how island transport systems have evolved to accommodate the car.

Jonathan L. Gifford is a specialist on transportation policy. His expertise includes highway and urban transportation policy, aviation policy, and advanced technology in transportation systems. Dr. Gifford directs the Master's program in Transportation Policy, Operations and Logistics at the School of Public Policy. He also teaches information technology, public policy analysis, and risk analysis in the Master of Public Administration program at George Mason University.

Genevieve Giuliano is Professor of Planning and Development at the University of Southern California and Director of the METRANS Transportation Center. Her research interests include land use and transport relationships, transportation policy, and travel behaviour. She serves on several journal editorial boards, and is a National Associate of the National Academy of Sciences.

Tomasz Komornicki has been affiliated to the Institute of Geography and Spatial Organisation as a researcher since 1989. His main topics of interest are transport geography, transport policy, foreign trade and political geography. In 1996 he worked in the Institute fur Landerkunde, Leipzig, Germany ('The West- East Axis'). In 1998 he obtained his PhD in Economic Geography. From 2000 he is the secretary of the Main Board of the Polish Geographical Society.

T.R. Lakshmanan is Professor, Department of Geography, Director of the Center for Transportation Studies and Executive Director, Center for Energy and Environmental Studies at Boston University. From 1994 to 1998, Dr. Lakshmanan served in a subcabinet position in the Clinton Administration as Director of the Bureau of Transportation Statistics at the U.S. DOT. He holds a PhD (1965) from Ohio State and an MA (1953) from the University of Madras.

Dhiraj Narayan holds a dual Master of Real Estate Development and a Master of Planning with a focus in Economic Development and Transportation Planning from the University of Southern California. He also has a Bachelors degree in Architectural Engineering from Regional Engineering College, Calicut, India and a Post-Graduate diploma in Urban and Regional Planning. He currently works as project analyst for a consulting company in Los Angeles.

Aisling Reynolds-Feighan is senior lecturer at University College Dublin, Ireland and Director of the Transport Policy Research Institute which is now part of the University's Institute for the Study of Social Change. Her research focuses on air and road transport, and in particular network aspects of firm behaviour and industry structure. She is an active member of the Regional Science Association International and the Air Transport Research Society.

Lars Sjöstedt is an engineering physicist with a PhD in traffic planning, specialized in systems engineering and related scientific disciplines. He was Professor of Transportation and Logistics at Chalmers University of Technology 1980–2000 and is now Professor of European Transportation and International Logistics Management at the Technical University Hamburg-Harburg.

Roger Stough is the Associate Dean of Research, Development and Outreach in the School of Public Policy. He holds the Northern Virginia Endowed Chair in Public Policy. Dr. Stough's primary areas of research expertise include: regional economic development policy, analysis and modelling; technology-led regional economic development and competitiveness; the relationship between transportation and economic development; leadership and governance in regional economic development; institutional barriers to technology deployment, and associated issues in transportation policy and intelligent transportation systems.

Dimitrios A. Tsamboulas is Associate Professor, Department of Transportation Planning and Engineering, National Technical University of Athens. He holds degrees in Civil Engineering and Transport from NTUA, MIT and University of Massachusetts. He is the author of more than 100 papers, with more than 30 years of academic and professional experience.

Barry Ubbels (graduated in transport economics) works as a researcher at the Department of Spatial Economics of the Free University in Amsterdam. His main research interest is with pricing and financing of mobility and infrastructure. He conducted various studies in this field for several institutions (such as Dutch Ministries, local authorities and the European Union). Besides this applied scientific research work, he is currently working on his PhD-research towards the effects of pricing policies on mobility behaviour in a multi-disciplinary context.

Erik Verhoef is affiliated as a full professor in Spatial Economics at the Free University Amsterdam. His research focuses on efficiency and equity aspects of spatial externalities and their economic regulation, in particular in transport, urban and spatial systems. He has published various books and numerous articles on these topics.

Roger Vickerman is Jean Monnet Professor of European Economics, Director of the Centre for European, Regional and Transport Economics and of the Kent Centre for Europe (a Jean Monnet Centre of Excellence) at the University of Kent, Canterbury, UK, and Visiting Professor in the Department of Economics at the Central European University, Budapest. He holds degrees in Economics from the Universities of Cambridge and Sussex and an honorary doctorate from the Philipps-Universität Marburg. His main research interest is in the relationship between transport, regional development and integration in the European Union on which he has published widely. He has been an adviser to the European Commission, the Department for Transport and the Home Office (UK) and many other public bodies.

ACCA	Association of Chartered Certified Accountants
ACI	Airports Council International
ALS	Area Licensing Scheme
ATC/ATM	air traffic control
ATM	air traffic management
CEFTA	Central European Free Trade Area
CIS	civil infrastructure systems
CPI	consumer price index
CTRL	Channel Tunnel Rail Link
ECJ	European Court of Justice
ECMT	European Conference of Ministers of Transport
EDI	electronic data interchange
ERP	Electronic Road Pricing
EU	European Union
FTA	free trade area
GATT	General Agreement on Tariffs and Trade
GDP	gross domestic product
HGV	heavy goods vehicle
HOT	High Occupancy Toll
HOV	High Occupancy Vehicle
IATA	International Air Transport Association
ICAO	International Civil Aviation Organization
ICC	Interstate Commerce Commission
ICS	information and communications system
ICT	information and communications technologies
ITS	intelligent transportation system
JIT	just-in-time
LCA	life cycle analysis
LTA	Local Transport Authority
NAFTA	North American Free Trade Agreement
NPTS	Nationwide Personal Travel Survey
NTS	National Transport Survey
OECD	Organization for Economic Co-operation and Development
PFI	Private Finance Initiative

PPP	Public Private Partnership
PSC	Public Sector Comparator
PTT	post, telephone and telegraph
RFF	Reseau Ferre de France
SCM	supply chain management
SNCF	Société Nationale des Chemins de Fer
SOV	single occupancy vehicle
SRA	Strategic Rail Authority
TEN	Trans-European Networks
TfL	Transport for London
TTF	transport and trade facilitation
UNCTAD	United Nations Conference on Trade and Development
WTO	World Trade Organization

Chapter 1

Institutional dimensions of sustainable transport

Roger R. Stough and Piet Rietveld

There can be little doubt that the primary barriers to sustainable transport are institutional. Certainly, there are technical and operational barriers to the creation of infrastructure and the vehicles that use it, but most of these are well understood over short and intermediate time horizons and involve fairly routine actions for implementation once institutional impediments are overcome. For example, in the United States, recent experience shows that transport projects costing more than $1 billion require at least 20 years of negotiation, proposal and counter-proposal discussions, to remove institutional impediments and thereby implement the project.

While the argument for the primacy of institutions is made in earlier work by Rietveld and Stough (2002) and Stough and Rietveld (1997), the importance of institutions can be easily appreciated when it is recognized that transport modes and supporting technology exist that, if used or adopted more broadly, could move countries and the world towards greater environmental and economic sustainability not to mention better commercial performance. For example, some modes are more fuel efficient in moving people and freight than others and more environmentally friendly, for example rail versus truck or public transport versus the private car. Further, commercially available, off the shelf as well as experimental technologies exist that could, if adopted, make an enormous impact almost immediately. It is getting beyond the decision to adopt, deploy, or use that is the primary bottleneck. And this journey depends on values, culture, interest group goals, laws and statutes, regulations, and entrenched and existing practices.

For example, the adoption of an ordinance in Delhi, India a few years ago required all public buses and taxis to use LPGs – Liquefied Petroleum Gases (hardly a new technology). This had an immediate impact on environmental quality that was not only measurable but witnessed throughout the city because of the improved visibility. Yet the decision to make LPGs compulsory involved a time-consuming debate that dragged on for years and the resolve to withstand some two weeks of intensive demonstrations against the measure (by taxi and motorized rickshaw operators and owners) after its enabling legislation was passed. Today, by all accounts, everyone is pleased with and proud of the outcome. This example is interesting and apropos here in that it demonstrates how important institutional variables are in making decisions that move a transport system towards greater sustainability, as it is institutional barriers to sustainable transport that are the concern here.

In this book we focus on how to move transport and transport systems towards sustainability. We make the assumption that actions that increase efficiency in transport and energy use and also improve environmental quality, at least relative to current conditions, are contributing to sustainability. Thus, the aim of sustainable transport is viewed as evolving transport systems towards states that are more efficient, use less energy, have better environmental quality, and are compatible with the general concept of sustainability.

This introduction describes aspects of the nature of institutions, defines them, and introduces a typology that illustrates various institutional dimensions and their impact, potential and real, on transport systems. In this regard it is a first ever attempt to bring some degree of formality to the understanding of the role of institutions and institutional analysis in transport. To further this aspect of the book institutional issues are illustrated with examples from the transport and sustainability contexts to demonstrate the scope and breadth of these issues and the thorny problems that they pose. From a research and policy perspective these and related problems in turn pose unique data and methodology issues that are therefore explored below.

This book evolved from a workshop sponsored by the STELLA-STAR[1] programme that has been examining differences in transport and institutions on both sides of the Atlantic. Consequently many of the chapters examine institutional issues from a comparative European and North American perspective which is also a unique contribution of the book. Further, it is surprising how thin the comparative transport literature is in general and in particular with respect to institutional differences and similarities between these two highly developed parts of the world. As a prelude to this aspect of the book, a subsequent part of the Introduction presents a brief comparative analysis of transport and sustainability differences between these regions. The penultimate part of the Introduction describes each chapter, placing them in the context of the institutional dimensions of sustainable transport analysis, while the concluding part ties the several themes of the book together in a futures oriented assessment.

Institutions and institutional issues in sustainable transport

Institutions are the rules and rule structures that guide both public and private action (North, 1990); they can be both formal and informal. From North's perspective, they are the rules of the 'game'. As such, institutions describe how society operates and is maintained. Organizations on the other hand are the agents that act and thus 'play the game'.

The new institutional economists provide a framework for analysing institutions and the ways in which they may either positively or negatively impact decisions and behaviour. Williamson (1994) views institutions as being of four types: informal, formal, governance, and resource allocation/ employment related. Examples of *informal institutions* are deeply embedded values, norms, practices, customs, and traditions. These are powerful conditioners of behaviour but for the most part change very slowly. However, when an informal institution does change, there may be rapid and profound behaviour changes, for example, the terrorist attacks of 11 September 2001 have significantly impacted privacy and accessibility norms in the US and other parts of the world, and these in turn are impacting the cost and ease of passenger and freight transport. This is a case where an extreme event impacted informal institutions almost immediately, and with significant and measurable impacts on the transport system and its operation.

Formal institutions are Williamson's second type of institution. These are codified statutes, constitutional provisions, laws, regulations, and high level administrative orders. They focus on such things as property rights, judicial, and administrative orders. Formal institutions may change more quickly than informal ones, but tend to be stable over fairly long periods (decades) unless there are radical changes in their environment. For example, civil and water rights legislation in the US and in other countries has involved decades of debate and multiple trial and error efforts at legislation that have at best produced modest incremental change. Efforts to alter land-use regulations to address the so-called inefficiencies of sprawl have been underway for many years in the US but again with modest outcome. In short, formal institutions tend to be quite resilient and resistant to change.

Governance institutions define the third type of institution. Here institutional change occurs with greater frequency, often measured in years rather than decades. Governance institutions are rules (minor laws, administrative orders, regulations, and policy directives) that function to maintain or change how government and related organizations, such as planning and zoning boards, conduct business and direct transactions with other actors and agents.

Finally, the *diverse actions and behaviour patterns of multiple actors in the decision environment*, ranging from government agencies to firms and to non-profit associations (for example, neighbourhood organizations) form the fourth type of institution. Institutions at this level are about allocating resources to operations designed to impact individual and organizational outcomes. These institutions are changing almost continuously because they have widely distributed consequences. However, the consequences at the societal level are small and often relatively insignificant in terms of long-run outcomes. They involve decisions and actions about production, delivery, resource acquisition and use, and process, and occur in a context measured in days, weeks, and months. Making decisions about a zoning variance request or a fare level change for a transit system are examples of the fourth level of institution.

Williamson's typology provides a framework for examining policy arenas as well as relationships between different arenas and, thus, a way to identify and understand the forces that are guiding action and behaviour in specific transport contexts. It also provides a way to identify and even define efficiency, effectiveness and equity problems, and policy intervention strategies. As such it provides a framework for sorting out the impact of various institutional variables, providing policy insight and offering a framework for helping define what the institutional approach is. Below we offer descriptions of a number of institutional issues in sustainable transport, and related data and methodological issues that are often different from those found in more traditional transportation analyses.

Thus far we have discussed institutions in a general way. Here we bring them into the form of specific values, beliefs, cultural parameters and regulations in keeping with Williamson's institutional typology. These rules and rule structures guide the way countries, regions and other jurisdictions implement, avoid implementing or thinking about concepts and actions related to liberalization, infrastructure financing, privatization, deregulation, the role of markets, the role of the state, technology standards and technological change, intergovernmental relations, and globalization. The institutions that define how these processes and roles are played influence greatly how a country or region 'does business' and thus, in turn, the nature of transport systems and how they are used and operated. In a sense, at any given time, institutions may be viewed as defining a crude equilibrium on how a country or region operates as well as where 'cracks' in the equilibrium are occurring.

There are several aspects, components and processes of (and related to) transport systems that are difficult to deal with and therefore resist change because of institutional issues. As such they contribute to the maintenance of less than optimal transport systems. The examples listed below provide the reader with a sample of these and the varied contexts within which they occur. They are derived from the multiple interviews the authors have had with their academic and public policy colleagues at the various STELLA-STAR sponsored research workshops. We have classified these examples according to the four types of institutions mentioned above, but also categorised them by the time dimension.

Long term (type 1 and 2 institutions)

- harmonizing economic development and environmental protection goals;

- institutional friction hindering cross border flows;
- territorialism and intergovernmental relations;
- barriers to adopting new technology;
- power conflicts among stakeholders;
- barriers to efficient pricing;
- achieving cooperation among actors to support intermodalism;
- decoupling the prestige of owning versus rational use of the private car;
- willingness to pay on part of public and users;
- consumer preferences for unsustainable lifestyles.

Short to medium term (type 3 and 4 institutions)

- achieving accountability among public transport operators;
- coping with ambiguous regulations;
- managing intergovernmental relations;
- managing freight and passenger transportation interaction;
- managing interest groups;
- adopting improvements based on research findings;
- goal definitions of organizations;
- land-use variances and managing land-use and zoning codes.

While these are problems within a country or region they are amplified when more than one country or region is part of the transportation issue because there often is considerable institutional dissonance when countries with their different values, regulations, standards, etc. are involved. This is easily understood when one considers the differences between North America and Europe on some transport related issues, and even between the United States and Canada! Some examples of the differences between North America and Europe are:

General institutional differences

- more national borders in Europe;
- lack of uniform 'rules' or institutions in Europe despite EU integration;
- decentralized decision-making is greater in the US;
- Europe is still figuring out integration – many problems derive from this;
- different histories of institutional development, e.g., public-private organizations;

- role of government is perceived differently, American exceptionalism (Lipset, 1996) versus stronger welfare state preferences in Europe;
- greater ability of government to implement in Europe;
- privatization approaches are different.

Differences in transport related institutions

- the US is more committed to road use and road access goals;
- Europe is more prepared to use transport pricing concepts;
- taxation of fuel is much higher in Europe;
- public transport availability is higher in Europe.

Differences in land use

- land-use planning has been devolved to minor units of government in the US;
- Europe is more densely populated;
- different urban location patterns, for example, sprawl dominates in the US;
- land-use regulation is stronger in Europe;
- differences in consumer preferences with respect to transport;
- levels of car ownership and related lifestyles;
- lower public transport demand in North America;
- barriers to sustainable transport greater in the US.

In summary, significant differences exist in how North Americans and Europeans use, create and operate the surface transport system. These differences are partly the result of different geographies and physical conditions but most are due to different histories and thus to different institutions that have evolved over time. For example, Europe has a medieval history while North America, a colonial frontier society, was heavily influenced by its revolutionary history. While a high impact revolution is clearly not solely a phenomena of the US, the American case differs from the revolutions in France, Germany and Spain in terms of impact on institutions and culture because the US revolution was coincident with the formation of the American state and its culture.

Methodological and data issues in institutional analysis

The role of institutions in transport analysis may be viewed in terms of independent variables that help to explain some dependent variables such as traffic congestion, infrastructure investment, operational procedures, policy intervention or lack of intervention, for example, pricing and privatization. Institutions also may serve as control variables from a planning systems and implementation research perspective. However, the institutional variable is very rich because of its complexity and its multiple forms as described above in the discussion on the institutional typology. Consequently, institutional variables tend to be seen as 'softer' and more difficult to quantify compared to other variables typically used in transportation analysis. For example, regulations are a major form of institution but to 'measure' or even inventory regulations the investigator must not only work through huge databases that define and describe them, but also interpret how they have been implemented and whether there is implementation consistency.

Further, in cross-national studies, context comparability or differences need to be established and validated. For these reasons the methodologies used in institutional analysis are broader than those typically found in transportation studies where regression and operations research models often dominate. For example, in-depth case studies and loosely structured policy-maker interviews, scenario analysis, qualitative modelling, focus group interviews, historical interpretive analysis are important methods where institutions are involved. Thus it should be no surprise that when institutions are an object of study in transportation research the focus is more interdisciplinary and, in addition to engineering and economics, includes fields such as political economy, sociology, psychology, social psychology, anthropology, and history.

Despite the complexity of the institutional variable and the need to focus on more interpretive and qualitative methods, the nature of institutions does not negate using more formal and quantitative analyses. Questions about institutional differences between countries often lead to hypotheses about differences in transportation flows and costs which can, of course, be examined using a variety of standard transportation models. Thus, despite the softer nature of institutions, it may be possible to structure institutional hypotheses using binary or categorical measures so that standard engineering, economic modelling, and analysis methods can be used and, therefore, the relative importance of institutions estimated. There are examples of both types of investigation illustrated in the chapters in this book. Thus, because it is possible to use both quantitative and qualitative methods, yet emphasize the latter more fully, it is possible to derive research questions that have been slow to surface in the past. The following list provides a few examples of the type of research questions that may be fruitfully approached from the perspective of institutional effects. These examples are:

• How can institutions be incorporated explicitly into transport models so that their explanatory contribution can be better tested?

- How can regulatory regimes be tested to determine which produces better network economies?
- What is the impact of multi-jurisdictional control of transport networks on network efficiency?
- How do public and private sector polices interact and to what level of social or economic benefit?
- What benefits are achieved through policies for re-allocating authority to different levels of government?
- What is the user's perspective on policy and procedural interventions?
- What is the role of lobbying in transport systems operations, modal split, efficiency and distribution of access to transportation?
- What is the impact of separating the building of infrastructure from its operation?
- How does an institution operate and how does its operation impact transport?

Research into some of these questions would probably require involving an almost totally interpretive or qualitative approach in order to obtain useful answers. Yet others hint at the possibility of adding an institutional variable into more traditional transport models to conduct policy modelling and evaluation. In summary, institutions are a different type of variable from most that have been traditionally used in transport analyses and thus trying to incorporate them into transport research poses methodological issues and problems.

The methodological issues and questions reviewed and discussed above immediately raise important and thorny data questions. For example, institutional databases are often maintained by the organizations that enforce or make the rules. Thus, there is potential for bias, perhaps unintentional, in such data. Obtaining data for in-depth case studies will often involve obtaining access to and interviewing senior policy-makers. Frequently, such interviews are difficult to set up in a way that produces answers with insight. Further, it is often difficult to identify what informal institutions are and thus comparative analysis is necessary to obtain a benchmark definition and understanding with depth and perspective. But cross-country data are notoriously inconsistent, incompatible, and unreliable. One way to deal partially with this would be to use privately purchased data sets but often these have confidentiality and propriety constraints. So these and other data issues are problems in the institutional approach to research, especially in transportation research.

Organization of the book

Following this Introduction, the book is divided into four parts. Part One focuses on transport policy and institutions. In Part Two some local and regional issues in sustainable transport are considered. This is followed in Part Three with an examination of international transport, while Part Four provides an analysis of freight transport issues and problems arising out of institutional issues and impediments.

Part One – Transport policy

In this part the relationship between institutions and public policy is examined. The chapters range from new types of initiatives in transport infrastructure provision to transport pricing and to both high- and low-level institutional issues. For example, Kenneth Button's chapter deals with informal, often hidden institutions, while Jonathan Gifford examines specific rule issues that trail down to the lowest level of the Williamson typology. Below we summarize and interpret the significant contributions made by the chapters in this part to the role of institutions in transportation.

In Chapter 2, Roger Vickerman examines some of the lessons learned in public and private sector provision of transport infrastructure. One of the themes that permeates this analysis is an examination of the conclusion that the private sector can provide infrastructure more efficiently and at less cost than the public sector. Vickerman argues that this conclusion has not been fully vindicated. Also, the question of the contribution that infrastructure makes to the overall economy is considered. More generally, Vickerman discusses the economics of infrastructure provision with a focus on opportunity cost, risk and transaction costs, and some of the implications of public and private sector funding of infrastructure for achieving efficiency and equity goals and thus sustainability. The institutional part of the analysis deals with the problem of providing effective transport networks and more specifically the problem of vertical integration of infrastructure and the services provided.

Transportation like many fields of inquiry has avoided certain topics altogether and interpreted others rather narrowly. Ken Button addresses this issue in his provocative chapter entitled 'Myths and taboos in transportation'. Button argues that much of the debate and policy discussion regarding transport takes place 'within a world full of superstition and voodoo' that is underpinned by assumptions that are not questioned and often not recognized. Some of these are: transportation is important; transportation is different from other goods and services; it is possible and appropriate to build a region's or nation's way out of transport problems, for example, traffic congestion; the market is the source of all evil; subsidized transportation helps the poor; telecommunications offer salvation to the congestion problem. Such assumptions or myths function as if they are institutions in that they often are the silent rules behind the friction in the process that leads to infrastructure and operations decisions.

In Chapter 4, David Banister discusses the impediments to the implementation of sustainable transportation measures. While this analysis examines a variety of physical and resource barriers, the dominant ones are institutional in nature. In the context of the analysis, legal, regulatory and higher level values and cultural dimensions are explored to provide a more focused understanding of how institutions and related impediments add friction to decisions that support sustainable transport. A large part of the chapter is devoted to measures or actions that may be employed to overcome these barriers.

Pricing or charging for the use of roads has long been supported by economic arguments. Yet adoption of pricing policies for the use of public roads has been difficult to achieve, despite the strong economic arguments that support it. In Chapter 5, Barry Ubbels and Erik Verhoef examine the barriers to transport pricing policies. Their analysis, including considerable case study material from the European context, finds institutional, political, and legal barriers to be at the centre of the friction holding back wider adoption of pricing policies. This again helps to confirm the primacy of institutional factors in transportation and related decision-making.

Marcus Enoch, in Chapter 6, argues that the nature of transportation and sustainability problems today is so great that radical transport schemes are required. Suggested strategies include measures such as compensating the losers, bribing motorists not to drive, marketing the benefits, and increasing choice. His analysis shows the importance of institutional issues in constraining the way and pace in which measures such as these can be more fully adopted. Enoch analyses the specific impediments to implementation of the proposed strategies and proposes additional strategies that could improve implementation efforts.

In the concluding chapter of Part One, Jonathan Gifford proposes a research agenda for institutional and market analysis in the provision of transport infrastructure. He identifies critical challenges for transport officials and decision-makers that form the basis of a twenty element research agenda. Chief among these elements are security and safety, system level planning, governance, innovation and technology transfer and regulatory lag. Strategically these and the other elements are consistent with the growing emphasis on operations versus physical infrastructure solutions to travel demand pressures that have emerged throughout most developed countries

Part Two – Local and regional aspects of sustainable transport

Part Two comprises two chapters. The first, Chapter 8 by Genevieve Giuliano and Dhiraj Narayan, is a comparison of various aspects of work versus non-work travel in the United States and Great Britain. The chapter examines the relationship between land-use patterns and individual mobility. Research shows that car ownership and use continues to increase in European countries despite considerably more restrictive land-use policies, more available public transport, and higher auto operating costs than in the US. Using a carefully constructed cross-national data set, the authors examine hypotheses about car use and ownership with respect to economic circumstances, land-use, and other policies. Through careful and rigorous analysis institutional issues are found to be important in explaining the general trends that transcend both countries as well as differences found between Great Britain and the US.

In Chapter 9, Edward Calthrop models the on-street parking market and also examines institutional issues that contribute to making this an imperfect market. The focus is on pricing policies for on-street parking and modelling institutional barriers that impact efficient utilization of such parking space. A model is developed for defining efficient on-street parking. This model accommodates consideration of such factors as time required to search for a space and the effect of under-priced road congestion. The model provides a formal way to examine the impact of institutional variables on operational efficiency of the on-street parking market. This is an initial model that builds on a modest literature base. Nonetheless, it is promising and offers insight into how institutional issues might be more formally examined not only in this case but also for the efficient operation of other transport-related markets.

Part Three – International transport

In this part of the book, three international topics are examined including air transport across the Atlantic, international trade, and border regimes. In Chapter 10, Aisling Reynolds-Feighan examines organizational and institutional issues in transatlantic aviation. The chapter begins by laying out the institutional and organizational structure that supports and manages aviation between North America and Europe. This is used to identify the central linkages and focuses of influence in the two different contexts, and thus lays the foundation for comparative analysis. The chapter examines influences that have contributed to and impacted recent developments in relations in the transatlantic aviation context, including such issues as market dynamics, market entry, and regulatory and legislative initiatives. Reynolds-Feighan also examines the impacts of the September 11 terrorist attacks on transatlantic aviation patterns and the ways in which institutions are facilitating or impeding progress in the adoption and implementation of joint safety and security measures. The chapter concludes with the identification of a set of research issues.

T.R. Lakshmanan and William Anderson examine the evolution of transport institutions and their role in international trade in Chapter 11. They note that the growth and impact of international trade since the end of World War II has been remarkable and, as a consequence, considerable institutional dynamics have occurred to accommodate this growth. Technology has also evolved significantly, for example, developments in aviation, the Interstate Highway System in North America and a similar infrastructure now nearly fully evolved in Europe, while modern logistics development has been enhanced by information technology and the knowledge revolution. These enabling and space-shrinking developments are transforming the space-time relations in all parts of the world. The authors find the institutional dynamics that have accompanied these changes to be of equal importance to the changes themselves. These dynamics have to do with changes in the economic rules impacting and governing transport, cross-border flows of people and freight, financial coordination mechanisms, and business logistics practices. Consequently these institutions have seen significant evolution and yet still are major impediments to achieving even more efficient flows and thus to continued higher transactions in the international movement of goods and people.

In Chapter 12, Tomasz Komornicki examines the impact of institutions governing border regimes in Central and Eastern Europe. The purpose of this work is to examine the influence exerted by border institutions on the development of transport in the context of the new socio-economic conditions in the Central and Eastern European context. These institutions include those that were designed to provide barriers to military aggression, support trade or the economic function, and to regulate social issues in general and migration in particular. Given the move of the countries in this part of the world towards more open and market-oriented regimes, related dynamics of borders and associated institutional issues make it an exciting research context, particularly after the expansion of the EU15 to the EU25 in May 2004.

Part Four – Freight transport

In Part Four two chapters address issues concerning institutions and freight transport. Lars Sjöstedt in Chapter 13 develops and applies a conceptual framework in an effort to analyse the roles of industry representatives and policy-makers in the context of sustainable goods transportation. The chapter begins with the observation that transportation and logistics are not the same and that they have different origins and, as a consequence, different institutions. These differences go to the heart of training and the nature of the professions and disciplines that define appropriate behaviours for freight transport actors and organizations. Sjöstedt develops a conceptual model and applies it in the context of several global logistics cases. Further, he examines the duality of transportation and logistics, and then charts a course showing how transport and logistics are integrating. In an interesting twist near the end of the chapter, he sets forth the concept of the emergence of a negotiated and collaboration-based economy as a framework for facilitating transport and logistics among other issues.

The final chapter, by Dimitrios Tsamboulas, is an examination of intermodalism in Europe with particular emphasis on markets and sustainability. He begins with an overview of freight transport in Europe and related but still emerging policies that are governing its evolution. The chapter is organized around the twin and interdependent topics of sustainability and intermodality. Policies to achieve intermodality are viewed as central to achieving sustainability. The chapter focuses most heavily on intermodality, what it means in practical terms, and the institutional changes needed better to achieve it.

Summary

This Introduction has described the topic of institutional issues in sustainable transport and their importance to policy, practice and managing a diverse array of transport related problems and issues. In support of this goal it first defined institutions and then offered a typology of institutions for placing issues and problems into a transport sustainability context. The four fold typology of informal, formal, governance and operational groupings was collapsed into a time dimension framework by sorting the institutional issues into long and short term issues. Thus, informal and formal institutional types form the framework for longer term issues and governance and operational categories for shorter ones.

To illustrate how institutions vary across world regions and countries a brief presentation was made of the short and long term institutional transport differences between North America and Europe and/or among their constituent countries. For example, although countries such as Canada and the US often seem to be quite similar there are significant and fundamental institutional differences between them, such as governance form and style (see Lipset, 1996) that consequently create relatively large barriers in finding collaborative transport solutions, especially cross border ones such as standards, immigration and trade documentation. The initial part of the Introduction that addresses these issues provides the reader with a frame of reference and tools for interpreting the larger significance of the various chapters of the book. The larger significance is that achieving sustainable transport always involves addressing significant and deep institutional barriers to change. But it is not clear whether institutions are more of a supporting vehicle or a barrier to solutions, even in the long run.

Following the perspective setting and typology part of the introduction a descriptive and interpretive summary description was supplied for each chapter. These are necessary to help guide the reader through the structure and importance of the contents and the role of the specific chapters with respect to the book theme. Despite the identification of the primary thrust of the chapters and the related institutional relevance there is still a need to better link the various elements of the introduction to the institutions and transport sustainability issue. Thus, in the next and concluding part of the Introduction several policy research themes are examined from the perspectives of institutional parameters and typologies, and sustainability and in a North American – European comparative context.

Some policy research agenda themes: comparisons across the Atlantic

Institutions and sustainability

In North America and Europe, institutional changes and regulatory reform have experienced some success during the past several decades. For example, institutional and regulatory reform have led to a large and measurable increase in efficiency and consumer welfare in aviation, whereas the railway sector experienced mixed effects, ranging from positive in the US to mostly negative in the EU. But it may be too early to draw final conclusions, because it appears that it may take many years before the fruits of regulatory reform fully emerge and are reaped. In efforts to eliminate trade restrictions at borders substantial welfare increases or benefits have been observed, although at the operational level there are still many impediments leading to inefficiencies in cross border transport.

A point of overall concern is the sustainability aspect of these institutional changes and regulatory reforms. Where it is possible to give several convincing examples of positive effects on efficiency, the environmental effects seem to be much less favorable, and often negative. The lesson is that institutions serve both as barriers to problem solutions and as vehicles for facilitating solutions, e.g., via helping keep transaction costs relatively low.

Institutional changes and regulatory reform had a strong focus on efficiency goals during the past several decades. Therefore, an important research question is how institutional change can be brought about that promotes sustainability. An example is the institutional change needed to make the Kyoto protocol effective. As a special point of attention we mention the problem of how to deal with conflicts between international transport efficiency and environmental goals in this context. Also the implementation of strategies for internalizing the full costs of transport in the aviation sector begs for attention.

Regulatory reform in specific sectors

An arena where regulatory reform has failed to produce fruitful results is in the European railway sector. The European share of rail in freight transport is much lower than in the US. Efforts to stimulate the emergence of efficient operators at the European level have had little effect thus far. One of the strategies to achieve greater efficiency was the separation of infrastructure ownership and operations. But this tended to have adverse effects on passenger transport, which has predominantly a national orientation. This leads to a question of whether or not complete separation of ownership and operations is necessary to achieve non-discriminatory access for freight. And more specifically, 'what can be learned from the North American experience of letting vertically integrated freight companies use each other's infrastructures'?

Deregulation of the aviation sector in the US and Europe have had clear and measurable positive effects on consumer welfare due to an increase in competition. At the same time substantial cooperative innovation took place in the form of the formation of a limited number of alliances. Further, deregulation of the transatlantic market may well lead to additional tendencies towards concentration. Of particular interest is the possibility that one of the current global strategic alliances might fail. This would imply that an alliances duopoly will evolve at the world level. In this case, deregulation may have substantial adverse effects on welfare due to an increase in monopoly power.

Institutional change and the role of borders

Borders and border transactions have changed considerably during the past decades due to the emergence of NAFTA, and the expansion and deepening of the EU. The recent entry of Eastern European countries in the EU has had huge impacts on waiting times for freight traffic at some borders with a purported reduction of total transport times up to 40%. However, there remain many more subtle institutional barriers to spatial interactions and their meaning and the consequences are not particularly well understood. These deserve serious attention from the border effects research community. Also, from a sustainability perspective it is interesting to observe that the reduction in border barrier effects seems to display some bias across the various transport modes. Cost reducing effects tend to be larger in aviation and road transport than in water and rail transport. Thus, transport modes that are generally considered to be more environmentally benign seem to benefit less from the reduction of border barriers than the modes that have strong negative environmental effects.

Subsidiarity: policy competition within the public sector

Subsidiarity is one of the cornerstones of the EU. Subsidiarity is a view that public sector tasks should be allocated to a lower level of government unless there are obvious reasons to arrange things at a higher level. From this perspective an economic analysis in the context of tax competition reveals that several problems can be identified that deserve more attention than they usually receive. For example, in the context of road tolls, there is the problem that tax burdens may be shifted to other parties with resulting adverse effects. In this context one may distinguish horizontal competition (between regions of the same level) and vertical tax competition (between a region and a larger spatial unit). Within horizontal tax competition two cases are possible: parallel and serial competition. Parallel horizontal tax competition in transport networks may lead to questions of how competition should be arranged to arrive at welfare improvements, although within this domain the problems seem limited. Serial horizontal tax competition leads to serious problems of the abuse of monopoly power. Also vertical tax competition in the form of local price setting, for example of parking charges versus regional or national toll price setting and fuel taxes, has not yet received the attention it deserves.

Barriers to the implementation of innovative transport policies

There are many examples of innovative transport policies that did not bear fruit due to various types of institutional barriers or where the success of such policies presenting themselves as beneficial is debatable. An important reason concerns the equity aspects of such policies, and this calls for a thorough analysis of the equity and efficiency of alternative funding mechanisms and compensation schemes. Also legal barriers against innovative policies deserve more systematic attention. Finally the appropriate arrangements of responsibilities within the public sector (central versus decentralized government) and between public and private sector are essential.

Private versus public roles in transport

Transport activities, and in particular the supply of infrastructure, usually lead to involvement of both the private and the public sectors. In many countries various arrangements of public and private roles have been tried, and it appears that the results are mixed and do not point at specific best arrangements or practices. Of particular relevance is the question how these arrangements can best be made at a network level, as opposed to the level of individual projects. Issues of risk shifting between the public and private sectors and the possibility of incorporating external cost pricing in these arrangements raise other relevant issues and questions. Also the theme of measurement of quality of infrastructure output is essential given its role in incentive setting.

Some final observations

The above research themes and questions have been presented to provide a broader perspective of some of the critical research questions that face the transport research community in general and more specifically those with a more institutional orientation. As the reader works through the various chapters not only are these themes visited again but others also emerge. This part of the Introduction is intended to provide a broader and deeper perspective on institutional issues both long- and short-term, sustainability in transport and the applicability of these for aiding analysis in a cross-Atlantic comparative framework.

Note

1   STELLA is supported by a grant from the European Science Foundation and STAR by a parallel grant from the US NSF. Transport Canada is supporting participation on the part of Canadian scholars and policy makers. The STELLA-STAR network is designed to support interaction among scholars and policy makers across the Atlantic leading to knowledge about similarities and differences between these regions and to create a cross Atlantic research agenda. There have been four STELLA-STAR workshops on Trans Atlantic transportation focused on institutional issues and impediments to achieving sustainable transport: (Athens (2004), Washington, DC (2003), Brussels (2003) and Amsterdam (2002). Each of the participating researchers and policy-makers have been surveyed and interviewed (formally and informally) in an effort to identify institutional issues, approaches to analysis, data and methodological problems, and differences between North America and Europe.

References

Lipset, S.M. (1996) *American Exceptionalism: A Double Edged Sword*. New York: W.W. Norton.

North, D.C. (1990) *Institutions, Institutional Change, and Economic Performance*. New York: Cambridge University Press.

Rietveld, P. and Stough, R.R. (2002) Institutions, regulations, and sustainable transport; a cross-national perspective. Paper presented at the STELLA kick-off meeting, Amsterdam.

Stough, R.R. and Rietveld, P. (1997) Institutional issues in transport systems. *Journal of Transportation Geography*, 5, pp. 207–214.

Williamson O.E. (1994) *Institutions and Economic Organization – The Governance Perspective*. Washington, DC: World Bank.

Chapter 2

Public and private initiatives in infrastructure provision[1]

Roger Vickerman

How to provide infrastructure remains a vexed question in the transport sector. Traditionally, provision has been the preserve of the public sector in most economies, but there has been increasing questioning of the rationale for this as the costs of both maintaining the existing infrastructure and making marginal additions to the infrastructure stock have escalated. Recent work on the contribution of infrastructure, and especially transport infrastructure, to the overall performance of the economy gives a mixed message. Similarly, the belief that the private sector can provide infrastructure more cheaply and efficiently than the public sector, has not been fully vindicated. The main focus is then to identify the conditions under which infrastructure does generate wider benefits than just to its direct users and whether this implicit boost to the productivity of private capital, provides a basis for shifting at least some of the responsibility for (and risk of) infrastructure provision to those who may benefit most?

Private infrastructure provision is not a new idea. Bridges have been privately owned for centuries,[2] the early turnpikes were privately provided and tolled; early railway development in many countries was purely private sector driven. However, government approval or licensing, regulation and eventually, in most European countries, state ownership became the norm. This state involvement was sometimes for ideological reasons, sometimes for military/security reasons, but more often for purely economic reasons as the private sector failed to meet rapidly growing or changing demands. The social benefit deriving from the infrastructure justified the state assuming responsibility for its maintenance and development.

Growing concern over state budgetary deficits, and an often ideologically driven concern over the inability of the public sector to manage complex infrastructure efficiently in an increasingly competitive climate, resulted in the reversal of this trend from the 1980s. Led by the deregulation movement in the US, enthusiastically picked up by the privatization movement in the UK, and fuelled by the availability of a highly liquid private capital market, there has been a fundamental change in the way infrastructure is viewed in the past two decades. But this has not been without its disappointments for the supporters of private initiatives or for governments wishing to see the off-loading of some of their financial responsibilities. In this chapter, we focus on the conditions under which transport infrastructure can be effectively provided by the private sector.

We first review key elements in the economics of infrastructure provision, concentrating on three elements, opportunity cost, risk, and transaction costs, before examining the implications and options for both public and private funding. From this we identify two key questions for further examination, the problem of providing effective networks, and the problem of the vertical integration of infrastructure and the services provided on that infrastructure. The chapter concludes with a short summary of key issues for future research.

The infrastructure provision problem

The problems in the provision of infrastructure identified above derive from the basic economics of infrastructure. The underlying conflict is that infrastructure has all the characteristics of a public good at levels of demand below capacity, but the lack of competition in infrastructure supply leads to the problem of a natural monopoly. The natural monopoly argument has been the underlying rationale for public involvement in infrastructure provision since the nineteenth century. The public good argument depends on the recognition that infrastructure is expensive to provide, and that the lead-time in construction requires large advance funding. Once provided, however, the short-run marginal cost of usage is zero (or close to zero) leading to the basic pricing difficulty. This problem has been recognized in the debate on 'fair and efficient pricing' for infrastructure conducted by the High Level Group for the European Commission.[3]

We face two linked, but separable, questions. Who should provide and manage infrastructure and how should that provision be financed? As we shall see, all four possible combinations of provision and finance shown in Table 2.1 are feasible. The conditions under which each combination is to be preferred will depend on opportunity cost, risk, and transactions costs.

Fixed infrastructure typically has a zero opportunity cost. Infrastructure providers, unlike transport service providers, cannot cover the risks of their investment by the residual value of the infrastructure. This is central to the notion that infrastructure should be priced at its short-run marginal cost, since there is no transfer price of the capital asset to be taken into account. But at levels of usage below capacity, the short run marginal cost is effectively zero and hence the infrastructure can make no contribution to its capital costs. However, the lumpiness and long gestation period of infrastructure prevents perfect marginal adjustments of capacity to demand. It is this characteristic which is seen as a valid argument for public funding as well as public

Table 2.1 Infrastructure provision and finance, possible combinations

	Public finance	Private finance
Public management	Traditional state ownership e.g. roads, national rail, local public transport	Public-private partnership deals where control remains with public sector: franchised operations with regulation
Private management	Public-private partnership deals where management control passes to private sector but public sector retains financial interest	Pure private provision

provision, since only the public sector will be able to take future needs into account adequately and ensure the correct level of provision at the right time, and this may imply cross-subsidy to cover the shortfall in revenues against full costs in an infrastructure priced at short-run marginal costs. At capacity, the situation reverses, however, and prices based on short-run marginal cost rise rapidly, making the infrastructure cash rich, implying the need for expansion. Such an expansion, however, even if it can be financed over its life, will pose problems in its early years when it will require subsidy.

Those financing infrastructure face three main types of risk that can affect provision: construction risk; revenue and maintenance risk; and planning and political risk. Construction risks arise because of the individuality of large infrastructure projects and their long gestation periods, both of which make costs difficult to estimate accurately. Large infrastructure projects frequently require detailed design to be carried out whilst construction is in progress, for example to overcome specific construction problems encountered.[4] Sometimes inadequate specification of the project compounds the expected construction cost risk. This compounds the problem of inefficiency in the actual management of the construction contract, which can make it easy for contractors to inflate costs and not appear to be responsible for these increases.[5] Flyvbjerg et al. (2002) report that infrastructure costs are underestimated in 90 per cent of transport projects and that actual costs are on average 28 per cent higher than estimated.[6] Despite these tendencies for costs to increase, there is a risk to the commissioning organization that contractors may systematically underestimate the costs involved. Lower costs increase rates of return and make it more likely that projects will be undertaken; although aware of this, the commissioning organization may also wish to see the costs underestimated in order to get a project accepted. Once large infrastructure projects are started, it becomes very difficult to abandon them completely.

Once completed, infrastructure providers also face operational risks. Where usage is below that expected there may be revenue risks.[7] These are the other side of the coin from construction cost risks, but may be associated with particular problems since the tendency systematically to underestimate costs is often seen to go together with the tendency to overestimate usage. The most difficult infrastructures, those with the highest costs, are likely to be those with the greatest risks from the combination of these two factors since they are the ones where previous experience is unlikely to be useful.[8] Where traffic forecasts are wrong in the other direction there can also be a problem since this may impose much higher maintenance costs on an infrastructure, both because of the need to repair structures designed for lower traffic levels and because of the loss of revenue during the repair periods, which will arise sooner and more frequently. This would be compounded by poor construction, which could arise if contractors were not responsible for its consequences.[9]

Finally, and most difficult to assess, are the policy and planning risks which any infrastructure provider has to take into account. Once again, the long gestation periods and the longevity of payback periods for major infrastructures make them vulnerable to changes of policy. Enthusiasm for private finance has been tempered where there is a risk that a change of government may lead to re-nationalization. Even more worrying can be the lack of consistency displayed by a government with respect to its own decisions.[10] When this becomes an open conflict between two levels of government as in the case of the mechanism for bringing private funding into London Underground it is difficult for the private sector to receive clear signals.[11]

Similar difficulties arise with the EU's Trans-European Networks programme (TEN). Direct EU funding for these schemes is only a small fraction of their total value; they depend for 90–95% of finance on member states and private sector finance. Although the European Investment Bank has played a major role in the development of TENs and other major infrastructures, often taking a proactive role, the EU has not been able to force the pace of development, such that only 20% of the planned network had been completed by 2001. Only two of the initial fourteen Essen list priority projects were in operation by 2003, and only a further three are expected to be in full operation by 2007.[12] Where international connections are concerned, different levels of commitment by member states can lead to continuing problems with incomplete networks.

Even without changes of policy which impact directly on the way infrastructure is operated, changes of policy which affect the competitive position of the mode to which the infrastructure relates can cause problems. Again, it is often uncertainty over future directions of government policy, which cause difficulties. The confusion that arose over the position of Railtrack in the UK caused serious problems for the rail operators and their commitment to co-finance infrastructure improvements. This was compounded in 2003 by a critical report by the Rail Regulator which suggested that Railtrack's successor, Network Rail could make substantial savings in its investment programme by deferring or delaying some aspects and renegotiating contracts.[13] Continual ambiguity over the attitude of governments towards some form of universal road pricing poses problems for potential investors in both road and competing modes.

Infrastructure is typically not consumed by the final user for itself, but rather for the service provided on the infrastructure. Thus, we cannot consider the economics of infrastructure provision in a vacuum without reference to the way it relates to the provision of service on that infrastructure. Transactions costs relate to the costs of trading intermediate services, which go to make up a final service. The issue that arises is whether these will be lower if the entire process is carried out within a single organization (vertical integration) or by separating out each element of the process (vertical separation).

The vertical separation inherent in the private finance of infrastructure implies that transaction costs become more transparent because the services are openly traded and therefore open to competitive pressure, which would be expected to lead to greater efficiency. However, vertical separation also implies that the services have to be provided under contract. Contracts will only be complete and efficient if the information required by both parties to the contract is symmetric. In most cases, the relevant information is asymmetric because one party will be in possession of facts, which are not available to the other party. This leads to each party to the contract needing to protect itself, by insurance and/or the threat of legal action, against the risk of default by another party. This is likely to raise effective transaction costs so that the potential efficiency gains from separation may be lost.

Hart *et al.* (1997) have shown that where contracts are incomplete private sector providers will have stronger incentives to engage in both cost reduction and improvements in service quality than public sector providers, but that there is a strong bias towards concentrating on cost reduction because the effect of this on non-contractible quality is ignored. Thus in order to obtain the desired increase in efficiency it is essential either to have effective competition in service delivery or clear contractual commitments over service levels.

Such a situation clearly characterizes the vertical separation imposed on the UK passenger rail system. The complexity of this is illustrated in Figure 2.1,[14] which relates to the situation just before the collapse of Railtrack. Each of the links between organizations in Figure 2.1 implies a contract in which information is less complete than would have been the case if the entire rail system were provided by a single organization. The need to provide compensation for failures in delivery, plus the problems of ensuring safety, contributed to the ultimate collapse of Railtrack, the privatized infrastructure provider. The situation has, if anything, become more complicated with the creation of Network Rail since it became clear in the latter days of Railtrack that a system in which all the payments were generated by track access charges, which depend ultimately on fares or subsidies to the train operators

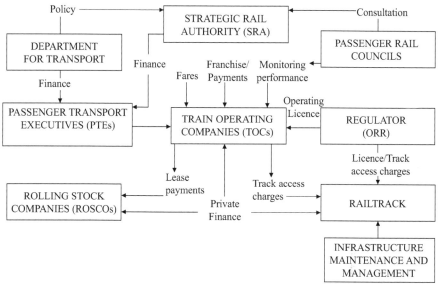

Figure 2.1 Organizational Structure of British Railways, 2001

via the Strategic Rail Authority (SRA), could not provide sufficient revenue to maintain the system. Hence, direct payments from government to the infrastructure operator became necessary.

We have emphasized here the problems associated with the provision of infrastructure, especially where this involves the private sector. Before we draw any conclusions about the overall economic implications of these problems, we need to retain some perspective over the relationship between infrastructure costs and total transport costs. Infrastructure is a problem because it is costly to provide, but the unit costs of that infrastructure per passenger or ton-km are relatively small, both with respect to total transport costs,[15] and even more so with respect to total logistics costs. One of the problems here is that the end users of infrastructure are taking a whole series of independent decisions about their logistics and transport needs for which demand for infrastructure is then a derived demand which it is expected will be available at the place and time needed.

The possible benefits of infrastructure go beyond the immediate user, however. A basic rationale for public involvement is that there are wider economic benefits from transport infrastructure that affect both the level and the spatial distribution of economic activity. The debate on the impact of infrastructure on economic growth and development, and how to capture this in project appraisal, is beyond the scope of this chapter.[16] However, the question of the balance between the competitiveness and the cohesion impacts of infrastructure remains crucial in the debate over funding since, if the primary economic impact of public infrastructure is on the productivity of private capital, then it is reasonable to expect that part of any surplus generated should be available to fund the infrastructure. Where that surplus would lead to infrastructure being built in the wrong place to secure the regional development/cohesion benefits desired, the public sector may need to intervene on redistributive grounds.

Perhaps the most difficult issue with respect to the balance between the market and the planning approaches to infrastructure development is the question of network planning. One of the requirements of infrastructure to be financed by the private sector is that it typically has to be broken into manageable sections in order to be able to define the associated risks. But transport infrastructure only works as a network, thus investors have to be assured that each relevant part of the network will be constructed and means have to be found of ensuring that appropriate external spill-overs can be identified and compensated.[17] This problem is compounded by the recognition of the need to provide interoperability, now enshrined in successive EU transport policy documents. This limits the scope of individual infrastructure providers to minimize costs by providing for access only for users imposing the least costs; for example the need for road operators to meet minimum axle weight and safety standards, new rail infrastructure to meet common loading gauge and signalling requirements. We return to this question below (see page 30).

We have set out in this section a range of the basic issues that arise in considering the provision of infrastructure. In the following two sections, we examine how far the public and private sectors are able to meet these requirements.

Public infrastructure and public funding

The principal rationale for public sector provision of infrastructure is through its public good characteristics. This would imply that infrastructure should be financed directly out of general tax revenues. However, infrastructure rarely meets all the criteria for a public good. In particular, mode specific transport infrastructure is excludable and, at levels of use approaching capacity, becomes rival. This shifts the argument towards the externality effects of infrastructure, and in particular the wider economic effects. Too frequently, these wider effects have been used as an assumption rather than as the outcome of a rigorous assessment.[18]

Concern over the validity of the traditional arguments, coupled with the need to reduce public sector budgets, led to a retreat from routine acceptance of public funding. The debate initiated by the Aschauer and Biehl studies in the late 1980s[19] showed that there were identifiable wider economic impacts which could justify public funding, but that these were not universal and needed to be justified on a case by case basis.[20]

If there is a case for arguing that there are identifiable external/spill-over benefits rather than just a general public good contribution, this may raise questions as to why most public sector funding comes out of general funding. Since users of infrastructure create external costs of congestion and environmental damage, there is a case for raising charges for the use of infrastructure to reflect this use of resources. The revenues from such charges should be regarded as the payment for a resource and not as general tax revenue and hence there is a case for these to be hypothecated to the transport sector, not on a mode-by-mode basis, but treating the transport sector as a whole. A case can hence be made for a self-financing, user-pays transport infrastructure network.[21]

The difficulty remains that many of the wider benefits of transport may accrue to individual firms and people, whose potential surplus could be expropriated to pay for the infrastructure, but disentangling private and social benefits is not easy.

We have referred above to the problems caused by the long gestation and construction periods of infrastructure. These frequently do not coincide with the planning horizons of public finance. Experience with railway investment in the UK has shown clearly the impact of public expenditure constraints and short-term horizons, which have led to levels of investment below that which would have been optimal for the system as a whole. Two related points are relevant here: infrastructure does not have an immediate impact on voting behaviour and thus is easier to defer than social welfare expenditure; likewise the perceived benefits are long-term and diffuse, and thus difficult to capitalize into voting behaviour.

Private funding options

The identification of a range of private benefits that are potentially able to be capitalized leads to the primary case for the private financing of infrastructure; it implies a re-evaluation of the balance of private and public interests in favour of the former. Although this argument for private finance has existed for some time, the renewed interest in the use of private finance in the 1980s occurred for two main, albeit secondary, reasons: increasing concern about the efficiency of the public sector in the management of large-scale projects, and the availability of substantial volumes of finance capital seeking projects. The first of these was part of the general argument about the inefficiency of the public sector and evidenced by the regularity of cost overruns and delays. The private sector would, it was argued, be more efficient in managing the construction projects, and this would be secured by ensuring that the private sector took an appropriate risk stake in projects. The second factor may have been of more practical significance in securing the change of emphasis since this also ensured that projects that would have been delayed in the highly constrained public sector could receive a rapid go-ahead in the private sector. These two factors combined would be expected to reduce the total cost of projects.

The main counter-argument to this expected cost advantage is that the cost of finance to the private sector would typically be higher than to the public sector given the higher degree of risk to the former. This raises the question as to whether the public sector should provide guarantees to ensure that any benefits are not lost through inability of the private sector to complete a project.[22]

The problem for the private sector remains that of identifying the beneficiaries from a project such that they can be appropriately charged. Since infrastructure operators will typically only have access to the direct users of the infrastructure this requires that the total benefits are sufficiently captured by user surplus. Such projects are likely to be those that are discrete, clearly bounded, and largely self-contained with no close competitor. For this reason the most common privately financed schemes have been bridges and tunnels.[23] Thus, private sector funding of infrastructure is likely to be associated with a degree of monopoly power.

If this is the case then the public sector may wish to consider exercising some control over pricing freedom through regulation. Most toll bridges for example do face price controls, but Eurotunnel, the operator of the Channel Tunnel was not subjected to such regulation given its competitive situation with the ferries, which are (largely) private sector operated, although it does face a degree of quantity regulation in having to provide certain minimum levels of service.[24] The issue for the public sector is the balance to be struck between seeking the expected benefits of private sector finance and maintaining a degree of control for public benefit reasons, including the key issue of maintaining appropriate safety standards.

In many cases, however, the difficulty in identifying beneficiaries directly leads to the public sector remaining involved as the main customer of the private sector infrastructure operator, as for example through the use of shadow tolls in road schemes or, less directly, through the payment of revenue subsidies to cover expected losses.[25]

A number of options for private finance are available, as summarized in Table 2.2. The most important distinctions are between the full-scale private provision of infrastructure and those that involve some form of contract between public and private sector. These involve schemes such as the Private Finance Initiative (PFI) and Public Private Partnerships (PPP) in the UK. PFI involves a long-term contractual partnership in which the private sector takes on the risks of a venture in return for payments dependent on agreed standards of performance. PPP is a rather more general arrangement between public and private sectors (often with legal force) for expected mutual benefit in the provision of services. The distinction between the two is rather blurred with PFI being a specific subset of PPP.

Generally, the conclusion from UK experience is that full privatization raises considerable difficulties. The purest private sector developed scheme, the Channel Tunnel, suggests that the expected cost savings in managing construction may not be as great as believed and that a PPP scheme such as the Channel Tunnel Rail Link (CTRL) and PFI road schemes may have offered better results.[26] The difficulties faced by Railtrack in managing and developing

Table 2.2 Schematic outline of private finance options

Type of scheme	Example scheme	Advantages to private sector	Disadvantages to private sector	Advantages to public sector	Disadvantages to public sector
Full private provision	Channel Tunnel	Full control of project; limited regulation	Full risk exposure; possible need to transfer project at end of agreed concession period	Transfer of all risk; retain some rights to asset at end of concession period	Residual risk of failure; Lack of control over prices etc unless regulatory structure.
PFI-scheme	DBFO Road schemes; Urban rapid transit (tram) systems	Greater control over project management; some risk retained by public sector	Value of project depends on correct forecasting of costs and revenue streams; need to return asset to public sector at agreed end of franchise	Transfer of (some) risk; lower overall cost of project; typically receive asset at end of agreed payback period	Retention of some risk; Need to fix payment for services to be delivered over long life of project
PPP-scheme	Channel Tunnel Rail Link; London Underground Modernisation	Agreed framework for payment received	Little or no ownership rights	Retention of ownership and control; all rights to asset revert at end of agreed payback period	Cost of payments; retention of risk elements
Service delivery agency scheme	New rail franchises	Agreed framework for payment received	No ownership rights	Full retention of ownership; possible benefits of private sector management efficiencies	Little sharing of risk; retention of responsibility for service delivery failure

the rail network in the private sector without increasing public sector support also cast some doubt on pure private sector provision.

The argument against this view usually takes the form that such private sector schemes have not worked because of the residual regulation preventing full competition. There are two responses to this. First, it can be argued that the competition does take place in the form of the competitive bidding for the rights. This is argued to be the most potent factor in reducing costs in PFI schemes.[27] Secondly, it has to be questioned whether a framework allowing for full competition, rather than competitive bidding, could ever be introduced for major infrastructure.[28]

PFI/PPP schemes, as well as allowing for lower costs of delivery, have typically delivered on time at a lower overall cost and thus meet the basic public sector test of value for money. The questions which are raised against such schemes are whether they sufficiently transfer risk to the private sector, given the agreement for the public sector to make certain contractual payments against a defined performance regime and the extent to which projects achieve cost savings, not through greater efficiency but through schemes which are inherently less safe. In the UK all PFI projects have to be set against a relevant Public Sector Comparator (PSC), the reference cost of a project in the public sector that defines the value for money of the private sector option. Defining the PSC then becomes the critical issue.

Grout (1997) suggested that the test was biased against the private sector because the PSC used the present value of the cash flow of costs whereas the implicit valuation of a private sector scheme by the government was of the present value of the revenue flows. This would not matter if the risks of each stream were accurately accounted for, but the same discount rate is typically applied to each and that would imply that risks were deemed equal whereas in practice revenue risks would be likely to be greater than cost risks. Grout suggests that this undervalues private sector projects whilst not adequately taking into account the scarcity of public funds. Whereas this argument may be generally valid for PFI projects in such cases as schools, hospitals and prisons, it is less likely to be true for large-scale transport infrastructure projects where there are much more substantial cost risks.

Recent evidence from the Association of Chartered Certified Accountants (ACCA) takes a different view and suggests that PFI projects have been poor value for money, implying that PSCs may have been consistently chosen to bias the evaluation in favour of privately financed schemes because of political pressure in favour of PFI. Only one in seven respondents to the ACCA survey believed that tests were objective and value for money tests had been described by the deputy controller of the National Audit Office as 'pseudo-scientific mumbo jumbo'.[29]

A battle has raged over the PPP scheme for London Underground, which sees the transfer of the management and responsibility for upgrading of the infrastructure (but not the ownership) to private sector consortia, whilst control remains firmly in the public sector through Transport for London (TfL). TfL and the London Mayor have argued strongly in favour of a public sector managed scheme financed by bonds. There seems to be little to choose in the relative costs of alternative means of finance, PPP projects do give savings over the agreed PSC (although bond finance appears to be more uncertain[30]), but there is a major political battle over the real degree of residual control retained in a PPP scheme.

The key question remains that of the distribution of risk in privately financed schemes. Although the principle of PFI-type projects is that there is a shift from the procurement of the assets involved in infrastructure to the purchase of the services provided by those assets, with the responsibility for provision and management of the assets remaining in the private sector, there is still a residual risk left with the public sector. As has been seen both with the early development of the Channel Tunnel Rail Link (CTRL) and the later problems with Railtrack, the public sector remains as the ultimate guarantor of a scheme.

The issue then is the appropriate length of the franchise/concession period. The usual basis sees the contract fixing a maximum period at the end of which the asset reverts to the public sector free of any encumbrances, but reversion will usually occur at the time that the asset is fully amortized. In this way the public sector tries to shift the downside risk onto the private sector whilst retaining the upside 'risk'. The adjustment of the concession period can be a bargaining issue, as for example in the case of the Channel Tunnel where the original concession of 55 years (including construction) was extended to 99 years to enhance the project's overall value at a time of crisis in the financing. Later projects have seen the transfer of a revenue-earning asset to a concessionaire to help provide a cash flow during the construction period as a means of easing the potential revenue risk in the early years.[31]

There appear to be two main sources of risk, which we term the network question and the vertical integration question. The network question relates to the problem of defining the private sector project. The vertical integration question relates to the transaction costs in a project.

The network question

Measuring network economies is a complex issue and one where it is difficult to separate the pure infrastructure economies from those of operation. Network economies comprise economies of scale, scope, and density. Network density economies are of two types. One relates to the density of the network, such that the infrastructure provides operators with the opportunity to supply services which link conveniently together thus lowering idle time of rolling stock and maximizing the number of passengers who face less disrupted journeys. The other relates to the average length of haul within a network of given density since the longer the average journey length the greater the economy from spreading the fixed terminal costs.[32]

Clearly fragmenting the network between different infrastructure operators presents problems in terms of ensuring that seamless journey opportunities can be provided to service operators and users. Apart from questions of the compatibility of the physical characteristics of the infrastructure network, slot allocation becomes more difficult.[33]

However, the problem then becomes one of whether it is ever possible to define an optimum network, and how far the optimal network from the point of view of the operators and users of services coincides with the optimum network from the point of view of infrastructure supply. Thus the question of financeability, which typically requires smaller, more manageable and identifiable networks, has to be set against network management from the point of view of the user.[34] Compromises may mean less than optimal solutions from both perspectives.

The vertical integration question

The vertical integration question is that of the extent to which infrastructure and service operation need to be combined, from the perspectives of both ownership and management. The traditional principle for railways was one of vertical integration whereas for most other modes of transport separation was practised. That was changed with the advent of EC Directive 91/440, which legislated for separation.

The main reason for separation was to ensure greater transparency in the accounting of operators such that clear evidence of the application of fair and efficient prices for the use of infrastructure existed, enabling comparison of modes. Greater transparency would lead to greater efficiency and the potential for competition, which would tend to lead to lower prices. This follows the experience of privatization in the electricity and gas industries where there was considerable pressure to create vertical separation between generation and distribution to minimize the monopoly power of the generators.

Competition here can be thought of in three forms: competition for infrastructure; competition on infrastructure; and competition between infrastructures (modes). We have already addressed the competition for infrastructure in terms of the relative merits of tendering and franchising competition. Competition on infrastructure is a means of ensuring greater efficiency in infrastructure provision through ensuring that there is no monopsony in the purchase of infrastructure services. Thus airports are typically limited in their ability to exercise monopoly power by the presence of many airlines competing for the slots available, but also able to take business elsewhere if charges become too high. The moderation of on-track competition in the case of railways in the UK, coupled with the ability of the operators to seek revenue support where track-access charges make services otherwise unprofitable has enabled Railtrack to escape this form of competitive pressure. There has only been one new open-access rail operator, and this is owned by another franchisee. Finally, the extent of competition between infrastructures is very limited, principally because infrastructure operators are shielded from end-user demand by service operators. Considerable effort was spent by rail operators and Railtrack in the UK to try and shift blame for poor service onto each other.

This highlights the importance of transaction costs in the analysis, in particular the conflict between transparency and contractual complexity. A major rationale for separation of infrastructure and service operation is to make the cost of infrastructure transparent. This transparency should lead to more competition for the provision of infrastructure and thus bring down the prices charged by infrastructure suppliers. This does not of course require private ownership,[35] but the latter does imply a greater degree of both vertical and horizontal separation to ensure financeability.

This is then the basic choice which confronts the analyst, whether any gains from the greater transparency and potential competition in the private provision of infrastructure will be outweighed by the increasing transaction costs associated with the administration and enforcing of complex contractual arrangements between independent organizations rather than within the same organization.

Some conclusions and issues for future research

This chapter has identified that, although we have a good understanding of the basic economics of infrastructure provision and the arguments for and against the use of private finance, there are still considerable areas of uncertainty surrounding the precise definition and measurement of key elements. Much of the research to date has tended to examine specific projects in a largely descriptive manner. Each of these tends to be highly specific, both in terms of the nature of the project and the mode of delivery chosen as governments have tried to learn from past mistakes and iterate towards a better structure for private involvement.

Success or failure of private finance initiatives has been argued to be related to three main factors: risk; transactions costs; and network economies. Each of these provides a topic where further research is required:

◆ Three major risk factors were identified relating to construction, revenue, and planning or political risk. The characteristics of major infrastructure mean that it will always be difficult to eliminate the first two of these which are inherent in any major construction project, but the clear apportionment of risk, and the relative ease with which parties have been able to shift risk-bearing in the provision of major infrastructure, remain problems. Revenue risk includes the problem of how far private providers of infrastructure are able to capture any wider benefits, other than to direct users of the infrastructure, which might be used as a justification for a project. The danger remains that these are seen as a public sector responsibility that is met either by a capital grant or continuing revenue support. The major factor is, however, the assessment of the policy and political risks involved in private provision of infrastructure. This represents a risk to both private and public parties to a project; the private sector needs to protect itself against changes in policy, the public sector perceives a risk in the private sector failing to fulfil its obligations. This has repercussions on both the willingness of the private sector to engage in such projects and the detail of conditions under which it will participate, not least in the determination of the length of any franchise or concession and the acceptance of a particular regulatory regime.

- ◆ The desire to avoid monopoly influences in the control of infrastructure and the need to provide more closely defined and specific projects for the private sector to evaluate has associated private provision with both vertical separation of infrastructure and service provision and with network fragmentation. Whilst transactions costs become more transparent in a vertically separated transport system, any hoped for increase in efficiency through greater competition appears likely to be lost through greater contractual complexity. Such contracts suffer in particular from asymmetry in the information available to the parties to the contracts where what might be taken as routine operational information in an integrated framework becomes commercially confidential in a separated framework.

- ◆ Network fragmentation to make private finance contracts viable and manageable risks the loss of network economies. The definition and measurement of network economies in the context of differing modes of delivery remains a problematic issue. This relates both to the wider benefits issue, discussed under revenue risk above, and to transaction costs between different infrastructure providers and the users of the infrastructure in order to determine the optimal organization of a transport network.

What conclusions can we draw from this analysis for the future use of private finance in infrastructure investment? First, it is clear that pure private provision is not the solution to the provision of infrastructure that governments hoped for in the 1980s. Secondly, private finance cannot step into an investment hole left by public sector neglect and rescue governments from their inability to manage the maintenance and development of infrastructure. Thirdly, where public-private partnerships of some form are used there has to be clearer specification of roles and risks; this is necessary both to encourage private finance into projects and to avoid the continuing battles over major projects. Fourthly, over-complex management structures for vertically fragmented industries lead to excessive transactions costs. One view is that the main problem has been the failure to introduce sufficient competition; certainly much of the problem comes from an excessive degree of regulation, as governments have been reluctant to allow competitive pressures to determine developments. Perhaps, however, the problem is one of inconsistent regulation between different sectors – is there really a need for individual regulators for each public utility? Finally, it has to be recognized that almost all large infrastructure investment projects are unique. There is not a single organizational model which can be expected to work universally; tailoring both organizational structure and financial structure to the specific needs of a project may be much more effective in the long run.

Notes

1 A first version of this chapter was presented at the STELLA Workshop in Brussels, 26–27 April 2002. I am grateful to participants for valuable comments and also to participants of the ESRC Urban and Regional Economics Study Group Meeting, Preston, July 2002 and of the Workshop on Applied Infrastructure Research, TU Berlin, October 2002 where the ideas in this chapter were further discussed.
2 Note that the original classic of infrastructure economics (Dupuit, 1844) referred to bridges.
3 See: European Commission (1999).
4 For example much of the cost increase associated with the construction of the Channel Tunnel was due to detailed design only being carried out as construction proceeded and despite detailed geological surveys problems of excessive wetness in the strata were unexpected. Another well quoted example is that of the south tower of the Humber Bridge which was unexpectedly located at a point where an underground stream was washing away concrete almost as fast as it was poured in.
5 The successive increases in the cost of the West Coast Main Line Route Modernisation in the UK appear to have been associated with an initial failure to specify the project accurately and then to control costs effectively.
6 This figure rises to 34% for fixed-link (major bridge and tunnel) projects and 45% for rail projects, and is around 20% for road projects. The data used in the study cannot determine whether private sector projects are more or less prone to such underestimation than public sector projects, but it does suggest that transport projects are not more susceptible to this problem than other large infrastructure projects.
7 These arise principally for the use of directly tolled infrastructures, but some road schemes can be provided on the basis of shadow tolls in which the provider is paid by the government or roads authority for the estimated usage. In the case of UK private road contracts this estimate is based

   on average traffic growth rather than the specific traffic usage of each length of road.
8 International infrastructures such as the Channel Tunnel and Øresund link have been particularly
   problematic.
9 One of the major reasons behind the DBFO contracts used in the UK highway programme
   was to try and secure higher construction standards if contractors were directly liable for the
   consequences of any construction failures.
10 The initial placing of Railtrack into administration in the UK, with no compensation for
   shareholders, displayed what was thought to be a reneging on a government undertaking not to
   re-nationalize because of the costs involved. Subsequent moves to provide the successor not-for-
   profit company, Network Rail with government funding sufficient to make compensation available
   to shareholders (though not explicitly given for this) have been thought to have been occasioned
   by fear of the drying up of private sector enthusiasm for funding infrastructure schemes in
   general.
11 See below for further discussion of the PFI versus bonds debate for the improvement of London
   Underground infrastructure.
12 See Report of High Level Group on the Trans-European Transport Network, European Commission,
   June 2003.
13 Office of the Rail Regulator (2003).
14 This shows the situation prior to the placing of Railtrack in administration. In 2002 Railtrack
   was replaced by a not-for-profit organization, Network Rail, but the same basic structure was
   retained.
15 For example it is estimated that infrastructure costs contribute between 18% and 23% of average
   road costs per vehicle km (including external costs, but excluding congestion) (Institute of
   Transport Studies, 2001) and see also Link *et al.* (2000).
16 See Vickerman (2001*a*) for a summary of the issues and SACTRA (1999) and Mackie *et al.* (2001)
   for a discussion of the relevance of this for evaluation procedures.
17 As an example see the question of the completion of the high-speed rail network associated with
   the Channel Tunnel; different attitudes to the network were taken in France and the UK. In France
   announcement of the construction of the TGV-Nord was made just ahead of the public flotation
   of Eurotunnel; in the UK concern over public opposition to construction of a high-speed line and
   recognition of the problems of separation of the marginal returns to high-speed line and tunnel
   (which had been instrumental in the abandonment of the previous scheme in the 1970s) led to a
   delay in even considering construction of CTRL which will only be completed some 13 years after
   the Channel Tunnel was opened (see Vickerman, 1995).
18 See the discussion in SACTRA (1999).
19 See Aschauer (1989), Biehl (1986, 1991).
20 See Gramlich (1994), SACTRA (1999).
21 This has been argued in more detail in Peirson and Vickerman (1993); see also the evidence for
   the UK in Peirson *et al.* (1995) and Peirson and Vickerman (1998).
22 The argument for a guarantee rests on the existence of difficult to identify wider economic
   benefits which would otherwise be lost, but also in relation to the planning blight which a
   partially completed infrastructure project would have on other potential projects. Against this is
   the argument that any public guarantee undermines the 'at own risk' element in private finance
   and thus interferes with the operation of capital market more generally.
23 This could include parallel road schemes reserved for specific types of traffic, e.g. express lanes
   or truck lanes on motorways, or roads aiming to offer a higher quality of service through price
   restricted access.
24 This is common with private sector urban transit schemes and it is interesting to note that even
   the early private sector railways were subject to some regulation over minimum levels of service
   at a maximum fare, the so-called Parliamentary train.
25 Besley and Ghatak (2001) suggest that ownership of a service with public good characteristics
   should lie with whoever values the service more highly; thus where there were substantial wider
   benefits which cannot be attributed the public sector should retain control.
26 The Channel Tunnel scheme was delivered at about a 100% overrun on its budget and one year

late (although much of this may be due to latent risk in changing government safety requirements and slow approval procedures); CTRL is currently on schedule and to budget (see Vickerman, 1995), although the National Audit Office (2001) has been critical of the likely returns to the public investment in the project. The Highways Agency estimates cost savings of about 15% on PFI road schemes; the National Audit Office (2003) confirms benefits in maintenance costs and management.

27 This is a similar argument to that of the benefits of franchising transport services: compare for example the experience of a franchising system for bus services in London with the full privatization in the rest of the UK (Mackie and Preston, 1996).

28 On a historical note, there was considerable competitive construction of railways in the UK, often leading to some of the residual problems of the network experienced today, and during the 1870s there were two rival Channel Tunnel schemes being constructed in parallel.

29 See *The Guardian*, 12 October 2002; ACCA Members' Survey: Do PFI Schemes Provide Value for Money, September 2002 (available at http://www.acca.co.uk/pdfs/miscellaneous/pfi_survey_report.pdf).

30 See Ernst and Young (2002).

31 An interesting debate has begun to emerge from the Dartford Crossing scheme in the UK which delivered a parallel bridge, doubling the capacity of the existing tunnels on the congested London Orbital Motorway (M25) route. The bridge was delivered on an expected payback period of a maximum of 20 years financed by regulated tolls; it is likely that this will have been achieved inside 10 years when it reverts as a free asset to the government, which has indicated that it will continue to charge tolls.

32 For a fuller discussion see Vickerman (2001b)

33 The lack of a Europe-wide air traffic control system is one of the causes of greater air traffic delays when compared with the US. Problems arise with Eurostar services through the Channel Tunnel where late running on one network causes problems of missed slots at the Tunnel and on the other main rail networks compounding the delays.

34 The proposal for the PPP scheme for London Underground envisages the setting up of three infrastructure companies, each of which would be responsible for a group of lines, but with coordination and the operation of services remaining integrated and in the public sector.

35 Many European railway companies have formally separated infrastructure and operations within the same State-owned organization, e.g. RFF and SNCF in France; Japanese railways were privatized on a vertically integrated regional basis; most US railroads are vertically integrated, with substantial mutual cross running, for freight services although the main passenger services provide by Amtrak are provided over other companies' rails.

Bibliography

Aschauer, D.A. (1989) Is public expenditure productive? *Journal of Monetary Economics*, **23**, pp. 177–200.

Besley, T. and Ghatak, M. (2001) Government versus private ownership of public goods. *Quarterly Journal of Economics*, **116**, pp. 1343–1372.

Biehl, D. (ed.) (1986) *The Contribution of Infrastructure to Regional Development*. Luxembourg: Office for Official Publications of the European Communities.

Biehl, D. (ed.) (1991) The role of infrastructure in regional development, in Vickerman, R. (ed.) *Infrastructure and Regional Development*. London: Pion.

Dupuit, J. (1844) De la mesure de l'utilité des travaux publics (On the measurement of the utility of public works). *Annales des Ponts et Chaussées*, 2nd series, Vol. 8; reprinted in Munby, D. (ed.) (1968) *Transport: Selected Readings*. Harmondsworth: Penguin.

Ernst and Young (2002) *London Underground PPPs – Value for Money Review*. Ernst and Young. Online. Available HTTP: <http://www.railways.dtlr.gov.uk/underground/ernstyoung/index.htm>.

European Commission (1999) *High Level Group on Transport Infrastructure Charging: Final*

Report on Estimating Transport Costs. Brussels: European Commission.

European Commission (2003) *Report of High Level Group on the Trans-European Transport Network* (Chairman, Van Miert). Brussels: European Commission.

Flyvbjerg, B., Skamris, M. and Buhl, S.L. (2002) Underestimating costs in public works projects: error or lie? *Journal of the American Planning Association*, **68**, pp. 279–295.

Gramlich, E. (1994) Infrastructure investment: a review essay. *Journal of Economic Literature*, **32**, pp. 1176–1196.

Grout, P. (1997) The economics of the private finance initiative. *Oxford Review of Economic Policy*, **13**, pp. 53–66.

Hart, O., Shleifer, A. and Vishny, R.W. (1997) The proper scope of government: theory and application to prisons. *Quarterly Journal of Economics*, **112**, pp. 1119–1158.

Institute of Transport Studies (2001) *Surface Transport Costs and Charge.* Leeds: ITS, University of Leeds.

Link, H., Stewart, L., Maibach, M., Sansome, T. and Nellthorp, J. (2000) The Accounts Approach: UNITE (UNIfication of accounts and marginal costs for Transport Efficiency). Deliverable 2, 5th Framework RTD Programme, ITS, University of Leeds.

Mackie, P. and Preston, J. (1996) *The Local Bus Market – A Case Study of Regulatory Change*, Aldershot: Avebury.

Mackie, P., Nellthorp, J., Kiel, J., Schade, W. and Nokkala, M. (2001) *IASON* Project Assessment Baseline: IASON (Integrated Appraisal of Spatial ecOnomic and Network) effects of transport investments and policies. Deliverable 1, 5th framework RTD Programme, TNO-INRO, Delft.

National Audit Office (2001) *The Channel Tunnel Rail Link. Report by the Comptroller and Auditor General.* HC 302 Session 2000–2001. London: The Stationery Office.

National Audit Office (2003) *Maintaining England's Motorways and Trunk Roads. Report by the Comptroller and Auditor General.* HC 431 Session 2002–2003. London: The Stationery Office.

Office of the Rail Regulator (2003) *Interim Review Of Track Access Charges: Third Consultation Paper,* July 2003. London: Office of the Rail Regulator

Peirson, J. and Vickerman, R. (1993) Environmental taxes and investment in transport infrastructure: the case for hypothecation. Paper to Royal Economic Society Conference, York.

Peirson, J., Skinner, I. and Vickerman, R.W. (1995) Estimating the external costs of UK passenger transport: the first step towards an efficient transport market. *Environment and Planning A*, **27**, pp. 1977–1993.

Peirson, J. and Vickerman, R. (1998) The environment, efficient pricing and investment in transport: a model and some results for the UK, in Banister, D. (ed.) *Transport Policy and the Environment*. London: E&FN Spon.

Standing Advisory Committee on Trunk Road Assessment (SACTRA) (1999) *Transport and the Economy*. London: HMSO.

Vickerman, R.W. (1995) The channel tunnel: the case for private sector provision of public infrastructure, in Banister, D. (ed.) *Transport and Urban Development*. London: Chapman and Hall.

Vickerman, R.W. (2001*a*) *Transport and Economic Development*. Report for 119th Round Table, European Conference of Ministers of Transport. Paris: ECMT.

Vickerman, R.W. (2001*b*) The concept of optimal transport systems, in Button, K.J. and Hensher, D.A. (eds.) *Handbook of Transport Systems and Traffic Control* (Handbooks in Transport Volume 3). Oxford: Pergamon.

Chapter 3

Myths and taboos in transport policy[1]

Kenneth Button

Transport policy has historically gone through periods of positive engagement by governments with active interventions by their civil servants followed by periods of almost benign neglect by the authorities.[2] Heavy and active policy interventions when adopted have varied significantly in their nature and local nuances. There is thus little by way of a standard period of transport policy, nor anything like a standard approach.

That the public is interested in transport policy, at least in recent history, is easily seen by counting the column inches in newspapers and the time devoted to it on the radio and on the television newscasts. Documentaries about some transport activity are often aired at peak listening and viewing times. Politicians regularly pontificate and take up air time and newsprint to advocate their pet projects, generally unfocused notions of how transport should be developed, and how large sums of public money should be used to support the transport system. That the academic community is engaged can be seen by the large number of learned journals and scholarly books devoted to various aspects of transport policy, and the array of courses that are on offer.

But much of the public debate on transport policy in the media is specific rather than general. It is often major accidents, the completion of large investments (usually displayed as a major political success story for the incumbent party), or the engineering failure of some piece of transportation infrastructure that attracts attention. Most recently, for example, matters pertaining to the environment have received attention often accompanied by graphic images of an oil-spill or exhaust fumes emanating from an automobile. Or it may be of deforestation for the construction of a superhighway in a developing country where 70% of the population is living on $150 a year and are almost certainly more in need of the infrastructure than those criticizing its construction in their air conditioned homes. Security issues have come to the fore since the events in New York and Arlington in 2001 and huge amounts of resources from other aspects of transport supply and elsewhere have been diverted as a consequence.

Much of the discussion and debate, however, takes place within a world full of superstition and voodoo. Even the more carefully thought through policy decisions are often made on less scientific grounds than those generated by Ouija boards. The aim of this chapter is to look (inevitably neither entirely randomly nor objectively) at some of the myths that seem to underlie much of the popular and often official policy debates of recent years. It also considers why it is that some fairly obvious policy approaches (at least obvious to many analysts) seem to be forbidden fruit for policy-makers.

The emphasis is also almost entirely on the wealthier, industrial countries of the world. In many ways this chapter may be underestimating the extent to which transport policy is ruled by myths and taboos. Leaders with fewer resources at their command and more interest in following somewhat different agendas from those of the industrial states have a greater incentive to create and perpetuate fantastic ideas.

What is perhaps surprising is that since the initial drafting of this chapter, which was seen at that time as an input to discussions at a rather informal seminar, I have had a number of invitations to talk to policy-makers and their advisors about some of the issues raised. What often seems self-evident to academics is clearly not so crystal clear to those that have to formulate and enact policy. It is perhaps appropriate to ask whether this situation extends beyond a matter of simple communication malfunction.

The list of myths[3] that we look at here is far from comprehensive and the comments terse rather than fully developed. It would need a full chapter on each to do anything like justice. The aim is to question some of the entrenched beliefs regarding what 'must' be done by transport policy and what is simply 'not possible', and to look at generalities and the broad views that are frequently found in transport policy debates and in the media. Ten are selected for discussion. It could have been nine or eleven or twenty-two, but ten is a convenient number, and also allows sufficient scope to cover some of the key myths and taboos. So here they are.

Transport is important

Perhaps this heading is slightly misleading. The issue is really not whether transport is important *per se* but rather just how important is it? And at a lower level, just how important are particular modes of transport or particular links in the system? The conclusion is also often reached (or much more often just 'posited') that since transport is important then it should not be left to the invisible hand of Adam Smith but rather be embraced in the iron fist of government. Indeed, even Adam Smith can be found to accept this in some instances where he felt inadequate transport infrastructure would be forth coming from the private sector for very large projects.

This interventionism is the cornerstone of the oft-called Continental Philosophy of regulation that has been central to much transport policy-making in the recent past. Basically, regulation is the norm with market forces only allowed to enter play when they are shown to be superior. The focus changed somewhat in the 1970s and 1980s as policy-makers began to entertain the notion that efficiency of transport provision *per se* was of considerable importance in its own right. The onus of proof moved to demonstrating that intervention could do better than the market, and also toward more bespoke regulation aimed at specific issues. But the change has been partially and certainly not whole-heartedly embraced by all.

The size of transportation in national income calculations has often been put forward as illustrative of the importance of the sector. In fact, any even cursory examination of the National Income Accounts of an industrialized country shows that transport constitutes only about 5% to 7% of the GDP. Where do the larger figures come from that show transport is responsible for 10% to 15% of the GDP – a not uncommon figure stated, for example, in advocacy statements?[4] These higher figures represent what is rapidly becoming known as 'Arthur Andersen' estimates. They generally combine data on final demand from the expenditure account with those of factor returns (aimed at capturing the intermediate goods nature of many transport services).

The simple fact is that national income accounts were designed and developed by Richard Stone, Simon Kuznets and others to provide information on the intermediate stage between aggregate public expenditures and employment in a Keynesian macroeconomic model of the world. They were never intended to be dynamic (they fitted into a comparative statics framework), nor to do they more than offer, in broad terms, guidance on the nature of the consumption function and other relationships in the Keynesian system. They have been manipulated and misused for many other purposes but they are internally consistent if used appropriately. In this manner, transport is a less important element in GDP than is often stated in public policy debates.

The notion of critical transport infrastructure has become a popular myth and, a little like the now somewhat shop-soiled idea of sustainable transport, has become a useful one on which to hang research grant applications, or for politicians to justify expending massive amounts of resources, generally for their own electoral gains. The seminal work of Fogel[5] indicated that the vast nineteenth-century investments in US railway infrastructure were not critical for that nation's economic expansion in the period. More recently, the initial work of Aschauer[6] purporting to show strong linkages between economic growth and the provision of infrastructure, of which transport infrastructure is a large component, has been dissected. Accepted problems of causality, model specification, data limitations, intellectual implausibility, and levels of aggregation have now generally taken this line of work out of mainstream thinking, although the idea of the centrality of infrastructure in economic growth still lingers in shadier corners.

But there are cruder, more empirical ways of looking at the situation. If transport infrastructure is critical, then by definition its absence would have profound effects on the social and economic systems. In fact, there is ample evidence showing that mankind is rather more ingenious than this would suggest. Going back to the Industrial Revolution in the UK, there is considerable evidence that growth in industrial productivity preceded any major changes in transportation. At a more meso level, the massive earthquake in San Francisco in 1989 that put such major transport arteries as the Oakland Bridge and the Cyprus Freeway out of action, certainly led to very short-term disruptions, but very rapidly ways were found to circumvent these.[7] Whenever there is a major concern about warfare, there is a seeming tradition in the US that large companies cease to allow executives to travel (presumably because they are critical for commercial success – although very rapidly expendable when profits fail to meet expectations) and other 'Ramboesque' figures follow suit. If transport were so vital, it would surely be the last thing that would be cut back on.

Does this all mean that transport is of no importance? Of course not. What it does mean is that importance in this case is more complex than can be found in manipulated accounts or in the simpler economic models. Its lubricating role in the system makes it difficult to assess, particularly at a time when policy debates have become increasingly reliant on numbers and cardinal assessments. The widespread use, and even wider misuse, of quasi-cost-benefit analysis in decision-making offers perhaps the most obvious example of this. But the problem is a little like that of trying to assess the importance of each component in a car. The engine oil may only constitute a very small fraction of the total expenditure on motoring but the car would soon grind to a halt without it!

Transport is different

One reason that is often put forward for adopting an interventionist approach to transport or in some way treating it differently to other goods and services that we buy is that, even if it is not quantitatively important in the economy, as it is significantly different in its nature to other goods and services there is a need for it to be regulated. The types of reason that are put forward for this include: the network features of the industry; the tendency for monopoly power to develop in its supply; the tendency for it to become excessively competitive and unstable; there are high fixed or common costs that cannot be recovered in market conditions; the high level of externalities associated with transport use; the public goods nature of the activity; the importance of transport in meeting wider economic objectives (e.g., regarding spatial equity); and the strategic importance of transport infrastructure.

Some of these are simply not valid. The oft-cited justification for public provision of roads, and the allowance of essential free access to them because they are what economists term 'public goods' is a case in point. It is actually very easy to stop potential users from entering a road where, if there is heavy use, congestion develops. Hence, they have neither the attributes of non-excludability nor non-rivalness that define public goods. Market structures are also often misused to initiate regulation. Fears of excessive competition in the road freight transport sector led the European Community some years ago to seek regulation of minimum tariffs, and just to be sure, it also set maximum rates in case monopoly tendencies emerged. This would seem to indicate a maximum of fuzziness in the Community's logic.

There are certainly fixed costs associated with the provision of many components of transportation, although certainly less than was traditionally believed. This can lead to either monopoly power arising or, when there are few barriers to entry, of an empty core emerging with associated instability and under supply (but not both at the same time). However, this is not a problem unique to transport. It is handled elsewhere within standard institutional frameworks of competition policy. This may involve regulation of power or, conversely in the empty core case, relaxation of certain laws. In some service sectors, self-regulation has been adopted. But the point is that these situations are not unique to transport.

Transport is often exempt from standard antitrust and competition policy and transport suppliers are given their own set of rules within which to operate. There have been bloc exemptions within EU transport policy for aviation and in the US, until recently, the Department of Transportation handled airline mergers rather than, as with most other sectors, the Department of Justice. But there seems little reason to separate in this way. There are broadly agreed principles of competition that are generic to all activities – for example, concerning the concentration of supply, the ease of market entry and exit, and the lack of predatory behaviour. Certainly there are specific industry characteristics, but only in the sense that context is important in each case, and that argument can be extended across each and every industry.

Turning to externalities, and first to environmental degradation. Surface transport has been likened to 'industry on wheels',[8] and I am sure that similar turns of phrase can be found in the maritime and aviation literature. Certainly, transport pollutes but so do very many other activities. One may quite legitimately argue that transport is somewhat more problematic because of the range of adverse environmental effects associated with it, that the source of the problem is mobile, and the fact that people actually want close proximity to transport for access reasons. But one can isolate the implications of power generation or agricultural activities by their characteristics. The crucial point is that a ton of carbon dioxide is just that, irrespective of its source. The issue is to limit carbon dioxide emissions not to think of environmental problems as being source specific. Indeed, efficient control would involve allowing flexibility in the way the emissions are reduced so as to minimize the overall costs. It does not take much to show that the most effective way to meet a target is through carbon taxation rather than *ad hoc* policies on vehicle fuel consumption, power plant design, etc!

The other form of externality (strictly a 'club good' problem) is that of traffic congestion. Roads do get congested, there is no question about that, but so do many other things, or at least many more would if they were not rationed out efficiently. Prices basically rise when there is a shortage of supply *vis-à-vis* demand in other sectors and congestion is largely averted. It was no accident that queues were the norm in centrally planned economies where prices were not fully used as an allocation mechanism.[9] Economists have advocated appropriate, officially regulated pricing to reduce congestion, and, some such as Pigou[10] who initiated the idea of road pricing to optimize road congestion, accept that private provision and free pricing of a competitive road network would resolve the problem. This is exactly what happens in virtually all other parts of Western economies.

You can 'build' your way out of problems

Engineering and physics got man to the moon but did so in a very inefficient and costly way. There have been some important technological advances in transport that have been primarily engineering/science driven.[11] Whether the same outcomes could have been achieved through other means is not clear but it would appear that there are important technology effects to be reaped. The two crucial issues would seem to be whether there are better ways of approaching problems than through the technology route and, even when technology is the optimal solution, what are the most efficient ways of getting it deployed.

One of the long-standing beliefs in transport was that one could build one's way out of congestion. This held in the 1960s with regard to urban road networks and still lingers in areas involving such things as airport congestion. Simple practical, but extraordinarily wasteful experience showed that laying tarmac will not in itself generate a solution to congestion. Downs' Law[12] reigns supreme. Traffic increases to fill the capacity available.[13] This has been superseded to a large extent by the idea that you can computerize your way out through such things as developing intelligent transport systems. Of course, in the right place there is the need for more capacity in the transport system. (And, on occasions there is the need for the removal of surplus capacity – for example of links in many rail networks in Central Europe – which can pose equal difficulties for policy-makers because some people will suffer.[14]) This may require older civil engineering technologies of laying tarmac or rails. But there is also the possibility that users and suppliers of transport services may be getting the wrong signals because of the lack of pricing and that better information about opportunity costs and more appropriate stimuli would be more effective in meeting social criteria.

There is simply a fundamental problem with trying to build one's way out of congestion problems either through constructing more physical capacity or by adopting more computing power. Like any factory, the transport system should be well managed (hence optimal traffic management and ITS systems) and should be of the appropriate scale (hence optimal investment) but any factory owner sells his output at an appropriate price to ensure that costs are recovered. This not only provides the revenue for investment and for operations, but also ensures that the users of the product are cognizant of the costs involved and makes consumption decisions accordingly. Without these signals, there are inevitable problems of excess demand. People will just keep consuming oblivious of the implications for the resources that they deplete. This applies to any situation from the long lines that formed in the Soviet Union where prices were low and irrelevant to the roads that are supplied on exactly the same principles in most parts of the world. Just supplying something without pricing for its use leads to overuse.

There are no such things as opportunity costs

The 1990s in the US was an interesting period for the observer of economic debate. The gurus of the day – generally individuals who had got most things wrong in the past, and will inevitably be wrong about everything in the future but have appropriate television persona – argued strongly that the days of the trade-cycle were now gone. The US economy was seen as heading towards the nirvana of perpetual economic growth. The actual situation has been somewhat different. One of the problems is that these much-publicized seers neglected the opportunity costs of events and actions. Political economy was not christened by Thomas Carlyle the 'dismal science' for nothing – economists take note of the costs of events and actions as well as the benefits. The notion of the 'double dividend' is an illusionary one for economists.

This is important in transport policy-making for a number of reasons but the focus here is limited. The first reason relates to the dynamic effects (or more accurately the lack of dynamic considerations) in virtually all policy interventions. In many cases the motivation for policy is more to do with distribution considerations – the sharing of the pie rather than its enlargement. In other cases, it is to limit allocative inefficiencies associated with such things as the potential monopoly power of some transport supplying entities. Whatever the form the intervention takes, in virtually all cases the underlying analysis is myopic. There is an inevitable inability, because of lack of perfect foresight, to see what technical developments would have occurred in a freer market. But there is an equal naiveté in many cases in assuming that those regulated will not innovate to circumvent the implications of policy instruments. This is not an optimal outcome in most cases but is an outcome that is seldom predicted by those doing the regulating.

Some examples. Looking at the UK local bus industry, it is clear that regulation until the mid-1980s stifled the development of mini-bus services as well as the more static inefficiencies of imposing out-dated route structures. The regulation of the US domestic passenger air transport market limited the development of computer reservation systems and managerial developments such as the integrated hub-and-route system. In terms of efforts, which are themselves resource consuming, to get around regulations, one can cite the growth of international airline strategic alliances to overcome the regime of air service bilateral agreements and the adoption of flags of convenience in the maritime sector to avoid national restrictions on crewing, etc.

But there are other opportunity costs besides those associated with limiting the efficiency of the transport industries themselves. The transactions costs of regulation, national ownership, and oversight can be extremely high relative to any potential benefits that are generated.

A final thought is, 'Should we be so surprised that policy-makers so often neglect opportunity cost?' I would argue not. At the most obvious level there is the inevitability that policy-makers underplay costs and overplay benefits to appeal to their constituents. But there is another, even more fundamental myth amongst the population that is important, namely that there is somehow a natural right to travel and have mobility. A fact that is actually accepted so widely that it is not even written into the constitutions of such countries as the US where virtually all aspects of life are centrally defined by the legal structure. If one accepts this universal right to mobility then, logically, it should be sought and supplied without regard to cost. The reality, of course, is that this is simply not practical, and probably not desirable.

The market is the source of all evil

A Jupiterian landing on earth would probably not unreasonably conclude that the welfare of mankind was highest in those countries where free markets played a predominant role in the economic structure.[15] But there still persists in many quarters a myth that things are more efficiently supplied if there is direction from the centre.[16] This type of attitude is one that has never been unique to transport. In medicine, for example, doctors continually applied remedies in the belief that they could out perform nature. The reality of the situation was that they probably killed more people than they cured; certainly, this was the case up to the early part of the twentieth century. But interfere they did.

Now one is not quite suggesting that transport policy-makers are of the same ilk as the leach-toting, blood-soaked, saw-bones of medical history, but their approach is often philosophically very much along the same lines. If there is a problem then the best approach is to become involved and to intervene. If the problem gets worse, then more intervention is the obvious approach. If intervention clearly fails then another layer is needed.[17] The incentive structure to do this is seen at both the political and bureaucratic levels. Politicians inevitably like to appear 'policy active' and seldom like to admit public policy failures. Civil servants and regulators have an incentive to expand the scale of their activities. To leave things alone is almost inevitable taboo.

Does this mean that markets are perfect, their outcomes are socially optimal, and that interventions inevitably lead to more problems than they solve? No. Markets do fail, for a whole variety of reasons, to provide optimal transport. Surely, the issue is rather one of whether intervention brings about a better outcome. At the most basic level of transport regulation, there will never be a perfectly competitive outcome, but the issue is whether the outcome will be workably competitive. The underlying consideration is whether the market failures that prevent the emergence of perfect competition are less socially costly than the intervention failures that accompany government involvement.[18] Government has a role to play, but the paramount concern is that the involvement acts as an improvement and not as a mechanism for intervention simply for the sake of it.

The simple fact is that the market is the most efficient mechanism that we have for handling complex information systems and decisions. It does it very imperfectly but in virtually all cases far better then even the most sophisticated planning system. This is true even when modern computing power supports the latter. The effects of any action on a system are ripple effects through that system and the full ramifications of these are, quite simply, still unpredictable. Many policy-makers fear markets because they do not foresee the outcome of any changes in the system – say a shift in demand. They feel that control gives them insights into this and the ability to react. The reality is that the models that are used are very imprecise at best and tend to capture only the immediate temporal, sector, and spatial impacts.

Subsidized transport helps the poor

Transportation, and in particular surface public transportation, has been subsidized in a variety of ways.[19] There have been many reasons put forward to justify this. One is that there is the need to take distribution effects of transport into account when enacting policy. These distribution arguments may take many forms. At one extreme, the notion of sustainability advocated in the Brundtland Report,[20] represents a concept of temporal and spatial equity, and this notion has been bastardized and subsequently corrupted to provide alternative notions. More parochial are arguments about social and environmental justice at the local level and, in particular, the need to ensure that everyone has at least an acceptable level of accessibility or mobility (whichever is the concept in favour at the time).

In practice, there is little evidence that subsidies always help the poor and in many cases, they may well be extremely regressive in their impacts. For example, mainly middle-income commuters, more often than not use subsidized sub-urban rail systems purportedly designed to offer transport for lower-income groups into cities. Even subsidies to bus services that are mainly used by lower-income groups are often captured by higher-income earners. A case in point is where subsidies were given to local bus services in the UK. Analysis by the Transport Research Laboratory found that 50% of these ended up as higher remuneration for those working in the industry rather than in more affordable fares.

None of this is to say that subsidies are bad. Rather, it is to highlight the misperception that subsidizing public transport, however altruistic the motive, automatically helps the more needy in society. The monies involved are easily captured. Economists have long argued that actual money transfers are a much more effective way of assisting the poor and, because the recipients have the ability to use the spending power as they feel fit, this avoids the excessive perception of paternalism associated with earmarked assistance.

But there is another aspect to this. Where do we find most of the dirty, noisy, unsightly terminals, interchange points, and maintenance depots that are essential in the modern urban transport system? They are seldom located in areas inhabited by the prosperous. Added to this, the public transportation that is used in poorer areas in a large numbers of cities is often more environmentally damaging in itself than the motor car. In the US, for example, the pollution per passenger-mile generated by buses has exceeded that of automobiles since 1992. The decision-making mechanism of transport planning is easily captured by the articulate and the more powerful and that does not often lead to them accepting the less attractive parts of the system in their back yard.

Telecommunications offer the salvation

Technology is often seen as the solution. In this vein, telecommunications has become a panacea to many politicians for solving most of the transport problems in urban areas. It would, following the advocacy line, fostering intelligent transport systems that allow the existing infrastructure to be used more efficiently, whilst teleworking and video conferencing would reduce congestion and the environmental damage associated with urban transport. There is obviously some truth in this. Better information, guidance, and communications systems can allow infrastructure to be better used. But it inevitably also means more central control over this utilization through those that control the information flows. This raises matters of priority and preference.

Even more of a concern is the politically attractive belief that traffic congestion in urban areas can be solved by substitution of telecommunications for travel. At one level, there is the macro evidence that telecommunications is a complement to travel and that the growth of the former simply produces more of the latter. This should not be too much of a shock since communications makes it easier to arrange physical contacts.[21]

But there is another dimension to this that has not been fully examined. Advocates generally see urban traffic congestion as a peak load problem (the 'rush hour') and telecommunications not only as a way of reducing traffic *per se* (which would seem doubtful) but also as a means of reducing the peak by redistributing traffic across the day. The difficulty is that adaptation to a wider telecommunications, information-based society is inevitably going to have complex outcomes. Over time there has been a very broadly observed constancy (often called 'Zahavi's Constant',[22] but with a longer pedigree going back to nineteenth-century German work) in individuals' travel time budgets. People travel at different times, over different distances, and by different modes but still spend about the same amount of time per day on travel.[23] Telecommunications can add flexibility to choices but if the travel time budget holds true, there may be fewer aggregate transportation benefits and even potential disbenefits.

Giving flexibility in the work place provides scope for making more complex trips through networks designed primarily for radial traffic. Again, looking at the empirical evidence we have, there is a tendency for unrestrained traffic flows in major cities to move asymptotically to an equilibrium flow of about 10 mph (16 km/h).[24] More complex travel behaviour, and the inevitable increase in cross flows of traffic that this entails would effectively reduce capacity even at this low speed. It also puts public transport at an even greater disadvantage not only in terms of having to compete on a congested system but also to meet the demands of less concentrated traffic flows.

This should not be taken to imply that teleworking, teleshoppping, videoconferencing, and so forth have no social benefits. They most certainly do. They provide individuals with more choices and through this offer enhanced welfare for the individual and for companies. Whether they solve traffic congestion and pollution problems is entirely another matter.

We need more data

Researchers always want more numbers. The enhanced ability to grind through billions of data points in front of your eyes in a nanosecond is irresistible. Software makes data analysis so easy that clearly more of it should be done. There is of course some truth in this. A better empirical understanding of the situation can help create better-informed policy. But there are quality issues. These come at several levels. More data do not always mean better data. The massive land-use transportation models of the 1960s and 1970s gobbled up vast quantities of data, churned them around in computers comparable in size to the Empire State Building and spewed out plenty of unreliable parameters. Disaggregate modelling,[25] in contrast, uses much less data and has generated a whole range of fresh insights into the motivations for and reactions to transport.

There is also another element to the data requirement debate. Frequently, the request for more research data is not entirely neutral. It often comes from policy-makers who do not like the conclusions drawn from the existing data – hence they argue there is the need for more data or, as discussed below, the requirement for more research. Data collection is generally expensive and time consuming and it is usually difficult for other parties to claim that more information would be a bad thing. Hence, there is delay and the group demanding more data gains time to regroup and reposition itself. There has been little research done on the extent that more (generally couched in terms of 'better') data actually results in a new technical conclusion being drawn. But the gathering of these data has certainly delayed many a policy change.[26]

There is also the issue of how the data are used. The common myth is that they are pushed through objective models in a scientific, or at least quasi-scientific manner, to generate parameters, forecasts, and predictions of impacts. But is this really how it is done? In practice the process is much less scientific, and over ridden by personal judgment. The evidence, at least from a cursory glance through the journals sitting on my desk, is that 'Button's First Law of Econometrics' applies. If regressions are used then, for example, the R^2 must fall between 0.64 and 0.89 to be deemed acceptable – if it is lower then the fit is 'poor'; if it is higher then there arise questions about whether the results are being fudged to get a 'good' fit;[27] and when outside of this range, other specification or estimation procedures are obviously needed to 'correct' the model. Now if one is simply selecting the model according to personal preferences – or more often the narrow technical expectations of editors or clients – then there seems no good reason to try to improve on the data. After all, if the result is essentially predetermined then the quality and quantity of data really become very much a secondary concern.

We need more policy research

We have a problem, then let us do another study. But is that really always an efficient way of thinking of matters or are there quality domains in research as well as matters of sheer quantity? Michael Beesley[28] made the point (and not a popular one amongst academics seeking tenure) that good research in transport economics (but the point can be extended to other disciplines) essentially serves two purposes. First, it serves the needs of policy-makers and is relevant for their needs. Second, it serves the needs of researchers in terms of meeting career objectives. Following an extensive review of the research on urban transport matters in the 1970s and 1980s he went on to say that much of the resultant focus was in fact on 'making research anticipate, rather than follow, policy needs'. Of course things may have changed, although I think not by very much, or he may have been misguided in his original judgment.

One problem is that the research findings that we have are often poorly brought together. They appear in a range of different academic and professional outlets – economics, engineering, geography, planning, and so on – and are often presented in different 'languages' that makes dialogue between the various disciplinary interests troublesome. This spread of material is in part the result of the way the academic world works. University tenure and promotion requires publications and kudos that are more often associated with publishing in narrow, disciplined outlets than in subject or topic based media. Applied work is particularly frowned upon.[29] Additionally, much of the analysis used in transport policy analysis is to be found in the grey literature of reports and mimeographs. Gaining accesses is often not easy. But all-in-all large amounts of work there are.

There have been attempts to synthesize in some sub-areas of transportation analysis. Some of this has been through standard review procedures, but more recently, attention has also been paid to meta-analysis and subjective qualitative assessment.[30] The mining of the existing literature has proved effective in other fields of academic endeavour such as medicine and management science. It can offer indications of the robustness of findings and highlight what factors are important in explaining local conditions. The myth is that there is a need for a full local analysis every time a policy is initiated. This may well be the case in some instances, but in many others there is a body of research findings that can be applied, effectively allowing the research resources to be concentrated in areas where there are genuine gaps in our knowledge.

Policy-makers aim to serve the public interest

'Why do these myths and taboos still exist?' One answer comes from the institutional fact that policy-makers and their supposed executives often find it convenient to initiate or perpetrate them. Those currently involved in the transport sector are often willing to go along, and indeed foster this situation. The notion of public interest was long up-held as the driving force of policy, but the advent of new political and economic models involving coalitions of interest rather than individual objectivity, and the ability to capture rather than be responsible to societal needs, has brought this into doubt.

There have been some switches in power as coalitions of interest have changed, their objectives have altered, or the power of individual members has fluctuated. Indeed, this has been a major reason why there have been policy shifts in recent years.[31] Nevertheless, the road construction companies, the computer soft and hardware suppliers, and so on are hardly objective in their views. But added to this is the problem that many of those in bureaucracies are less familiar with wider public policy issues than with the technicalities of the modes over which they have policy responsibilities. (An interesting – but almost inevitably doomed – research agenda would be to look at the backgrounds of those who are making decisions.[32])

A related point that I have made elsewhere is very germane to this situation.[33] One thing that is very noticeable is that those concerned with transport industries have an active liking for their product. Go to the office of virtually anyone working in transport and you will find models or pictures (but mainly both) of planes, or trains or trucks (but very seldom more than one mode). Go to a civil engineer's office, and my personal and rigorous visual analysis assures me these must be decorated by framed shovels on the wall and small blocks of asphalt set in acrylic on the desk to serve as paper weights. I pass no judgments on images that appear on the neck-ties that I have seen. Casual empiricism suggests that this is not normal outside of transport. Venturing into the office of the chairman of a pet food company does not reveal pictures of offal on the wall or model cans in the display cabinet. Not even a chicken bone set in acrylic with which to stir the coffee. Whenever you visit a transport undertaking, it is almost inevitable that you enjoy a tram ride or a tour of a ship. Again, at pet food plants, sampling is not common and tours of plants unlikely. The providers and regulations of transport are too often advocates and lovers of their product rather than rational business people.[34]

Conclusions

So where does all this leave us? Actually very much where we always are. Humans, despite their supposed quest and thirst for knowledge, like the firm security of widely held beliefs. There is as much religion in transport policy as in every other aspect of human life. The past from which these myths came is often as murky and lost in time as that of any religion. As with religion, they also have positive virtues and limitations. They provide certain parameters and signals that ensure an overall consistency in the way affairs are conducted and a degree of temporal continuity. They are also seldom beliefs of a fundamentalist kind. They do evolve and they often have some flexibility although there are inevitably diehards who remain committed to some particular myth or refuse to violate a taboo.

Has this situation damaged the development of transport policy? That very much depends on the areas that one looks at. The lack of sensible pricing of roads over time almost certainly has imposed very significant costs on society and on the larger environment. Attempting to build one's way out of congestion has diverted massive amounts of resources from other, socially more useful, purposes. The resources wasted in the collection of largely unused data sets or to conduct what, even at the time of funding, was very peripheral research were in the larger order of things probably minimal (and even provided a Keynesian incentive by keeping otherwise unemployed researchers in jobs). Will the myths continue? Inevitably.

Notes

1   This chapter has been through a number of revisions and I would like thank those, including the referees of this volume, for their very helpful comments, even if I am not in agreement with some of them. The chapter remains my responsibility.
2   Button and Gillingwater (1986).
3   For example some interesting but excluded myths include; 'Public transport is good for the environment'; 'The private sector should not be interfered with' (something of the opposite of one myth that is discussed below); and 'That there is such a thing as 'fair' and 'efficient' pricing'.
4   I was recently asked at an air transport conference what would happen to US GDP if air transport were not included. My answer, essentially saying 'Not a lot', did not go down too well!
5   Fogel (1964).
6   Aschauer (1989).
7   Much travel is also discretionary in nature – for example in the US only about 15% of trips are for commuting reasons, down from 25% in 1969, with the bulk being for such activities as shopping.
8   Thomson (1974).
9   The inefficient way road space and other transport infrastructure is allocated can be seen as a confirmation of the well-known Gresham's Law – that bad money (here wasted time) drives out the good (currency).
10   Pigou initiated the idea of road pricing in Pigou (1912), and refined it in Pigou (1920). After an interchange with the American economist, Frank Knight, however, he dropped it from all other editions of the book accepting Knight's view that congestion was the result of public ownership of roads.
11   Although even the Wright Brothers, who had enormous enthusiasm for flight, rapidly patented their technology and defended the patent strongly. The financial motive often goes in conjunction with successful engineering.
12   Downs (1962).
13   Linked with this is the way that transport forecasting was traditionally done. The four-stage-model assumed that traffic generation was unrelated to changes in generalized costs, which was only considered to affect, O-D, mode and route choices. The 'discovery' of latent demand (i.e., that the aggregate demand curve for trip-making is not vertical) by modellers in the 1990s

despite the fact that in the 1850s French engineers appreciated its importance highlights a lack of appreciation of some very simple principles that transcend transport matters.

14 Despite the fact that within the EU only 8% of freight tonne-kilometres are carried by rail (and only about 15% if we limit the analysis to road and rail), rail accounts for over 50% of the core track. But if one thinks in value terms (and this seems to be reasonable since welfare depends on value not bulk) railways account for about 2% to 3% of the total – less than 6 months growth in the value of goods moved in the EU. Despite the obvious limitations of rail freight transport, the EU White Paper on European transport policy (European Commission, 2001) argues that transition economies should aim to carry 35% of their tonne-kilometres by rail. Since most of their traffic is coal moving to power stations, a more efficient and environmentally benign means of transport would seem to be to take the power stations to the mines and move the energy through a distribution grid. At a recent conference in Berlin on appropriate transport policy in the EU accession countries, most of the discussion was about rail and my intervention suggesting that one should look at the value of what they moved, rather than the bulk, seemed never to have occurred to most there.

15 If not then, a casual glance at the tables produced by the World Bank and more accessible calculations that regularly appear in the *Economist* should be sufficient to convince.

16 In a speech some years ago I suggested that privatization of the road system would be a good idea. Several members of the audience pointed to all the problems of congestion and coordination on roads and how these were getting worse and that this logically meant there should be more public sector control. I pointed out that all these problems were actually associated with a system that was already publicly owned and controlled and that more public ownership would not seem to be the logical solution. Unfortunately, I could tell from facial expressions that I was not convincing. Mind you, the speech was to the civil engineers of the Dutch Transport Planning Colloquium.

17 The classic case of this is the decision to put airport security under public control in the US after the tragic events of September 11, 2001. The fact that it appears the weapons taken aboard planes conformed to legal restrictions set by the public sector and that it appears from the evidence to date that the private security firms met their remit is ignored.

18 In terms of policies attempting to limit the environmental costs of transport there is ample evidence that many interventions are at best counter-productive, see Button (1992).

19 The fastest growing mode of public transportation, air transport, is subsidized much less and by decreasing amounts.

20 World Commission on Environment and Development (1987).

21 Button and Taylor (2001).

22 Zahavi (1977).

23 Mokhtarian and Bagley (2000) give some underlying support to travel time budgets in that they find commuters have preference for particular commute times.

24 Thomson (1997).

25 McFadden (2001).

26 For example, the European Union congratulated itself on gradualism in its liberalization of the internal air transport market as it learnt from US experience. This meant, however, that Europeans were deprived of many years of benefits from freer markets and, given current market developments, still have to endure the instabilities of the transition process.

27 A careful look at the seven journals sitting on my desk dealing with transport, economics and, regional science find that those with regressions all have final R^2s within the range I cite. In three cases, initially models had lower R^2s but suitable 'scientific' reassessment caused the authors to respecify the model.

28 Beesley (1989).

29 Some years ago I was involved in a survey of UK economists to elicit information about how much prestige they felt they obtained from publishing in various journals. Four fictitious journals, two with titles implying a theoretical bent and two with applied sounding titles, were included in the list. Quite a large number of respondents assumed they existed. Interestingly, they put the

theoretically sounding titles near the top of their lists and the applied ones at the bottom (Button and Pearce, 1977).

30 Button (1977).

31 Keeler (1984).

32 Linked to this is a point made some years ago by Stewart Joy, namely that on the railways, management worked their way up within the system and often when reaching the top spent their time dealing with some long defunct issue (Joy, 1973).

33 Button (1993).

34 I recently attended a high level conference on air transport capacity. After listening to the initial three speakers, they showed some puzzlement when I asked how they could present their papers without any mention of passengers or freight. It was all about how many aircraft could be squeezed into the skies. The number of passengers that could be carried (or wanted to be carried) or tons of freight that could be lifted apparently did not fit into their calculations.

Bibliography

Aschauer, D.A. (1989) Is public expenditure productive? *Journal of Monetary Economics*, **23**, pp. 177–200.

Beesley, M.E. (1989) Transport research and economics. *Journal of Transport Economics and Policy*, **23**, pp. 17–28.

Button, K.J. (1977) What can meta-analysis tell us about the implications of transport? *Regional Studies*, **29**, pp. 507–517.

Button, K.J. (1992) *Market and Government Failures in Environmental Policy: The Case of Transport*. Paris: OECD.

Button, K.J. (1993) *Transport Economics,* 2nd ed. Cheltenham: Edward Elgar.

Button, K.J. and Gillingwater, D. (1986) *Future Transport Policy*. London: Croom Helm.

Button, K.J. and Pearce, D.W. (1977) What British economists think of their journals. *International Journal of Social Economics*, 4, pp. 151–158.

Button, K.J. and Taylor, S.Y. (2001) Towards an economics of the internet and electronic commerce, in Brunn, S.D. and Leinbach, T.R. (eds.) *The Wired Worlds of Electronic Commerce*. London: Wiley.

Downs, A. (1962) The law of peak-hour express congestion. *Traffic Quarterly*, **16**, pp. 393–409.

European Commission (2001) *White Paper. European Transport Policy for 2010: Time to Decide*. Brussels: European Commission.

Fogel, R.W. (1964) *Railroads and American Economic Growth, Essays in Econometric History*. Baltimore: Johns Hopkins University Press.

German Ministry for Transport, Construction and Housing (2003) *Transport Political and Economic Transport Strategies of EU Enlargement*. Berlin: Deutsche Verkehrswissenschaftl iche Gesellscaft.

Joy, S. (1973) *The Train that Ran Away*. London: Ian Allan.

Keeler, T.E. (1984) Theories of regulation and the deregulation movement. *Public Choice*, **3**, pp. 399–424.

McFadden, D. (2001) Economic choice. *American Economic Review*, **91**, pp. 351–379.

Mokhtarian, P.L. and Bagley, M.N. (2000) Modeling employee's perceptions and proportional preferences of work locations: the regular workplace and telecommuting alternatives. *Transportation Research, Part A*, **34**, pp. 223–242.

Pigou, A. (1912) *Wealth and Welfare*. London: Macmillan.

Pigou, A. (1920) *The Economics of Welfare*. London: Macmillan.

Thomson, J.M. (1974) *Modern Transport Economics*. Harmondsworth: Penguin.

Thomson, J.M. (1997) *Great Cities and their Traffic*, London: Gollanez.

World Commission on Environment and Development (1987) *Our Common Future*. Oxford: Oxford University Press.

Zahavi, Y. (1977) Equilibrium between travel, demand, system supply and urban structure, in Visser, E.J. (ed.) *Transport Decisions in an Age of Uncertainty*, The Hague: Martinus Nijhoff.

Chapter 4

Overcoming barriers to the implementation of sustainable transport[1]

David Banister

Barriers to implementation

At one level, public policy-making on sustainable transport is straightforward, as it is more or less taken for granted that once a policy decision has been made the policy will be implemented, and the people will respond with the expected changes in behaviour. When the results of a policy fall short of their expectation, the people are blamed. Individuals regularly refuse to behave in ways that the policy-makers would prefer. This gap between the assumptions underlying policy measures on the one hand, and the behavioural responses by individuals on the other, is normally referred to as the policy behaviour gap. With reference to the gap between policy measures and behavioural responses to congestion, Salomon and Mokhtarian (1997) point to the large set of alternative strategies that individuals have at their disposal to avoid the expected behaviour. But 'non-rational' behaviour by the public may also be reinforced by poor implementation whereas the measure does not accomplish what was intended.

In the process of policy-making, there are not only expectations about the behaviour of the public, but also about the way a measure can be implemented. According to Smith (1973, p. 199), 'problems of policy implementation may be more widespread than commonly acknowledged'. If the programmes are of a new, non-incremental nature, difficulties with implementation may occur. One can imagine that this is the case with measures that try to introduce a sustainable transport policy. For example, fuel costs may be raised substantially to reduce the use of the car, but demand has been found to be relatively inelastic in the short term and in the longer term purchasing patterns may change. There is little evidence that car use has actually been reduced.

Part of the explanation is that there are several forces that prevent a measure from being implemented in its ideal form. These forces (or barriers) could either reduce the potential of a measure once implemented, or even make implementation impossible, at least in a form that might be effective. Barriers can be divided into six main categories:

1 Resource barriers are in essence very simple. To implement a measure, an adequate amount of financial and physical resources have to be available. If these resources are not available in time and in the right amount, implementation will be delayed. Lack of money for implementation is closely linked to institutional barriers, as local, regional, and governmental authorities are unlikely to provide money for schemes that do not concur with their policy priorities.

2 Institutional and policy barriers relate to problems with coordinated actions between different organizations or levels of government, and to conflicts with other policies. A large number of public and private bodies are involved in transport provision and this means that it is often difficult to achieve coordinated action by the implementing agency. Sometimes, this is due to differences in cultures between departments (for example, bureaucratic versus market orientated). In other cases, the distribution of legal powers between governmental bodies affects the implementation of measures and schemes. Also, the implementing organization itself has to be well equipped to accomplish the implementation job properly. An unstable administrative organization and unqualified personnel may reduce the capacity to implement (Smith, 1973).

3 Social and cultural barriers concern the public acceptability of measures. While some measures may theoretically be effective at promoting sustainable transport, their effectiveness is minimal if people do not accept their introduction or implementation. Social acceptability may often depend on whether the proposed strategy compromises 'push' or 'pull' measures (i.e. whether it is a strategy of discouragement or encouragement). On the whole, pull measures tend to be popular and may encourage, for example, an increase in the use of more sustainable modes of transport. Conversely, many people are reluctant to give up the perceived freedom associated with owning and using a car and so these push policies tend to be unpopular. Social acceptability involves the travelling public and local businesses and other organizations that will be affected by the implementation of a new measure.

4 Legal barriers. Many transport policies and measures need adjustment of laws and regulations, within or outside the realm of transport. If implementation is complicated by legal requirements or even made impossible by law, legal barriers are raised. They can occur at several levels. For example, in almost all countries the design and signposting of transport schemes are circumscribed by government regulations and directives. While many of these are beneficial in ensuring reasonable standards, others can impose restraints on innovative solutions. When good implementation requires changes in rules or regulation

outside the transport domain, one can expect that more effort must be put to facilitate these changes.

5 Side effects. Almost every measure has one or more side effects. If implementation of a measure has serious side effects, this may hinder other activities to such an extent that implementation becomes too complicated, even though these side effects may have only limited effects on the success of the measure itself. For instance, traffic calming does not only reduce the speed of cars, but also causes inconvenience to public transport, and it may bring about a change in the frequency and severity of traffic accidents. It is often difficult to anticipate both the positive and negative side effects, for example, of road pricing. But these side effects and the positive demonstration effects both play an important role in determining whether policies will be implemented more widely or not.

6 Other (physical) barriers could take the form of space restrictions or are related to the topography of an area. For example, there may not be adequate space on the outskirts of an urban area for the introduction of park and ride facilities, and the large parking areas they require. Hilly terrain may make the promotion of cycling impractical.

An empirical investigation of a wide range of policy measures has been undertaken (Banister and Marshall, 2000) to assess the scale of the barriers to implementation for public policies aimed at making transport more sustainable. Barriers, which occurred during policy-making and prevented measures from being implemented, are excluded from this analysis. Information was gathered by interviews with decision-makers and implementing agents. In a few cases, studies about the implementation process were available. These studies either consisted of pilot projects, which were implemented to gather information about how the measures were introduced, together with their results, or they were successful measures, which can be demonstrated as examples of good practice to other cities.

It was found that only one of the 61 policy measures reviewed was implemented without any form of a barrier (Figure 4.1). This was the handicapped bus stops measure in Aalborg (Denmark) – a good example of a very cheap 'pull' measure. The other measures had to cope with one or more barriers. There were two measures that encountered all barrier types. These were the development at public transport nodes in Bucharest (Romania) and traffic calming in Zürich (Switzerland).

Barriers may occur in various forms. Sometimes they are of limited importance, but in other situations, they can seriously hinder implementation. For each measure and barrier type, the influence of the barriers on the

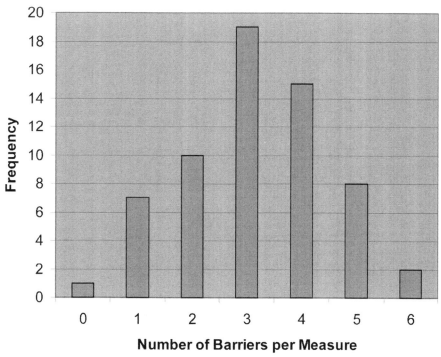

Figure 4.1 Frequency of the number of barrier types per measure

implementation process was assessed as to whether barriers had occurred or not, and if so why (Figure 4.2). The histogram presents the frequencies by the level of seriousness for each barrier type. This kind of visualization shows us the seriousness of barriers to implementation.

The results suggest that resource barriers occurred most frequently, followed by institutional/policy and social/cultural barriers. Side effects and physical/other barriers were the categories with the fewest entries. Looking at the seriousness of the barriers, it appears that most of them are real but were overcome. Within the resource category, the seriousness of the barrier hindered good implementation in 18% of the cases. Side effects hardly affected the implementation process at all.

It is easy to make an extensive list of barriers that occurred during implementation, but politicians have to balance various interests and spend money in the 'public interest'. A scheme is part of a wider policy or a package of measures, which is aimed at a particular goal, such as sustainable development, and transport is only one element in that policy. To achieve sustainable development, methods of analysis have to be extended beyond single sector analysis to explicitly include the effects of policy decisions. This lack of interaction between sectors is seen by Banister (1998) as one of the main

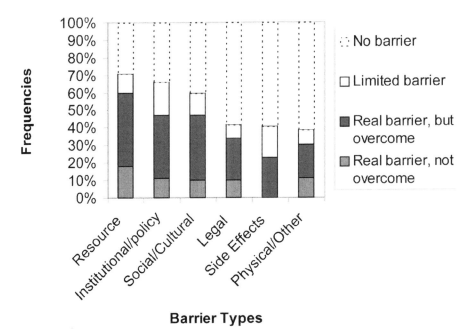

Barrier Types

Figure 4.2 Level of barrier seriousness per barrier type

barriers to achieving urban sustainability. A second set of barriers mentioned by Banister relates to the responsibilities of the decision-makers themselves. They do not seem to have a real political commitment to introducing measures to address the key issues in a comprehensive and consistent approach. In the next section, we elaborate on some of these issues as they relate to the means by which barriers to implementation can be overcome.

Overcoming barriers to implementation

The achievement of successful policy implementation requires leadership and a commitment to change. This thinking is particularly important where there are so many potentially conflicting interests, and where there is extreme complexity together with uncertain outcomes. Transport and spatial policies illustrate well all these concerns. Five framework conditions need to be addressed so that successful and consistent policy implementation can take place.

1 A national policy framework on spatial development should be established, which takes a long-term perspective and provides consistency within which individual decisions can be placed. This policy framework should be related to international and pan-European perspectives where similar complementary

statements should have been made. Such a requirement gets away from much of the fragmentation of decisions that is seen at the national level, and it would provide stability through a vertical integration within government, and a horizontal integration across sectors.

2 A sustainable transport strategy would form an important element within this national policy framework. As stated in the recent ECMT/OECD (2002) report, the key elements of such a strategy are now reasonably well known – maximize the use of public transport and green modes of transport; manage the private car through integrated transport and mobility management; minimize urban sprawl; and improve air quality through less fuel use and reductions in the emissions of pollutants.

3 Decentralization of powers and responsibilities for transport should be commensurate with the level of implementation, together with the necessary resources or revenue raising powers. To some extent, this change has taken place in many countries with governments providing national planning guidance for local authorities and other agencies to use in determining their own priorities. However, such a flexible and supportive national framework has been compromised by the limitations on the powers for those local agencies to raise funds for investment. The centre still controls the revenue raising mechanisms and the means by which the funds are distributed. Such action concentrates power at the centre and gives little incentive to innovate locally.

4 Consistency in policy direction is needed to prevent 'perverse effects' from occurring. Even though there may be strict limitations on where development can take place, peripheral greenfield development is still permitted, as there is a need for local authorities to increase their revenue base from local taxation on businesses and properties. As options are limited, local authorities are often keen to encourage development to improve local employment. These decisions have implications for the generation of traffic, and in the longer term on housing and other services and facilities. The land market may operate very effectively in determining different land-use values, but it needs to be placed within the clear framework of the national policy for spatial development and the sustainable transport strategy.

5 Public and private acceptability of policy underlies successful implementation. If controversial transport and spatial policies are to be introduced with outcomes that lead to behavioural change, then the issues of communication and involvement become a key concern. It is only when the implementation of a sustainable transport strategy, within the national policy framework on

spatial policy, is presented to the public (in a general sense) and accepted (at least in principle), that success is likely (but not guaranteed). This means that participation must move from the low levels of information and manipulation, to the higher levels of information and empowerment so that decisions relating to transport and spatial policy become accountable to the users (Putnam, 2001).

The implications of these five framework conditions are profound. They must be seen as a coherent whole or a package in themselves. Unless such an approach to implementation is taken, a range of outcomes will emerge that does not match up to the policy intentions. Such a conclusion can be illustrated with respect to travel reduction strategies that may lead to counter-intuitive outcomes (Marshall and Banister, 2000).

1 Non-complementary policies. These include cases where measures have been unsuccessful because of a lack of complementary policies or the presence of directly conflicting policies. For example, free tickets were introduced for students on public transport in the Netherlands (1991), and this led to a reduction of cycle travel in Enschede between 1991 and 1994 of about 14%.

2 Direct incentives to travel more. These include cases in which a particular measure directly encourages more travel. For example, subsidies (82% for buses in Bucharest in 1997) may be devised to increase travel by public transport but, unless there are any disincentives to travel by other modes, travel overall simply increased.

3 Improving system efficiency. These include cases where travel reduction is activated to some extent, but the very act of removing traffic or journeys frees up more road space or vehicles to be used by others. Thus, the initial travel reduction feeds back to generate a net increase in travel.

4 Contradictory outcomes. These include cases where more travel was generated despite the intention of the measure to reduce travel. In Aalborg (Denmark), a parking information system was introduced (1995) to reduce the distance travelled to search for a parking space and improve the overall efficiency of the road system. But it seems that as it is now easier to park, more people may be using their cars.

5 Change without improvement. These include cases where measures have achieved some change, but where no improvement in terms of travel reduction has been achieved. For example, mode switching from bicycle and walking to public transport, or destination switching that does not reduce trip distance.

6 Absence of evidence or negligible impact. These include cases where the

travel reduction impact of a measure is negligible, or the evidence is weak or inconclusive and effects cannot be attributed explicitly to the measure. In Edinburgh there are new car free developments and innovative car sharing schemes, but in both cases as the (successful) experiments are so small it is very difficult to measure their impact on the city as a whole.

7 Non-acceptance or lack of uptake by users. These include cases where the measures have not been accepted or used by the public. In Zürich, the bicycle lanes have not been used, perhaps because of the high quality public transport, or the hilly terrain, or the incompleteness of the bicycle network, or because of the lack of secure storage, or because the traffic signal system does not give cyclists any advantage, or a combination of these (and other) reasons.

More generally, these types of outcomes can be grouped together and linked back to the barriers identified above, and these limitations are summarized in Table 4.1.

Table 4.1 Classic tactics for ineffective implementation

Indecision	Outcomes	Example
1 Inadequate funding – fiscal constraints.	No implementation, or delayed or partial action.	Package of measures for a city accepted, but only partially introduced for financial reasons. Important to provide investment in public transport as an alternative mode prior to restrictions on the use of the car being imposed.
2 Ill-defined legal and regulatory rules – legal constraints.	Legal challenges and delays in implementation.	Road pricing could be introduced, but challenged in the courts on the basis of lack of consultation, or human rights concerns over privacy and use of information.
3 Sectorization of policy-making – no coherence.	Lack of awareness of indirect effects of policy actions.	City centre strategy of car restraint works well, but growth allowed in peripheral areas so net effect is more travel.
4 Opaqueness of responsibilities for decisions between agencies – conflict.	Partial implementation and no clear rationale for action.	Construction of new housing in peripheral locations leads to longer car based work journeys. Closure of local schools and hospitals lead to longer journeys.
5 Partial implementation – no commitment.	Unclear or inconsistent messages.	Package of measures for a city accepted, but only partially implemented for political (or other) reasons, thus reducing its effectiveness.
6 Lack of debate and involvement – no consultation	No change in behaviour and public resentment.	Plans introduced to encourage modal shift from car to public transport or cycle, but little change takes place due to inappropriate implementation or non acceptance by users.

As with much of the research in this difficult area, it is relatively easy to identify implementation failures, but progress can only be made if good practice is combined with the five framework conditions outlined above. The five conditions all really relate to structural problems, and the allocation of responsibilities to the key decision-makers. It is here that there are also problems relating to inertia, professionalism, and a general resistance to change, as particular stakeholders might perceive that they would be in a loss situation. There are further questions relating to the capabilities of decision-makers in terms of technical skills and resources available, and in terms of their motivations.

The net result of these constraints would suggest that it is remarkable that any policy change is actually ever implemented. But the structural problems must be seen in their social and cultural context. It is argued that in addition to being explicit about the five framework conditions, the *process of implementation* must be examined from its formulation, through its enactment, to the monitoring of outcomes so that we can learn from the demonstration effects. This is the approach adopted in TRANSPLUS (2002*a* and *b*), where a difference has been drawn between actors, areas, and instruments in their compatibility analysis. A framework has been developed to ensure that comparison between policy objectives is valid in the sense that there are similar contextual factors in operation. Policies can only be *translated* from one situation to another if there is institutional compatibility. If there is no institutional compatibility, then policies can be *transplanted*

Table 4.2 Checklist approach to overcoming barriers

1 Responsibilities	Overlapping responsibilities – spatial, organizational, planning. Underlapping responsibilities – gaps. Need for clear allocation of tasks.
2 Coordination	Vertical and horizontal coordination – within government at all levels, across sectors and modes, between agencies and professionals – must involve all relevant actors.
3 Technical	To cover analysis, complexity, forecasting, monitoring and evaluation. Agreement on technical case for package of measures, not just individual measures.
4 Traditions	Technical quantitative and discursive qualitative approaches to be reconciled. Compatibility between long-term and short-term policy objectives.
5 Financial	Centralized control with distribution to localities and locally raised resources. Availability and control of budgets, and phasing of investment and accountability.
6 Innovation	Risk taking and interest in radical policy or incremental change. Commitment to real change and achievement of national spatial policies and the sustainable transport strategy.

with the necessary institutional change (TRANSPLUS, 2002*b*). In addition to issues relating to compatibility, the *checklist approach* might help anticipate potential implementation barriers (Table 4.2).

As part of the evaluation carried out on a package of measures to be introduced, there would be two types of *barrier analysis* carried out. One would identify the type of barrier (see above) and the other would consist of a checklist of issues to be addressed (Table 4.2). Not all of these issues would be relevant in each case, but they would help identify where possible difficulties might arise and anticipate where there is a high probability of effective action or a possibility of ineffective action (Table 4.1). The way the checklist could be used would be in a *policy forum* where the proposals are discussed with all relevant stakeholders and the barriers to effective implementation are discussed in turn. This is a continuing process that involves a partnership between the public and private sectors and the users.

Congestion charging in Central London

Such an approach has been adopted in London with respect to the most controversial transport policy package to reduce levels of traffic congestion and to make the centre of London a 'liveable city'. The core of that strategy is congestion charging, which is a fairly straightforward (if radical) policy intervention, yet it provides an excellent example of the numerous barriers to implementation and how they have been overcome through extensive consultation on the transport strategy (GLA, 2000*a*), the scrutiny committee's review (GLA, 2000*b*), an extensive programme of public consultation (Table 4.3), and culminating in the London Plan (GLA, 2002).

The process of consultation first addressed the questions of the principles of congestion charging. This has formed part of government policy (since 1998) and the Mayor of London's campaigning strategy (2000). Since then there has been a wide debate on the scheme in London, including the charges, the area covered, the time when charges would be enforced, and improvements in public transport. Once the principle had been accepted, questions of detail were then discussed. These included exemptions and discounts, monitoring and enforcement, entrances to the cordon area, and the schedule for implementation. These questions are summarized in Table 4.4.

The pathways to successful implementation are outlined in this table, but even after this extensive process has taken place, there were still barriers to be overcome prior to implementation (for example, testing the reliability of the technology, the level of registrations on the database, and reliability of the different payment systems). Interactive planning (in the Netherlands) or community participation (in the UK) combines the decision-making and implementation processes through the involvement of both politicians and

Table 4.3 Overcoming barriers to successful implementation – the London congestion charging example

Congestion Charging
Single sector policy, but a key part of a complex range of strategies for transport in London and the desire to make London a liveable city.

Rationale
Mainly to address the problem of congestion in Central London, but also to raise revenue for investment in transport and to achieve environmental objectives on air quality.

Barriers
1   Resource barriers – level of charges: effectiveness of charging and use of funds.
2   Institutional and policy barriers – potential very high, but powers devolved to Mayor from central government: Still threat of legal challenges and need to involve all major stakeholders in London.
    (a)   Social and cultural barriers – equity: reinvestment of revenues in public transport, but adverse impacts on shift workers and low-income car users.
    (b)   Social and cultural barriers – business impacts: greater efficiency and reliability, and can pass on costs.
    (c)   Social and cultural barriers – public acceptance: hypothecation of revenues and extensive consultations to gain acceptability.
3   Legal barriers – requirement for vehicles to display licence: legislation changed.
4   Side effects – boundary pressures: eventually to be overcome by a full road pricing scheme and a flexible boundary, but at present traffic management to ease increase in traffic at boundary and to accommodate diverted traffic.
5   Physical barriers – not that important, but some debate over whether the area for congestion charging should extend south of the River Thames or end at the river (a natural barrier).

Implementation Issues
1   Principle of congestion charging: accepted politically and publicly, and by business interests.
2   Area of charging: limit number of entry and exit points and turning movements.
3   Boundary effect: north of River Thames or to the South as well, and congestion around the edge of the cordon.
4   Charges and time of scheme: flat rate or vehicle related rate, and time of scheme operation, including weekdays only or weekends as well.
5   Exemptions and discounts: residents: reduced rate of charging at 10% of full rate. Exemptions include – cleaner vehicles, cycles and motorcycles, taxis and buses.
6   Monitoring and exemptions: Fine of £80.
7   Timing: introduced in Spring 2003 during school half term and historically when traffic demand in London is at an annual low.

Longer Term Issues
1   Property market effects, including land values, rent levels and returns inside and outside the charging area.
2   Development effects, including pressures inside and immediately outside charging area.
3   Employment effects inside and outside charging area.
4   London wide impact on image of city

Note: The barriers section of the table relates back to the six barriers raised (pages 55–56) and the implementation issues relate forwards to those highlighted in Table 4.4.

other stakeholders, including the general public. This is done not by a formal public inquiry procedure, but by creating awareness and debate with all parties

Table 4.4 A summary of the means by which barriers to implementation have been overcome

Barrier	Original proposal July 2001	Consultation – issues raised	Final proposal March 2002
Principle of congestion charging	Central part of London's Transport Strategy	Widespread support – alternatives suggested included massive improvement of public transport or workplace parking levies – still a funding shortfall.	No change, but the scheme 'go-live' date will be reviewed in October 2002. If improvements in public transport not ready, then the Scheme may be delayed.
Area of charging	Zone is 21km^2 or 1.3% of of Greater London – Inner Ring Road with 174 entry/ exit points	Scheme should have wider boundaries (e.g. the North and South Circular roads) or be restricted to the area North of the Thames	No changes made – one minor modification to allow access to a petrol station in Park Lane – in the longer term extensions may be made.
Boundary effects	On Inner Ring Road where no charge will be levied	Increased flows on Inner Ring Road from diverted traffic and local roads affected. Modelling suggests that there is the capacity available, even around the hotspot of Tower Bridge	No change, but the traffic changes will be monitored.
Charges and time of operation	£5 for cars and van, £15 for lorries 07.00-19.00 on weekdays	Hostility to higher charges for lorries as many of their journeys are unavoidable. A standard charge may be regressive. But technical problems of intro-ducing a full road pricing scheme as in Singapore. This may happen later. No discounts for weekly, monthly or annual passes.	£5 for all vehicles. Charges apply to each vehicle for each day, so allowing more than 1 trip by the same vehicle within the day. 07.00 – 18.30 on weekdays.
Exemptions and discounts	Some 16 categories of exemptions and discounts	Caused huge difficulties. Some wanted no exemptions and others many more categories. Essential journeys cannot be defined individually. Some changes to help schools, voluntary bodies, some NHS staff and patients, firefighters and disabled people (Disabled blue badge holders).	Some changes in the categories and residents (90% reduction) discount area extended to 3 small areas outside the charging zone. Private hire vehicles and minicabs on hire will also be exempt, as will alternative fuel vehicles (not just mono fuelled gas vehicles), breakdown and recovery vehicles, and emergency service vehicles.
Monitoring and enforcement	Penalty charge of £80, reduced to £40 if paid within two weeks and raised to £120 for non payment after 28 days	Enforcement cameras at boundary points and monitoring cameras throughout the charging zone.	No change – number plate recognition cameras at entry points will match vehicles coming in with the database and photo-graph those in violation for penalty charges.
Timing of scheme introduction	To be introduced by early 2003	Assured that the technology will work and that the scheme will be effective. Extensive trials of the full system in Autumn 2002.	Implementation of Congestion Charging in Central London 17 February 2003.

involved. The goal of interactive planning is to bridge the gap between politics and citizens, to democratize decision-making and to create public support.

Congestion charging in Central London provides an excellent example of how a radical and potentially unpopular policy can be successfully implemented. Full consultation and debate took place with all stakeholder interests over a 24 month period, and certain concessions were made (Table 4.4 and Banister, 2003), but crucially, there was support from businesses, most local authorities, the transport operators, some of the general public, with reservations coming from small businesses, retailers, some leisure interests (for example, hotels and restaurants), and some low paid car dependent workers. Implementation would not have taken place without the guaranteed hypothecation of the revenues for transport investment and the general support from businesses and other key interests. Implementation (17 February 2003) has resulted in increases of 10–15% in Central London speeds (including a 15% increase in bus speeds) and a 20% reduction in traffic levels. In terms of acceptability, a MORI poll in March 2003 showed 50% of Londoners backing the scheme, with some 34% against it. This was a mirror image of a poll carried out in December 2002, which showed 50% of Londoners against the scheme and only 34% in favour of it.

Comments

Macro level policies (often outside the transport sector) can have substantial impacts on transport. Transport is a unique sector in that it links together activities carried out by individuals and firms. This means that it should not be dealt with in isolation, but as part of any composite evaluation. Decisions made in each sector have transport implications – these include the housing sector, the location of businesses, recreational facilities, shops, schools, health services, and a multitude of other factors. It is also an argument for taking a holistic approach to evaluation and not just looking at the costs and benefits to the funding agency, but to include the broader implications on transport and other sectors.

A clear set of relationships is required that links the policies to those directly and indirectly affected by them. At present, too much policy-making is taken at a level that is remote from those affected by it. This means involving not just the general public in the debates about transport, but those other decision-makers that have an influence on it. Many decisions are taken within one particular sector without any serious attention being given on the impacts across sectors. In some cases, these decisions have major effects on the transport system, not just in the immediate term but also in the longer term. It could be argued that many of the transport solutions are really only 'fire fighting' as the cause of the problem lies in decisions over which those in the transport sector have no control. It also suggests that there is a need for new thinking on how policy-making can be made more complementary between sectors as well as mutually reinforcing within sectors.

Most analysis hypothesizes rather simple linkages, but the reality is much more complex and subtle in its effects. Pricing strategies, for example, may result in little apparent change in travel, leading to the conclusion that travel demand is inelastic. Yet, in the longer term people may use more efficient cars and make many other adjustments to their travel patterns. Similarly, land-use strategies may result in shorter journeys for those living in higher density urban locations, but this effect may be overwhelmed by the movement of other people out of cities to lower density locations with longer trip lengths.

Where empirical evidence is available (Banister and Marshall, 2000), the impacts may seem small, as many changes take time to impact and the adjustments are in several directions. Some people may travel less, but others more. Much analysis tries to assess the net effects rather than identifying and measuring the different types of linkages. Analysis must therefore begin to move away from cause and effect as a simple representation of reality to developing the full range of effects (or chains) that actually take place.

Public policy should enhance the reasoning ability of the population through enlarging the scope of public discourse. This in turn will enhance and reinforce democratic processes. All through this chapter, the importance of the involvement and commitment of all actors has been emphasized to raise their awareness, to gain their support, and to empower them to take action. Within transport, there is an acceptance that not all decisions are market based, and that even if the market did operate efficiently in transport, it would not be democratic. Markets operate well in certain well-specified situations, but they are subject to many distortions from powerful corporate and governmental institutions. Institutional approaches to public policy-making encourage community and corporate involvement and empowerment.

Overcoming barriers to effective implementation requires interactive and participatory processes, so that intentions and outcomes of policy interventions on sustainable transport coincide. This means that individualism needs to be moderated and there must be an increased acceptance of collective responsibility in decisions related to transport. This would result in modal shifts to public transport and green modes, less use of the car, higher vehicle occupancy levels, targeted programmes for companies, shops and schools, car free areas in cities, and strong media and governmental support.

As part of the change in values and attitudes, there should be a clear and open debate on the issues, linked with positive actions to create choices. The broader issues related to sustainability and the environment need to be linked to individual travel decisions and lifestyles. There must be an awareness of the benefits and a willingness to change. If these vital elements are not present, then it is very difficult in a democratic society to pursue a policy of sustainable transport, and decision-makers should recognize what is possible and what is not possible to achieve.

Note

1. This research was carried out by the EU DGVI DANTE Consortium in six European cities – Aalborg (Denmark), Bristol (UK), Bucharest (Romania), Enschede (Netherlands), Rome (Italy) and Zurich (Switzerland) – and is published in Banister and Marshall (2000). An earlier version of this chapter was presented at the STELLA Focus Group 5 meeting on Institutions, Regulations and Markets in Transportation, Brussels, April 2002. Stephen Marshall helped with much of the conceptual thinking behind this chapter.

Bibliography

Banister, D. (1998) Barriers to implementation of urban sustainability. *International Journal of Environment and Pollution*, 10, pp. 65–83.

Banister, D. (2003) Critical pragmatism and congestion charging in London. *International Social Science Journal*, **176**, pp. 174–190.

Banister, D. and Marshall, S. (2000) *Encouraging Transport Alternatives: Good Practice in Reducing Travel*. London: The Stationery Office.

ECMT/OECD (2002) *Implementing Sustainable Urban Travel Policies*. Paris: ECMT/OECD.

Greater London Authority (2000a) Transport Strategy for London, London: GLA. Online. Available HTTP: <www.london.gov.uk>.

Greater London Authority (2000b) Congestion Charging. The London Assembly Scrutiny Report Number 1. London: GLA.

Greater London Authority (2002) *The London Plan*. London: GLA. Online. Available HTTP: <www.london.gov.uk>.

Marshall, S. and Banister, D. (2000) Travel reduction strategies: Intentions and outcomes. *Transportation Research, Part A*, **34**, pp. 321–338.

Putnam, R. (2001) Social capital measurement and consequences, in Helliwell, J.F. (ed.) *The Contribution of Human and Social Capital to Sustained Economic Growth and Well Being*. Proceedings of an OECD/HDRC Conference, Quebec, 19–21 March 2000. Quebec: OECD/Statistics.

Salomon, I. and Mokhtarian, P. (1997) Coping with congestion: reconciling behavioural responses and policy analysis. *Transportation Research, Part D*, **2**., pp. 107–123.

Smith, T.B. (1973) The policy implementation process. *Policy Sciences*, **4**, pp. 197–209.

TRANSPLUS (2002a) *Assessment of Barriers*. Deliverable 4.1 from the DG TREN Project on Transport Planning, Land Use and Sustainability, June, Restricted.

TRANSPLUS (2002b) *Methodological Framework for Compatibility Analysis*. Deliverable 4.2 from the DG TREN Project on Transport Planning, Land Use and Sustainability, July, Public. Online. Available HTTP: <www.isis-it.com/transplus.htm>.

Chapter 5

Barriers to transport pricing[1]

Barry Ubbels and Erik Verhoef

Road transport is known to generate considerable external costs, in particular in the form of congestion, noise, and emissions of pollutants. Economists have often advocated that these costs should be properly reflected in prices, otherwise over-consumption of road transport would generally result. In recent years, considerable theoretical research has been undertaken regarding the effectiveness of implementing urban transport pricing projects. It has been shown that various pricing measures may give rise to substantial welfare benefits for urban populations. According to standard welfare economic theory, prices should equate marginal social cost throughout the economy to obtain maximum efficiency (see also Ubbels, 2002). However, in addition, other (second-best) pricing measures may lead to considerable welfare benefits. For example, applied congestion pricing schemes may not fully reflect all social costs of the trips involved, but may lead to considerable congestion reductions and overall welfare gains to society. Traditional forms of pricing policies in road transport, such as vehicle taxes, will often be too crude to achieve anything near the welfare gains that a more targeted and refined system of road pricing would yield.

Despite this transport economists' preference for more refined road pricing, it is only rarely implemented in practice. Apparently, the implementation of congestion pricing (let alone marginal cost-based pricing) is not as straightforward as it may seem after calculating the welfare gains. Indeed, significant barriers can be identified that may prevent a smooth and easy implementation of pricing policing. As a result, all sorts of constraints can be identified that prevent a regulator from charging the prices that it ideally would like to set. For instance, it is still technologically difficult (and hence expensive) to charge drivers according to the marginal social costs caused. Nevertheless, electronic road pricing has been successfully applied in various places, demonstrating that it becomes increasingly possible, at least technically, to differentiate road prices over time and place. Other barriers are still relevant, acceptability being one of them. Congestion pricing schemes have the double consequence of discouraging transport use, at least at certain times on certain parts of the network, and of transferring cash from private persons to other (often public) parties. Especially the latter fact is likely to be a major impediment to its public and hence political acceptability. Therefore, to render pricing schemes politically and publicly acceptable, it is probably necessary to 'recycle' the revenues in certain ways.

Apart from public acceptability, institutional barriers have also received increasing attention over recent years. An important sub-set of institutional barriers arises through the conflicting interests that different governments may have amongst themselves, as well as through differences between governments and other organizations.

This chapter deals with these issues, and focuses on acceptability of road transport pricing and the role of revenue use, both in relation to each other and institutional barriers to implementation of transport pricing. We start with an overview of barriers to road pricing. Then, we focus on the acceptability of road pricing schemes, with particular attention for the role of revenue use in this. There follows a discussion on institutional barriers, and in particular the interactions between institutional (organizational) barriers and public acceptability, and finally some concluding remarks.

Barriers to road pricing

Prices provide signals to buyers and users about costs. This will affect the demand for the good or service, and for its substitutes. Increasing costs in private road transport may, for instance, induce people to use public transport instead. There is a well-developed transport economic theory to determine appropriate prices, including justifications for subsidies in public transport, and for the introduction of point-of-use road pricing to encourage greater efficiency. The concept underlying optimal transport pricing is that of marginal cost pricing. In principle, an efficient transport system requires users to pay the full costs of their travel, including any external costs. A primary motivation for the use of marginal cost pricing is thus that individuals, when confronted with prices that reflect the marginal social cost of their choices, would exhibit behaviour that not only maximizes their own utility given the prices they face, but also results in an equilibrium that maximizes the social objective (Verhoef, 2002). These optimal charges should then vary along with variations in marginal external costs caused by individuals.

Since transport externalities include a large variety of effects, first-best optimal individual charges may have to vary over many dimensions (see Verhoef, 2000). This would in practice require the use of electronic road charges, ideally using sophisticated technologies that can monitor actual emissions, place and time of driving, driving style and prevailing traffic conditions. It is clear, therefore, that there may be various barriers that would hinder the implementation of such first-best pricing policies in practice. First-best pricing is therefore mainly used by researchers as a benchmark, to compare the results of more realistic second-best pricing measures with that of the optimal situation.

An additional complication is that the optimality of marginal social cost pricing only holds under certain further conditions, which often do not hold in reality. These include assumptions on perfect information, but also that other markets do not show distortions. Clearly, these assumptions will not normally be met in reality. An example is that labour markets are typically distorted as a result of taxation.

In conclusion, it is one thing to compute first-best prices for a transport model and calculate the resulting social benefits; it is quite a different thing to design an efficient pricing scheme for a real-world situation, as required for actual implementation. The transport analyst has full control over his model, whereas a regulator faces all sorts of constraints that may prevent him from designing and implementing the desired pricing scheme. Under such conditions, the government has to resort to second-best pricing. We will now discuss most prevalent barriers to the implementation of first-best pricing, many of which also apply to pricing measures in general (this draws on Verhoef, 2002). We will distinguish three main categories of barriers, indicated in Table 5.1 (adapted from Verhoef 2003), and some sub-categories.

Table 5.1 Classification of barriers to transport pricing

1	Technological and practical barriers
2	Acceptability barriers
2a	Public
2b	Political (see also below under 3b)
2c	Business
3	Institutional barriers
3a	Organizational structures
*	On the 'regulator's side'
*	On the 'regulatees' side'
3b	Political (see also above under 2b)
3c	Legal

Technological and practical barriers

As indicated, road pricing prices should ideally involve charges that vary continuously over time, place, route chosen, driving style, type of vehicle and its technical state, etc. It is clear that the resulting pricing scheme may be too complex to be understood by car drivers, and may require more sophisticated pricing and monitoring technologies than currently available. For instance, for realistic road pricing schemes, one would expect differentiation over user classes to be possible only for a crude distinction into passenger cars, vans and trucks; over time up to the level of a few steps during the peak and one level outside it, at a maximum; and tolls to be charged on a few key-roads (for example, main highways) in the network, only.

From a recent study in the Netherlands, it appears that the technology for a nation-wide kilometre charge is in principle available (see Ubbels *et al.*, 2002). However, the study foresaw that it might take some additional time to test the reliability even for a relatively simple nation-wide system that 'only' determines the time and location of the vehicle. The development of systems that would vary charges over other aspects, such as driving style and emissions, would of course take longer. It is presumably a good strategy, when starting with a relatively simple system (allowing for a crude time and place differentiation only), to choose a technology that would in principle allow for further sophistication of price differentiation in the future.

In some sense, technological barriers as sketched above can, of course, be interpreted as 'financial barriers': the required technologies may exist, but may as yet be too expensive to offer attractive possibilities.

Other practical barriers that can be distinguished would be insufficient knowledge on marginal external cost figures, inadequate transport models and procedures for predicting equilibrium levels of second-best optimal road taxes, and so forth. Provided tax levels do not have to be fixed for a long period of time, it is to be expected that deviations between predicted and actual behavioural responses may lead to adaptation of initial tax levels for these reasons.

Acceptability barriers

It is broadly believed that probably the greatest barrier to implementation is the public, and linked to this political, acceptability (Jones, 1998). These issues will be discussed further below (see 'Acceptability and revenue use'). In brief, public attitude surveys have identified a wide range of concerns about innovative proposals to charge drivers more directly instead of the current taxes on ownership and purchase of cars. For instance, drivers find it difficult to accept that they should pay for congestion. Furthermore, the public often thinks that it is not needed, unfair and not effective. In addition, local businesses may be opposed to the implementation of (congestion) charging schemes, mainly motivated by a fear of losing patronage. These concerns may lead to the abolition of schemes (as happened in Stockholm and Hong Kong). Alternatively, acceptability concerns may create a situation in which, for instance, a constraint on the maximum level of charges is pre-specified.

Finally, there is a clear correspondence between public and political acceptability in a democracy – where the chances of being re-elected depend on the extent to which voters appreciate the policies implemented. Politicians' perceptions of the public acceptability of transport pricing schemes – in particular for their specific voter population – may of course affect the position they take in transport pricing issues.

Institutional barriers

Various types of institutional barriers can be distinguished. One category of institutional barriers arises when the organization of government bodies is such that there is no single regulator that can set all transport (related) prices and taxes so as to maximize social welfare throughout the system. An example is where a local or regional government either cannot affect some transport charges that are set by a higher level government (e.g. fuel taxes), or has to accept lower and/or upper limits on charges allowed, set by a higher level government. Another example is when the government in one jurisdiction cannot affect the prices charged by a neighbouring jurisdiction, while trans-boundary traffic and/or externalities are relatively important. The two governments may then end up in some form of tax competition.

Comparable problems may arise when public transport is operated by a private party who is relatively free in choosing prices and service levels but does so in a socially non-optimal way, or when private toll roads exist in an otherwise publicly controlled road network.

Furthermore, the efficiency of transport pricing can be maximized only if other government bodies – for instance, the Ministry of Finance – would adjust taxes (e.g. on labour) and subsidies (e.g. on commuting cost tax deductions) that are outside the control of the transport authority in charge of the transport prices – for instance, the Ministry of Transport. Indeed, transport has – arguably more than any other economic activity – direct links with numerous other economic sectors and markets. This means that the transport regulator will have to take into account that (changes in) transport prices may affect the equilibria of numerous other markets, many of which will be distorted and might thus call for an upward or downward adjustment of those transport prices. Among the most important of these other markets would typically be the labour market, where relatively high marginal tax rates may lead to a serious under-supply of labour, calling for a downward adjustment in transport taxes when its price effect dominates the labour supply decision, or an upward adjustment when the revenues are used to lower labour taxes and this revenue effect appears to dominate. Another example would be freight transport for goods that create environmental pollution in their production process, typically calling for an upward adjustment in transport prices as this might offer an indirect way of taxing a polluting firm's output. The existence of inefficiencies in the various markets 'served' by transport thus create constraints that should be taken seriously in setting transport prices. Institutional barriers arise when these other taxes – and related policies – are the domain of government bodies other than the transport authority in charge of the transport pricing scheme.

In all such cases, institutional barriers may prevent optimal pricing from being attainable.

But institutional barriers may also arise on the 'regulatees' side'. In particular, the regulatees may be organized in powerful lobby organizations such as automobile associations, labour unions, chambers of commerce, etc. Moreover, these organizations may join forces in their opposition against transport pricing implementation. As we will see below ('Interactions between acceptable and institutional barriers'), this may create further institutional barriers to its implementation.

Political barriers

Political barriers were mentioned above as a sub-type of acceptability barriers. Of course, political barriers can also be viewed as a specific type of institutional barrier. This underlines that the distinction between the different types of barrier need not always be crystal clear, in particular not when there are interactions between different barriers. In any case, it is not inconceivable that in democracies, especially where coalition governments are in office, the level of charges and the design of a pricing scheme become political issues much more than economic questions. In such cases, deals between political parties accepting the implementation of marginal cost-based pricing may create limitations on the types of charges and the flexibility that can be implemented.

Legal barriers

One may finally distinguish legal barriers as a specific type of institutional barrier. It may not always be possible to charge the ideal prices on the basis of legal arguments. For instance, suppose that the law implies that the level of taxes should be predictable to the tax payer. However, congestion is to some extent unpredictable (for example, due to weather conditions or road works). Therefore the optimal congestion charge would vary not only over the day, but also between days. A legal barrier might then exist preventing the implementation of this latter type of variation.

Acceptability and revenue use

Economists have often demonstrated the benefits of road pricing measures. The increased efficiency means that everyone can potentially be made better off, and that the winners are in principle able to compensate the losers. Nevertheless, practical implementation is only rarely the case. Over the last 40 years many attempts have been made to introduce urban road pricing around the world, and most of them have failed. Examples of schemes that have never been implemented include Stockholm, Hong Kong and the Netherlands. In most cases extensive studies had demonstrated the technical feasibility and economic benefits of introducing the scheme, but the problem was public and political acceptability. This aspect has received inadequate attention, in the apparent belief that a scheme which shows strong social and economic benefits would sell itself.

It is vital for the design of any transport pricing measure that, in addition to devising a technically robust system, the public and politicians need to understand the reason for implementation. Despite the fact that politicians and the public regard traffic problems in cities as a very important and urgent issue, people may have several concerns about road pricing. These concerns are very much related to the previous constraints, but specifically refer to the notions and opinions of the public. The policy-maker should consider these before implementing pricing measures of any kind. The concerns often mentioned include (Jones, 1998):

- It is difficult for drivers to accept the notion that they should pay for congestion, it seems irrational and inappropriate.

- Car users feel that urban road pricing is not needed, it is a publicly provided good that is free at the point of use.

- Pricing will not lessen congestion, it is an ineffective measure because drivers will be inelastic to road charges.

- The measure will result in unacceptable privacy issues. This issue played an important role in the discussion on kilometre charging in the Netherlands.

- Road pricing will face implementation problems such as unreliable technology and boundary issues.

- Road pricing is considered to be unfair.

In order to meet these concerns so as to obtain some level of acceptability and make a transport pricing measure more likely, the spending of revenues is likely to play an important role. For example, Verhoef (1996) asked morning peak road users their opinion on road pricing. An overwhelming majority (83%) indicated that his or her opinion depended on the allocation of revenues.

The opinion of businesses on the other hand seems to depend very much on the perceived effectiveness with regard to time savings. An analysis of the economic effects of road pricing in Utrecht (the Netherlands) indicates that companies are positive as long as time savings are expected to compensate for road pricing costs (see PATS, 1999). However, businesses do have their doubts whether road pricing would be really effective in decreasing the level of congestion. Results from four case study cities (Athens, Como, Dresden and Oslo) in the EU study AFFORD (2001) show that factors determining business acceptability may depend on local circumstances. The criterion of 'business patronage' turned out to be the one that most strongly influences the preferences of interviewees in Athens and Dresden. For Oslo it was the 'cost' criterion, while 'business operation' dominated in Como. In all surveys, the majority of interviewees appeared to perceive that in order to solve urban mobility problems, measures other than pricing strategies should be used, i.e. park and ride facilities, improvement of the level of service of public transport, enlargement of parking facilities, improved traffic management, parking fee policies.

It seems that we have now reached the situation where the major barriers to the successful implementation of transport pricing strategies relate largely to lack of stakeholder and political acceptability, rather than to technical or administrative problems. Since raising prices is generally disliked by the respective user group, the acceptance of pricing policies is often low. But pricing also generates revenues, which one can use for many purposes, including influencing the public acceptability of pricing. This section discusses public acceptability and the role of revenue use. Political and institutional issues will be discussed more explicitly in the next section.

Fairness and the use of revenues

It may be clear that in practically all public decisions relating to transport, there are winners and losers. Pricing in particular may be perceived by the public as only causing losers. Congestion alleviating arguments do not seem to be convincing, and the effectiveness of the measure is not undisputed. Fairness is another issue that has to be treated with care. Taxing measures and the spending of the revenues generated have distributional consequences that might affect some groups in society more than others. Substantially raising the costs of using the car may be distributionally regressive, politically unacceptable, and seem a major infringement on the motorist's freedom (Banister, 1994). Compensating measures may be required to ensure fiscal neutrality and to avoid undesired negative distributional effects. Hypothecation of revenues may aim to address these issues, for instance by investing in public transport or by compensating particular groups (for example, low-income car-owning households). This should then be clearly communicated, in order to reach some level of acceptability.

Different concepts of equity can be introduced when looking at the distribution of road pricing revenues. Horizontal equity requires governments to treat like persons alike in decisions concerning funding, the distribution of benefits, and compensation (Banister, 1994). Vertical equity relates to fairness in the distribution of wealth among different income groups, for instance travel concessions for the poor and elderly. Road pricing is usually considered vertically inequitable since it is generally argued (e.g. Litman, 1996) that the low-income car owners will suffer the greatest detrimental impact from road pricing, particularly if adequate public transport is not available. This effect is however tempered by the fact that lower-income people drive less on average than those with higher incomes. A flat toll may be horizontally equitable since everybody pays the same charge. On the other hand, non-car drivers may benefit from increased reliability and greater productivity of public transport, which can now operate under less congested conditions. A negative consequence may be caused by overcrowded vehicles due to new demand from former car drivers. The vertically inequality of road pricing may be compensated by the distribution of revenues.

Acceptability and the use of revenues

The previous sections indicated that the use of the revenues from pricing instruments may strongly influence acceptability. There are various options how to use the revenues. Literature suggest that the revenues may, for instance, be used for capacity improvement, highway maintenance, investment in public transport, reduction in road taxes or other taxes (e.g. Small, 1992; Higgins, 1997). Empirical questionnaire results reported in several studies confirm the finding that acceptability is influenced by the way revenues are used.

Verhoef (1996) asked for the public opinion on a number of possible allocations of revenue spending on a five point scale, varying from a very bad allocation of revenues to a very good allocation. The allocation objectives that are in the direct interest of the road users received most support, as may be expected. Road investments, together with lower fuel and vehicle taxes ('variabilization') received the highest average score. General purposes, such as general tax reductions and the government budget in general, obtained least support from morning peak road users.

The importance of the use of the funds in gaining or losing public acceptance for a pricing measure has also been shown by a survey in the UK. The attitudes of people to a series of measures that would reduce urban traffic problems were sought. When asked independently (road pricing as a stand alone measure), only 30% responded in support of charging road users to enter highly congested urban areas (Jones, 1998). The respondents were then offered a package that included a charge on entering a zone that was then used to fund better public transport, traffic calming, and better facilities for walking and cycling. This resulted in a support of 57% for the package. A similar result was found in particular for London. A single measure was supported by 43% of the public, whereas 63% accepted the scheme when revenues were used for purposes approved by respondents. Hypothecating revenues thus increases public support.

The AFFORD study (AFFORD, 2001) conducted an empirical survey on public acceptability of different pricing strategies in the four European cities of Athens, Como, Dresden and Oslo (see also Schade and Schlag, 2000). Also respondents' attitudes on revenue use were investigated. It was again found that using money for transport purposes, like traffic flow and public transport improvements, are favoured by a vast majority of respondents. While a lowering of vehicle taxes is also supported by modest people, a lowering of income taxes is not a very popular way of using road pricing revenues. Apart from preferences on different types of revenue use, also expectations were investigated. It turned out that around 70% of the respondents expect that the money will be used for state or municipal purposes, which is not a very popular way of using the revenues (Schade and Schlag, 2000). This study has also analyzed the factors influencing the degree of acceptability of pricing measures. In contrast to previous studies, revenue use does not seem to be a very important factor. Instead, variables such as 'social norm', 'perceived effectiveness' and 'approval of societal important aims' were found to be positively connected with the acceptability of pricing strategies.

An interesting study by Small (1992) suggests that public and political support can be reached for road pricing, even without using all the revenues to compensate travellers since higher user charges are accompanied by reduced travel times. He searched for a strategy that funds programmes with such a variety of distributions of impacts that nearly everyone affected will find at least some offsetting benefits, and a majority will perceive the entire package as an improvement. Seven interest groups were distinguished ranging from the travelling public and public transport users to low tax advocates. It was suggested to keep money in the transportation sector. Funds should be allocated about equally between monetary subsidies to travellers, substitutions of general taxes now used to pay for transportation services, and new transportation services. Small illustrates this by designing a politically feasible (in terms of support from the earlier identified interest groups) congestion pricing package for Southern California. His equity analysis indicates that this programme makes every class of traveller better off (combination of travel time saved, financial improvements, and transportation improvement), with the greatest gains for higher income drivers and public transport users.

The idea of using revenue raised from pricing measures for predetermined purposes calls in the concept of earmarking. Earmarking may be justified to satisfy distributional or acceptability objectives, but it has little relation to efficiency (which is generally served best in absence of restrictions on the use of government funds). The concept also reduces the flexibility of governments to design efficient general budgets, therefore treasury departments normally avoid earmarking (PATS, 1999). On the other hand, public acceptance of taxes may increase if they are earmarked for a connected purpose. Note that hypothecation in the transport sector is not common, but nevertheless sometimes exists, for instance when the funding of public transport relies on revenues from local taxes and charges (see Ubbels *et al.* (2001) for an overview of case studies world-wide).

There is a downside to using revenues solely to improve acceptability. From a broader perspective, it becomes important also to consider explicitly the interaction (or trade-off) between public acceptability and efficiency. Clearly, when a scheme is adopted too easily so as to meet public acceptability requirements, its efficiency properties may be undermined – even by so much that the efficiency considerations motivating the scheme in the first place would then call for its cancellation. Two examples mentioned in the literature are:

◆   Pay-lanes. The use of tolls on only a part of a highway's capacity will generally induce inefficient route split effects: the unpriced part becomes more heavily congested. The second-best price for a pay-lane is accordingly low. If this is ignored, and 'quasi first-best prices' are used instead, efficiency losses instead of gains may result. So, a gradual, piecemeal introduction of marginal cost pricing to gain public support may at least temporarily create efficiency losses rather than gains. From the efficiency viewpoint, such a 'gesture to acceptability concerns' can be justified only if the foreseen end-state would be one in which marginal cost pricing is implemented at the vast majority of links in the network.

◆   Public transport subsidies. The use of road pricing revenues for subsidies in public transport is another often mentioned strategy to enhance public acceptability. Insofar as public transport is priced inefficiently low already, this may induce further efficiency losses – apart from the possibly negative impacts of subsidies on the efficiency of management. So, at least, such subsidies should be targeted to those cost elements of a transit system that indeed should be subsidized from an efficiency viewpoint. These may include the infrastructure and possibly the 'rolling stock', the fixed costs of which may be impossible to recapture using marginal cost pricing principles. But in general, the point is that public transport subsidies may have different efficiency impacts, depending on the shape they take, and this should be accounted for in the design of a scheme.

A final conclusion that can thus be drawn is that acceptability concerns would often suggest amendments in road pricing schemes that may at least partly undermine its efficiency impacts – which form the primary motivation of the scheme in the first place. When dealing with these issues in the design of actual policies, it is therefore important to keep in mind that the goal to be pursued should not be the implementation of pricing *per se*, but rather the improvement of the efficiency of transport (and related) systems.

Road pricing and acceptability in practice

Practical experience with road pricing has been rather small, mainly due to low acceptability levels. For many years, the only example of congestion pricing was Singapore. But today there is more experience to draw from, since other cities have implemented or drawn up quite detailed plans that made progress towards political approval. Below we will discuss some of these cases and their experiences in obtaining sufficient (or insufficient) support.

The Oslo toll ring. Toll cordons have been operated in three Norwegian cities for some time (Bergen, Oslo and Trondheim). A fourth cordon toll scheme, in the Stavanger-region, started operation in April 2001 (Larsen and Østmoe, 2001). Oslo was confronted with unsatisfactorily high traffic flow levels (significant delays) and local environmental problems. For the purpose of dealing with these problems by constructing new infrastructure, the authorities decided to seek the additional resources needed from users.

The toll ring was designed primarily to generate revenues to finance desired transportation infrastructure improvements (with a minor share going to public transportation). Congestion management was not among the objectives underlined by low and flat tolls. Differentiating the toll rates by time of day has been proposed in Oslo, the only city in Norway where congestion at present will make it worthwhile to use pricing as a measure to affect demand. These proposals have been turned down by politicians in power, even though it is now technically very easy to implement.

The political process towards implementation was difficult in Oslo. Four years before implementation, agreement between Oslo City Council and Akershus County Council led to the approval of tolls to finance roads and other transport infrastructure. Formal political approval was obtained two years later, just before the Norwegian Parliament had changed the law. After this principal political approval, the discussion continued on local issues such as fairness and location of toll booths (who should pay for entering the city centre?). Moreover, the spending of revenues was an issue because the Labour Party demanded more funding for public transport. In the end an agreement was reached due to two different factors (CUPID, 2000):

◆ Supporters of road users were satisfied by the availability of new road infrastructure, while those against road construction agreed with the limitation of the number of cars entering the city caused by the toll charges.

◆ The fear that national government might terminate investments in case of local disagreements made municipal politicians willing to make a compromise.

While political acceptability took some time, public acceptability was not immediately acquired either. Despite the fact that tolls already existed in Norway before the opening of the Oslo toll ring (tolls on bridges and tunnels connecting islands to mainland were common), the attitude of the majority of the population towards the proposal was negative (around 70%, see Table 5.2). This initial opposition was also expressed by threats of sabotage. However, this picture changed after opening. When the system had been operational for a year, the opposition reduced to 64%. The proportion in favour of the toll system has steadily increased over time, from 30% before opening to 46% in 1998. Most people now seem to accept the cordons as a fact of life, like parking fees and other restrictive measures, but still opposition is substantial. A contributing factor to the high initial opposition may have been a belief that the tollgates would be new bottlenecks in road systems (Larsen and Østmoe, 2001). This turned out not to be the case, and opposition dropped some percentage points.

Table 5.2 Development of public attitudes towards the Oslo toll ring (numbers in %)

	1989 (before tolling)	1990 (after tolling)	1991	1993	1996	1998
Positive attitude	30	36	38	41	45	46
Negative attitude	70	64	62	59	55	54

In the end, the main explanations for feasibility of this Norwegian example lie in its simplicity, and the political support from the central government. The only purpose of the tolling schemes has been to raise money locally for projects. Hence, the benefits (improving infrastructure) were quite obvious both to politicians and the public. These objectives have been clearly communicated to the public and were easy to understand (well articulated and widely shared). This was facilitated by the existing experience with tolling. Moreover, local political feasibility benefited from (financial) central governmental support.

The Dutch experience.   The implementation of road pricing type of instruments has been considered seriously over the last decade in the Netherlands. Peak-hour permits (*spitsvignet*), toll plazas (*tolpleinen*), electronic peak-hour cordon pricing (*rekening rijden*) and, most recently, electronic kilometre charging have all been mentioned as a possible solution to the severe levels of congestion in the densely populated Randstad area. Nevertheless, none of these considerations have (so far) led to implementation. According to current discussions, the kilometre charge is now favourite among politicians when it comes to new road transport pricing measures dealing with congestion. Revenues should be used to lower (or even replace) current fixed vehicle taxes, making taxes dependent on actual kilometrage, which seems to improve acceptability levels. After sufficient experience with flat rates, the technology should be possible at a later stage to allow differentiation of taxes according to the place and time of driving.

Boot *et al.* (1999) assessed the different types of barriers distinguished in the attempts to introduce the peak-hour cordon pricing. They discuss studies indicating the promising efficiency gains of the proposed scheme. In addition, the technical feasibility was not regarded as a major obstacle to implementation. Hence, the problem is not so much the calculated effectiveness, but more the people's perception of these results. People may often not really believe the computations, and fears of private welfare reduction dominate perceptions. Another important factor negatively affecting the broad social feasibility in the Netherlands has been the strong opposition voiced by a number of respectable institutions (such as the Dutch Automobile Association). This latter organization claimed that introduction would not be effective (in reducing congestion), and only cost money for drivers. The plan was withdrawn by the Minister, in particular after this campaign and the positive feedback it received from the public at large. Institutional feasibility was the major obstacle and communication failed in this Dutch case. The motivation for pricing, the projected effectiveness, and the economic rationale have apparently not reached or convinced the opponents.

Value Pricing in the US: SR 91 express lanes.   The first site of congestion pricing in the United States is a section of highway in California, which opened to traffic in 1995. State Route 91 (SR 91) was selected for expansion with the help of private capital. Two lanes were added to the original four lanes in each direction. While the original freeway lanes remain untolled, users of the new express lanes must pay a fee, except for motorcycles and high-occupancy vehicles (HOV). The SR 91 operating company chose to implement a variable toll schedule, which was called 'Value Pricing'. From a marketing point of view, the name of the scheme has the advantage of hinting at its positive aspects. Whereas all other value pricing projects in the US are operated by public organizations, a private company ran the SR 91 project until the beginning of 2003 (when the SR 91 franchise was sold to the public transportation authority of Orange County). The only public sector influence over the tolls was a prescribed upper limit on the company's rate of return on investment. Once the agreement with the State was signed (to the requirements of AB 680), the private operator needed no further public approvals, since environmental clearances for construction had already been obtained by the State. The revenues generated from the tolls financed the construction of the pay-lane.

Initially, the project met some resistance from people living in Riverside County, who will pay most of the tolls, even though it added new capacity and the original lanes remain free of charge (Small and Gomez-Ibanez, 1998). The reason is that it substitutes for an originally planned single HOV lane in each direction. This objection was partially ameliorated by the decision to make the lanes free of charge for vehicles with three or more occupants. But in general the project received favourable ratings in opinion surveys carried out among peak period travellers during several different periods in time. The surveys addressed the public's opinions about travel conditions, variable toll pricing, and the other innovative technical and institutional features of the project (see Sullivan (1998 and 2000) for an overview).

It is shown that commuters in the SR 91 corridor generally approve toll-financed lanes to bypass congestion (approval percentages in the 60–80% range), starting with the survey conducted just before opening. The approval percentages for toll lane users were 5–10% higher than for non-users, with different variation among vehicle occupancy categories. However, approval of variable tolls (depending on the severity of congestion bypassed), which has consistently lagged approval of toll financing in general, decreased significantly from its high point of 55–75% in 1996 (just after opening) to the 30–50% range in 1999 (Sullivan, 2000). This approval of variable tolls depends very much on the method of travel of commuters, and not so much on income differences. For instance, among single occupancy vehicles, a very large difference in approval (53% vs. 28%) was observed between recent toll lane users and non-users. However, no similar difference was observed for HOV commuters. In addition, firms in the area of the toll lane were asked for their opinion. Overall, the companies' view was that the new lanes improved ease and reliability of travel, not only for employees but also for customers, suppliers and the firms' own work-related travel. For the most part, respondents to the business survey expressed levels of approval for the various features of the toll lanes in the same range as the commuters.

A more general review of all value pricing projects, which were successfully implemented in the United States, suggests that such projects often share several key attributes. Many of these are likely to play a role in enlarging the level of public acceptability (Sullivan, 2002):

- Considerable attention was paid to effective advertising and public relations;

- Project advertising and public relations emphasized the benefits to be gained by travellers, primarily time savings and improved reliability, creating superior travel options not previously available.

- Benefits to the public were identified in simple, tangible terms, and evidence of their existence was clear after implementation.

- Traveller participation has been optional; if people did not want to use the pay lanes, they could avoid them.

Communication has been an important tool in creating public acceptance. For instance, at the national level it was recognized that using the rather academic title 'congestion pricing' elicited negative emotions. 'Value pricing' provided a more positive way to identify the same notion. Another illustration is the positive labels of the toll collection technologies such as Fastrak (Californian projects) and Quickride (Houston). In addition, extensive marketing and public relations initiatives were conducted.

Lessons for governments

Governments that want to implement some form of pricing should pay attention to several aspects to overcome the acceptability problem. A number of guidelines to a more successful implementation, taking the previous mentioned issues into account, have been suggested (see also CUPID, 2000):

- Pricing strategies should be perceived as very effective solutions. The effectiveness of road pricing may be high but this is not guaranteed and depends on the definition of objectives. These objectives must be highly valued by the public. Moreover, people must also believe that their change in behaviour will contribute to reaching these objectives.

- Revenue spending is of crucial importance in gaining acceptance. People want to get something for their money. Jones (1998) even states that road pricing is not publicly acceptable unless the money raised is hypothecated for local transport and environmental projects. But, it is important not to undermine the efficiency impacts of the scheme when distributing revenues to gain acceptance.

- Fairness issues have to be considered, the system must be perceived as fair in terms of personal benefits and costs. The use of revenues together with the charging structure is important to influencing the distributional impacts in the desired direction. Governments could use the revenues to reduce taxation, or they could target particular disadvantaged groups or locations, as is done in Switzerland (Banister, 1994).

The empirical examples, together with the above-mentioned issues, stress the necessity of developing an intelligent communication strategy. Clearly describing the problem (the presence of externalities in the case of road pricing) and the solutions to this problem with the objectives seems appropriate.

Interactions between acceptability and institutional barriers: a simple conceptual framework

As explained above, besides the views and intentions of individuals affected by the measure, responsible political groups and institutional organizations also have to be taken into account. The range of relevant actors potentially affecting or being effected by pricing measures includes all organizations and institutions likely to play a significant role in the design and implementation of a transport pricing system. This means not only the involvement at the different policy-making levels (local, national, EU), but also other relevant actors such as public administrative bodies, and various organizations in the private sector with varying levels of formality (e.g. financiers, interest groups such as automobile associations, media etc.). These actors all have a different role in getting from policy that is justified in technical terms, through a formal planning process to a political decision. Although institutions may initiate and facilitate the implementation of new pricing measures, they can also place limits or constraints on the available and feasible policies. Institutional barriers may appear on the charging side and the revenue use side. Discussion may, for instance, arise over the actual price level and the spending objectives of the revenues.

Although it is common to study acceptability and institutional issues rather independently, these two aspects need not be unrelated in reality. In contrast, they may be strongly interrelated and in fact mutually reinforcing. It is of considerable relevance to obtain further insight into such interrelations when the eventual purpose is to overcome barriers to transport pricing, as it may help identifying why some barriers exist or are particularly high, and may thus give insight into the question of how to overcome them. Some of the main interactions between acceptability and institutional feasibility of transport pricing were therefore illustrated in the AFFORD (2001) study by means of probably the simplest possible framework of interrelations between acceptability and institutional issues suited to this purpose. In particular, the conceptual framework predicts, on the basis of a number of rather plausible assumptions and qualitative reasoning, that social acceptability and institutional feasibility of pricing measures would typically be two mutually reinforcing barriers against its implementation.

Let us turn to the conceptual framework. First, we restrict attention to 'institutions' in the meaning of 'organization', and will distinguish between 'government institutions' and 'non-government institutions'. Secondly, we assume that the behaviour of each institution can be characterized as pursuing the interests of two groups of individuals: those working for the institution (which we will call the institution's representatives) and those whose interests are represented by the institution (the institution's population). In some cases, the institution itself has some freedom in defining and attracting the population it represents, and at the same time decides not to represent other groups. The population may even have created such an institution in the first place which, for example, is the case for unions, employer's organizations, or automobile associations. Government institutions, on the other hand, serve a population that is more or less exogenously given, and that is normally defined by the geographical boundaries of the jurisdiction. Governments have an incentive to serve the population's interests as well as possible for electoral reasons; non-government institutions have a similar incentive through the necessity of maintaining long-run membership. An important difference will be that government institutions typically have a relatively more heterogeneous population than a non-government institution's population, which has selected itself through voluntary membership or – if membership is obligatory – at least shares important characteristics that define their eligibility for membership (such as enterprises in case of Chambers of Commerce). We will not enter into more detail of the relationship between voters and politicians. There is extensive public choice theory available that focuses on behaviour of representatives (during campaign and while in office) and of voters in choosing representatives (see for an overview Mueller, 1979). These theories would be interesting to apply in a more elaborate analysis, but we deliberately keep things simple so as to be able to highlight some key aspects that are likely to remain relevant also in more advanced models.

In the previous paragraph, we deliberately stated that an institution pursues, not maximizes, the interests of its representatives and population. These interests may often diverge among relevant individuals, both within the population, and between population and representatives. The theoretical option of maximizing some joint utility function reflecting the representatives' and population's preferences would be a rather artificial assumption to make. More likely is that in reality, a rule-of-thumb type of behavioural function characterizes an institution's behaviour, where it satisfies rather than maximizes. Most satisfying rules would in any case include the objective to prevent too great individual losses for even a minority of the representatives or population, as soon as interests would diverge among relevant individuals (despite the fact that sometimes decisions are made that, in the short term, are against the majority's interest, e.g. support for the Kyoto protocol). An underlying reason would be that the degree to which individuals would support or object to a certain arrangement may often increase more than proportionally to the size of the perceived welfare change due to this arrangement. Small welfare changes, below some threshold level, may make individuals simply not bother to get fully informed, and shape and voice a clear opinion. Disproportionate welfare gains or losses in contrast, make it worthwhile to invest time and effort trying to influence the arrangement.

As suggested implicitly, the representatives' short-run objectives need not always coincide with the population's objectives, even when the population was homogeneous in the first place. Central representatives' personal opinions may rather strongly affect the institution's attitude towards pricing in transport – if anything because these are the spokesmen – but possibly in a way that deviates somewhat from what could be expected when identifying the population's interests. In the longer run, however, such representatives are less likely to survive in their position. Therefore, although we emphasize that personal opinions of central representatives may have an important impact on the institution's attitude, we believe that the expected institution's attitude should more or less reflect the population's interests (although this may be too simplistic, the median voter theorem, for instance, suggests that the policy chosen is the one preferred by the median voter). The distinction between an institution's population and representatives may thus explain some 'noise' in the institution's attitude, but should probably not be a driving force in predicting or explaining the institution's behaviour.

A next important observation to make is that institutions typically have the equivalent of what in standard economics is known as market power. Institutions may thus actively try to – successfully – affect market or political outcomes. As a result of such 'market power', institutions may exhibit strategic behaviour in order to try to influence such outcomes to serve their representatives' and populations' interests as much as possible. Typically, the institutions' longer-run viability would even not allow any other type of behaviour. A government not satisfying the population's interests sufficiently might well face electoral damage in a relatively short run. A non-government institution would face increased competition (or the creation) of competing institutions serving the same population. So even if an institution does not succeed in affecting fully market or political outcomes to the representatives' and population's satisfaction, a failure to attempt to do so may affect its viability likewise, or perhaps even more strongly.

These ingredients, in fact, are sufficient to explain many of the institutional barriers that may prevent the implementation of road pricing in transport in a country's main urban areas (e.g. through toll cordons), as well as the existence of a mutually reinforcing process between a limited social acceptability and a limited institutional feasibility, for the following general reasons:

1 Road pricing, accompanied by a system of tax recycling, typically may lead to relatively pronounced welfare losses for a well-defined group of individuals, while creating relatively small benefits per individual for others (those that benefit from a reduction of other taxes, or from reduced environmental externalities – a substantial share of which may even be enjoyed only by as yet non-existing individuals). The probability that institutions representing the 'losers' object, and the intensity of objection, are therefore larger than for the 'winners'.

2 The implementation of such a policy will lead to a redistribution of welfare. Prior to implementation, institutions have an incentive to exaggerate expected losses or neglect possible gains, in order to try and realize a share in the revenue allocation as large as possible, should implementation materialize. In other words, resistance may seem even greater than it actually is, due to such strategic behaviour. Support for the measure may bear the risk of signalling likely acceptance of a smaller share of the revenue allocation.

3 The failure even to attempt to influence the scheme as much as possible in the institution's population's interests is unattractive when the institution's representatives are judged by the extent to which they serve their population. So strong opinions voiced by institutions during the phase of negotiations on any scheme's details should be the rule rather than the exception. If this is true, institutional barriers of the kind considered in this section can also be expected almost with certainty, and should not be treated as a 'surprising disappointment'.

4 Individuals may often find justification in their opposition against road pricing when a comparable view is expressed by established, respectable institutions. Insofar as the institution's population's negative perception of the pricing concept thus becomes more pronounced, the institution's representatives would subsequently face an increased incentive to oppose road pricing, etc. publicly. Acceptability and institutional barriers may then be mutually reinforcing.

To these general reasons, we can add the following considerations for some specific institutions:

1 For local governments and political parties, a local tax with a national recycling scheme is a particularly unattractive scheme to support. Moreover,

regardless of whether the rather abstract goal of efficient transport is served, the threat that the city may become a less attractive business location, or even only be perceived to be so, may be sufficient to prevent support. A change in firms' locational behaviour may be perceived as a clearer measure for political success than a more efficiently operated transport system.

2 Local governments of cities just outside the main urban areas where road pricing is to be applied will realize that their inhabitants are particularly likely to be net losers, and will therefore oppose.

3 Local Chambers of Commerce, representing firms, will realize that the 'solution' of traffic congestion by extra road space, financed through the national government's budget instead of through local transport charges, is a more attractive option from the local businesses' perspective. Those initially paying for these national taxes typically gain less, per individual, from a policy change, and are less likely to become involved in the debate. Local governments will be inclined to value the local businesses' opinions, to secure the image of an attractive business location.

4 Local and national unions may represent both winners and losers. However, the intensity of welfare changes for the losers, again, is likely to be bigger than for the winners, suggesting that opposition may be a safer strategy.

5 National employees' organizations are likely to make a similar trade-off.

6 For automobile associations, only full recycling of the revenues to car owners would leave their population as a whole financially equally well off. But even then, the intensity of welfare changes for the losers, again, is likely to be bigger than for the winners, suggesting that opposition may be a safer strategy. When revenues are used for more general goals, such opposition would only increase further.

7 Public transport agencies may have the following considerations. First, it is questionable whether they would have enough capacity to serve the increase in peak hour demand that may result from road congestion pricing in the short run. The inability to do so may lead to damages to the often already vulnerable image. Moreover, capacity expansions catering only for additional peak hour demand may be relatively expensive for transit agencies, who instead often seek to spread demand. Secondly, the agency may be in doubt as to whether appropriate (marginal cost based) pricing, once applied to public transport too, would be in its interest.

Institutional barriers to the implementation of road pricing of the type considered here – opposition by government and non-government organizations – are unlikely not to arise. The key therefore is to keep this at a minimum, if the goal is to be seriously pursued. How this should be done will probably vary strongly by site. On the basis of the Dutch experiences with the failure to introduce cordon pricing, we formulate the following lessons:

1 In presenting innovative pricing measures, great care should be taken in communication. In particular, the motivation for pricing, the projected effectiveness and the economic rationale may otherwise not reach or convince the opponents. Also, justifications of fairness, which are in fact relatively easy to make – the 'user pays principle' – should be spelled out clearly, in particular because fairness seems so much more important than economic efficiency in public debates.

2 Institutions will not easily change an opinion after ventilating it publicly, so an early involvement in the policy design procedure, and an early explanation of the goals and details of the policy to relevant institutions, seems very important.

3 Particularly detrimental for the implementation of new pricing measures could be the joint opposition of a coalition of institutions of different backgrounds. This increases the perceived reliability of the argumentation, and the number of channels through which opposition can be made public. If possible, the formation of such coalitions should at least not be encouraged, which may require that a balanced recycling scheme should, from that perspective, be an integral part of the scheme.

4 A central government that is dedicated to the introduction of some form of road pricing should either have enough power to impose the system upon cities, or should be prepared to offer compensating measures to 'bribe' cities and other key institutions into acceptance. This may make some possible allocations of revenues impossible. When pricing and funds for transport investments are offered as a package, competing cities may in fact fear a 'lagger disadvantage' in not accepting the package. From the economic efficiency perspective, the main task would be to secure, at the same time, that the tax allocations do not imply imperfections or worsen market functioning elsewhere.

Finally, we add the following hypothesis. Opposition to road pricing may sometimes be motivated partly by the fear of becoming relatively worse off. Although there may be advantages in using demonstration projects and experiments, an integral implementation of marginal cost pricing may in contrast have the advantage of taking away such feelings of injustice. Which of the two strategies would eventually work better remains an open question.

Concluding remarks

Most countries rely on existing pricing mechanisms such as fuel duties, registration fees, and parking charges. However, this current charging regime is not very efficient. Economists have advocated the use of more appropriate pricing tools for a long time by demonstrating the welfare gains. Nevertheless, these more efficient road pricing measures have until now only seldom been implemented in practice. The low level of implementation is due to various barriers. Barriers may be practical in nature, but also public acceptability, and institutions may prevent smooth implementation. Road pricing nowadays faces not so much technical or administrative problems. It is generally acknowledged that pricing measures meet public resistance and that acceptability is nowadays one of the major barriers to successful implementation of new and more efficient pricing measures. Moreover, institutional issues are also seen as an important hurdle to be overcome. This chapter focused on these two issues by analyzing the low level of public acceptability and the role of revenue use in this, and in discussing the interrelations between acceptability and institutional barriers.

Despite the fact that politicians and the public regard transport problems as very urgent and important, people do have concerns about road pricing. These doubts are related to the perceived effectiveness of the measure, the feeling that roads are free to use, and that it is an unfair measure. People seem to understand the concept, but are against the imposition of an additional tax, particularly if the revenue raised is paid to the general tax income. Decision-makers should take these concerns into account when preparing implementation of such a measure. Several guidelines have been proposed to come to a more successful implementation strategy.

Besides an intelligent communication campaign (confirmed by the US experiences), the role of revenue spending seems to be a key issue, especially in relation to the argument of fairness. Research has shown the importance of the use of funds in gaining or losing public acceptance. This also appeared from the Oslo experience. Revenues could be targeted to those persons affected by road pricing and remain within the transport sector, but also other objectives may be thought of such as new infrastructure or lower income taxes. In general it has been found that allocation objectives in the direct interest of the road users received most support. Car drivers mainly favour a redistribution in transport (for example, lower fuel taxes or public transport investments) and refuse general tax deductions. A clear communication strategy revealing the spending objectives increases the acceptability rate even more. Despite the fact that transport is an attractive way of spending revenues from an acceptability perspective, it does not immediately mean that it is efficient.

Besides the difficulties in gaining public acceptance, institutional barriers may also create a considerable problem to implementation. Institutional constraints (for which both policy-making bodies as well as institutional (private) organizations are responsible) may take several forms. Successful preparation and implementation of new road pricing schemes may often require that different government and non-government agencies cooperate and agree both on the goals of the policy and on politically important issues such as the question of which government body (and at which spatial level) will receive the tax revenues, and which laws need to be adjusted.

Such cooperation becomes even more important if one takes into account that acceptability barriers and institutional barriers may be mutually reinforcing. Under some reasonably mild assumptions, this was readily shown to be the case in a conceptual framework. Formalizing such a framework and enhancing its degree of realism would be a challenging task, which may, however, yield interesting and rewarding further insights into the viability of transport pricing implementation in democratic societies.

Note

1 This contribution draws from research carried out within the NWO/Connekt VEV project on 'A Multidisciplinary Study of Pricing Policies in Transport – An Economic Perspective', and the EU funded projects AFFORD, MC-ICAM and IMPRINT. Financial support is gratefully acknowledged.

Bibliography

AFFORD (2001) *Acceptability of Fiscal and Financial Measures and Organisational Requirements for Demand Management Final Report*. Helsinki: VATT.

Banister, D. (1994) Equity and acceptability question in internalising the social costs of transport, in OECD/ECMT, *Internalising the Social Costs of Transport*. Paris: OECD/ECMT.

Boot, J., Boot, P. and Verhoef, E.T. (1999) The long road towards the implementation of road pricing: the Dutch experience. Unpublished manuscript, Free University, Amsterdam.

CUPID (2000) State of the Art – Frequently Asked Questions. Deliverable 3, project funded by the European Commission under the Growth Programme, Brussels.

Higgins, T.J. (1997) Congestion pricing: public polling perspective. *Transportation Quarterly*, 48, pp. 287–298.

Jones, P. (1998) Urban road pricing: public acceptability and barriers to implementation, in Button, K.J. and Verhoef, E.T. (eds.) *Road Pricing, Traffic Congestion and the Environment: Issues of Efficiency and Social Feasibility*. Cheltenham: Edward Elgar, pp. 263–284.

Larsen, O.I. and Østmoe, K. (2001) The experience of urban toll cordons in Norway. *Journal of Transport Economics and Policy*, Part 3, 35, pp. 457–471.

Litman, T. (1996) Using road pricing revenue: economic efficiency and equity considerations. *Transportation Research Record*, 1558, pp. 24–28.

Mueller, D.C. (1979) *Public Choice*. Cambridge: Cambridge University Press.

PATS (1999) State of the Art Synthesis on Price Acceptability. Deliverable 1. Project funded by the European Commission under the Transport RTD Programme of the 4th Framework Programme, Brussels.

PROSAM (2000) *The Toll Cordon – Public Attitudes 1989–1999*. Report 67. Oslo: Public Roads Authorities.

Schade, J. and Schlag, B. (2000) *Acceptability of Urban Transport Pricing*. AFFORD publication, Research report 72. Helsinki: VATT.

Small, K.A. (1992) Using the revenues from congestion pricing. *Transportation*, **19**, pp. 359–381.

Small, K.A. and Gomez-Ibanez, J.A. (1998) Road pricing for congestion management: the transition from theory to policy, in Button, K.J. and Verhoef, E.T. (eds.) *Road Pricing, Traffic Congestion and the Environment: Issues of Efficiency and Social Feasibility*. Cheltenham: Edward Elgar, pp. 213–247.

Sullivan, E.C. (1998) *Evaluating the Impacts of the SR 91 Variable Toll Lane Facility*. San Luis Obispo: California Polytechnic State University.

Sullivan, E.C. (2000) *Continuation Study to Evaluate the Impacts of the SR 91 Value Priced Express Lanes*. San Luis Obispo: California Polytechnic State University.

Sullivan, E.C. (2002) *Implementing Value Pricing for U.S. Roadways*. Paper presented at the IMPRINT workshop Brussels. San Luis Obispo: California Polytechnic State University.

Ubbels, B. (2002) *The Economics of Transport Pricing*. Colloquium Vervoersplanologisch Speurwerk: De kunst van het verleiden? Delft: CVS, pp. 201–219.

Ubbels, B., Nijkamp, P., Verhoef, E.T., Potter, S. and Enoch, M. (2001) Alternative ways of funding public transport. *European Journal of Transport and Infrastructure Research*, **1**, pp. 73–89.

Ubbels, B., Rietveld, P. and Peeters, P.M. (2002) Environmental effects of a kilometre charge in road transport: an investigation for the Netherlands. *Transportation Research D*, **7**, pp. 255–264.

Verhoef, E.T. (1996) *Economic Efficiency and Social Feasibility in the Regulation of Road Transport Externalities*. Amsterdam: Thesis Publishers.

Verhoef, E.T. (2000) The implementation of marginal external cost pricing in road transport. *Papers in Regional Science*, **79**, 307–332.

Verhoef, E.T. (2002) Marginal cost based pricing in transport: key implementation issues from the economic perspective. Unpublished IMPRINT discussion paper, Free University, Amsterdam.

Verhoef, E.T. (2003) Phasing and packaging of pricing reform: the MC-ICAM approach. Unpublished IMPRINT discussion paper, Free University, Amsterdam.

Chapter 6

Alternative implementation strategies for radical transport schemes[1]

Marcus P. Enoch

This chapter arose from an off-the-cuff closing remark at a STELLA FP5 meeting in Brussels in May 2002. Broadly, the seminar was felt to have covered a wide area of institutional issues but had missed out the crucially important one of implementation – and in particular the need for transport practitioners to know how best to go about introducing transport schemes that probably would not be very popular with politicians or the public. Accordingly, the following notes are more practical musings on how existing examples of radical transport schemes might be classified according to a very simple implementation strategy framework than an academically rigorous exercise.

The mobility explosion

Since the early 1950s, all developed countries have witnessed a 'mobility explosion'. Indeed, across the fifteen countries in the European Union (EU-15), overall passenger transport use (in cars, buses, coaches, trams, trains and aeroplanes) rose by 121% between 1970 and 1996. This translates to an increase in the average distance travelled by each EU citizen per day from 16.5 km to 35 km over the same period. Transport demand across the EU was calculated to be 4700 billion passenger-kilometres in 1996 (EC, 1999).

The majority of this increase is almost entirely due to a rise in car use, although air transport is experiencing the fastest increase of all, albeit from a lower level than for cars. Over the 1970–1996 period, car use increased by 136%, with the modal share increasing from 74% of passenger-kilometres in 1970 to 79% in 1996. This has been facilitated by increased road capacity, with income and population growth viewed as the major drivers behind increasing vehicle ownership and use (Marshall *et al.*, 1997; Marshall and Banister, 2000). In the EU-15, there was a 34% increase in the number of vehicles owned between 1985 and 1995, with the number of cars on EU-15 roads growing from 60.77 million to 165.54 million, an average growth rate of just less than 4% a year. Thus, by 1996, there were 444 cars per 1000 EU-15 inhabitants (European Commission, 1999). OECD (1995) predicted that this would increase by a further 50% between 1995 and 2020, bringing vehicle ownership levels to more than 600 per 1000 people in many EU-15 countries.

Such growth is frightening enough, but at the moment 80% of the 550 million vehicles (including 400 million cars) registered worldwide are owned by the richest 15% of people living in the 'mainly developed' and industrialized OECD countries. Unsurprisingly therefore, the number of vehicles and traffic levels are growing much faster in developing countries than in the developed world. Two-thirds of the rise in vehicles is forecast to occur in non-OECD nations particularly in Eastern Europe and Asia. If historic rates are maintained, the global vehicle population will exceed one billion by 2020 (Potter, 2000).

The need for radical solutions

Such a depressing prognosis requires radical treatment, but political factors have generally precluded such actions. And so the transport crisis continues to worsen.

However, there are towns and cities that have managed to adopt radical car restraint policies without the sky falling on their heads. Using data from some of these schemes, this chapter develops a number of potential implementation strategies that may be adopted by transport policy-makers in the future. In short, eight strategies are suggested, four focus on 'sweetening the pill' of potentially unpopular measures, and three aim to convince the motorist that the new policy is actually quite a reasonable response to the traffic problem. The final strategy suggests that transport policy goals be met through the sympathetic introduction of other ostensibly unrelated policies – surely the purest manifestation of joined-up thinking.

Compensating losers[2]

The introduction of road user charging in Singapore in 1975 has long been seen as a 'one off' event, which was only possible because of unique circumstances in that the citizens are generally law abiding, and there are no similar alternative cities to which businesses may relocate. But, while this certainly played a large part in the introduction of the original very simple and low-tech Area Licensing Scheme (ALS), which used paper windshield stickers enforced through visual inspection by traffic inspectors within a single cordon, it was less important when it was decided to adopt an Electronic Road Pricing (ERP) system in 1998.

Instead, what is less well publicized is that the Singapore government made a policy decision to ensure that most people benefited as a result of the change, and that as few people as possible lost out, at least in the short term. This was achieved by granting rebates to certain user groups. For example, taxis were given road tax rebates for the first three years after implementation, while businesses were given four years of rebates. In addition, a S$60 a month levy imposed on owners of non-residential parking spaces was replaced by a nominal S$1 per space per month licence fee in the same year. In other words, the government 'bribed' the public to give the scheme a chance of working in the first year, and gambled on the scheme being accepted by the time the rebates were withdrawn.

Such an approach was possible because the main objective of the scheme was to manage traffic levels rather than raise revenue. The cost of the 'subsidies' could thus be written off as a necessary implementation cost.

Bribing the motorist not to drive[3]

Certainly, the most overt way of 'incentivizing' drivers out of their cars is by paying them not to use their cars for certain trips – i.e. effectively bribing motorists to use an alternative mode. One application of this principal – the parking cash out – is becoming increasingly common in the UK. Annual schemes operate at Southampton General Hospital and at telecom firm Orange's new Bristol office, while a monthly pass system operates at the Vodafone offices in Newbury, Berkshire.

Still more radical, the pharmaceutical giant Pfizer began operating a parking cash out scheme that rewards non-car commuters on a daily basis among staff at its research and production facilities at Sandwich in Kent in June 2001, and at Walton Oaks near Reigate in Surrey in December 2001. This works by using staff-personalized security pass 'proximity card' technology. An employee's card is credited with enough points to 'pay' for one month's parking. The card opens the parking barriers and records how many points are used. If not used for parking, staff then cash in these parking points at the end of each month and these are credited to them through the payroll. Staff at the Sandwich site receive £2 per day for leaving their car at home, while at Walton Oaks the incentive is £5 a day – a reflection of the far tighter parking standards set by the local planning authority at the Reigate site.

Overall, the value of cash outs given to staff amounts to around £0.5m a year, and currently around a third of staff travel to work by modes other than the car.

It is not only parking spaces that motorists are paid to give up – in some cases they are paid to give up their cars. For example, during Green Transport Week in June 1999, public transport operator First Glasgow's 'Swap a banger for a bus' scheme led to more than 500 residents of Glasgow swapping their car for an annual bus pass worth £560. In the United States, too, a car cash out project is being tested by the State of Washington and public transport operator King County Metro in Seattle, through funding from the Federal Highway Administration value pricing programme.

Highlighting the benefits[4]

By contrast, in Oslo, Norway, road tolls were introduced in the city to raise money to pay for new transport infrastructure, and not to reduce traffic congestion. This meant that the 'rebate route' might exempt too many people for the required amount of money to be raised. Indeed, the charges introduced were relatively low and were spread across the 'population' as far as possible so as to maintain traffic levels and maximize revenue.

In the Norwegian case therefore, the important objective was to convince the public that the money they were being charged was being used to directly benefit them as motorists. Accordingly, much effort was spent on a well-targeted and publicized information campaign, which was certainly helped by the charge being implemented only 14 days after the Oslo Tunnel (later renamed *Festningstunnelen* – the Castle Tunnel) was opened to traffic.

Offering more choice to the road user[5]

The key reason for drivers accepting the High Occupancy Toll (HOT) lane facility on Interstate 15 to the north of San Diego is that drivers are offered a genuine and informed choice – they can use the general purpose lanes for free with the likelihood of being delayed, or else they can pay but enjoy a hassle free and predictable journey time. This is a major factor missing from area charging schemes.

The HOT facility originally opened in 1988 as a High Occupancy Vehicle (HOV) lane for buses, vanpools and two-person carpools. While it was suggested that the lanes be opened to Single Occupancy Vehicles (SOVs) on payment of a toll in 1991, as only 50% of the two lanes' capacity was being used while adjacent general-purpose lanes were experiencing severe congestion during peak periods, it was not until December 1996 that the HOT lane became reality.

As drivers approach the HOT lane, variable message signs advise them of the toll to use the lanes. The level of this toll depends on how much spare capacity is available in the HOV lane, and varies from US$0.50 (€0.56) to US$4 (€4.5) in normal circumstances, with drivers paying more the busier the lanes. Around US$430,000 (€481,000) of the annual US$1.6m (€1.8m) toll revenue covers operating costs, and US$60,000 (€67,000) pays the California Highway Patrol to enforce the lanes. State law requires the remaining money to be spent on developing the express lanes and improving the public transport service along the corridor; specifically, the express bus service known as the Inland Breeze, which began operating in November 1997. While initially there were concerns that the lanes would become 'Lexus Lanes' – i.e. only used by the rich – this has not been borne out in practice.

It might have been worse . . .

A similar tactic was used to herald the introduction of London's Congestion Charge in February 2003, whereby hostile newspaper reporting prior to the introduction of the charge and predictions of traffic chaos by the London Mayor, combined with a lessening in traffic due to a half-term school holiday, meant that for the first week at least the charge performed far better than expected and was consequently seen as a success.

The lesser of two evils[6]

A strategy used in a similar vein is the idea that the public be provided with two choices, one of which is more politically unpalatable – yet just as logical or reasonable – as the favoured one. A recent example of this approach occurred in the City of Durham before the introduction of the congestion charge there in October 2002.

In summary, traffic was causing problems for the World Heritage Site of the city's cathedral and castle, as well as for pedestrian shoppers in the city centre. Accordingly, a transport study demonstrated that action needed to be taken – a position appreciated by almost everyone – that cars were charged to drive in the area or else banned altogether. Given the alternatives, it became the less controversial route for the council to adopt the access charge.

Adapting tried, tested and accepted methods

Despite the recent press surrounding the launch of the London Congestion Charging Scheme in February 2003, two of the largest cities in the United States – San Francisco and New York City – have effectively been charging vehicles to enter or exit downtown areas for many years with virtually no political acceptance problems. Specifically, drivers must pay tolls to cross eight 'Caltrans' bridges in the Bay Area of California, including the four bridges to enter San Francisco (Caltrans, 2000). Similarly in New York City, drivers crossing into Manhattan must pay to use seven of the city's bridges and two tunnels (MTA, 2003). This apparent public acceptance indicates that drivers are happy to pay to use a facility such as a bridge or a tunnel, whereas the idea of paying to enter the downtown area of a city would be extremely controversial. The lesson here would therefore seem to be that 'traditional' charges that have been in place and accepted for many years might still do just as effective a job as something seen as new, radical and threatening, but with rather less opposition.

The Trojan Horse

Perhaps the classic case of a transport policy being introduced by a 'trigger mechanism' – i.e. on the back of a totally unrelated policy – is that of the so-called 'Ring of Steel' imposed on the City of London in 1993. This policy was executed almost overnight in response to a terrorist bomb attack in Bishopsgate, and involved restricting access to the central core of the city to a small number of roads. In addition to the closure of 17 minor streets and the conversion of 13 roads to one way, traffic signals were altered at 23 junctions and public transport and pedestrians were given greater priority (Cairns *et al.*, 1998). Overall, as a result of what was a security policy – in the eyes of the public at least – traffic entering the restricted area fell by a quarter from 160,000 vehicles a day, and pollution levels were 15% lower. However, there was a slight increase in traffic levels on the zone boundary.

Interestingly, the bomb exploded only a month before a traffic scheme known as 'The Key to the Future' was due to be implemented that was also designed to restrict traffic for environmental reasons, and so significant elements of this proposal were incorporated into the security operation. It is probably fair to say that resistance to such a radical policy would have been far greater had the bomb not gone off, simply because the public is far more accepting of policies 'forced' on policy-makers due to 'circumstances beyond anybody's control' or by 'safety concerns'. Therefore, similar conditions could perhaps be created by taking advantage of particularly bad weather or some other 'Act of God', or more predictably by maintenance problems closing roads, bridges or car parks (for example, Hammersmith Bridge in London). Essentially, it may be worth transport planners becoming more involved with Emergency Planning sections at local councils.

Lessons to be learnt

Overall, there are important lessons to be learnt from the successes and failures of radical demand management schemes to date. These are not about the technology of road pricing, which has attracted much attention, but about how schemes are designed, the effective inclusion of user concerns, and political sensitivity. Major factors that appear to be associated with success are:

+ having clearly defined and complementary objectives;
+ not trying to achieve too much in the early stages;
+ achieving at least some of the benefits promised as quickly as possible;

- being supported by politicians of all persuasions;
- being seen to work properly and reliably;
- gaining the support of the public;
- being understood by the public;
- having flexibility to develop as circumstances, public attitudes, objectives, and technology change, and of being tweaked to react to 'unexpected' events;
- offering realistic alternatives to travellers who wish to switch from driving into the cordon;
- paying attention to details.

However, it also clear that in many of the more radical schemes adopted around the world there are additional strategies that have been employed, either deliberately or as an act of circumstance.

Firstly, the public is often willing to wait and see if a scheme will work provided:

- They can perceive there is a problem and the policy seems a reasonable way of solving it.

- They benefit from the scheme, are compensated in some way for any disbenefits, or are provided with a viable and acceptable alternative means of travel.

- They feel that other organizations or individuals are convinced the scheme is the right way to go.

- They feel they have been properly consulted for their opinions, and these have at least been listened to and ideally acted upon.

  Secondly, the public will often accept a scheme if:

- They feel there is no alternative (or that it is the least worst alternative).

- The scheme is not so different from existing schemes or if they have had experience of similar schemes.

- The scheme is implemented as a response to some kind of crisis that is beyond the government's control – for example, an act of terrorism or a national emergency – or that is obviously for the public good – for example, drink driving, security.

- The scheme delivers what it set out to achieve.

Clearly, the strategies suggested are already implemented to varying degrees in most transport projects, but have possibly not been set out quite so bluntly in the past. It is also obvious that the appropriateness of some or all of these strategies is strongly dependent on the particular circumstances of a proposed scheme. Finally, there is scope for combining suitable strategies in order to increase acceptability still further.

In summary, in many countries it is increasingly problems with the implementation of a project – and in particular in convincing the public and by extension the politicians – rather than the planning or even the financing of a project that determine whether it goes ahead or not. It is hoped that this chapter might provide a slightly different way of looking at the implementation process so that future schemes may benefit.

Notes

1 Thanks are extended to those who were interviewed, and to Dr Sarah Wixey at the University of Westminster for her comments.
2 This section is based on Wong et al (2002).
3 This section is based on information reported in Enoch (2002).
4 This section is based on Waerstad (2002).
5 This section is based on Enoch (2001).
6 This section is based on Ieromonachou et al., (2003).

Bibliography

Cairns S., Hass Klau, C. and Goodwin, P. (1998) *Traffic Impact of Highway Capacity Reductions: Assessment of the Evidence*. London: Landor Publishing.

Caltrans (2000) *The Bridges on San Francisco Bay*. San Francisco: California Department of Transportation. Online. Available HTTP: <www.dot.ca.gov/dist4/calbrdgs.htm> (accessed 27 February 2003).

Enoch, M. P. (2001) Lessons from America: the San Diego HOT lane. *Traffic Engineering and Control*, **42**, pp. 260–263.

Enoch, M. P. (2002) UK parking cash out experience, and lessons from California. *Traffic Engineering and Control*, **43**, pp. 184–187.

European Commission (1999) *Panorama of Transport: Statistical Overview of Road, Rail and Inland Waterway Transport in the European Union 1970–1996*. Eurostat, Theme 7 Transport. Luxembourg: Office for Official Publications of the European Communities.

Ieromonachou, P., Enoch, M. P. and Potter, S. (2003) All charged up: Early lessons from the Durham congestion-charging scheme. *Town and Country Planning*, **72**(2), pp. 44–48.

Marshall, S., Banister, D. and McLellan, A. (1997) A strategic assessment of travel trends and travel reduction strategies. *Innovation, The European Journal of Social Sciences*, **10**, pp. 289–304.

Marshall, S. and Banister, D. (2000) Travel reduction strategies: intentions and outcomes. *Transportation Research Part A*, **34**, pp. 321–338.

MTA (2003) *Bridges and Tunnels*. New York: Metropolitan Transit Authority. Online. Available HTTP:<www.mta.nyc.ny.us/bandt/index.html> (accessed 27 February 2003).

OECD (1995) *Motor Vehicle Pollution: Reduction Strategies beyond 2010*. Paris: OECD.

Potter, S. (2000) 'Travelling Light', Theme 2, Course T172, Technology Level 1, Working with our environment: Technology for a sustainable future, Milton Keynes: The Open University.

Waerstad, K. (2002) Telephone interview, City of Oslo, 18 July.

Wong, K., Lim, L. C. and Chan, S. H. (2002) Personal interview, Singapore Land Transport Administration, 5 July.

Chapter 7

A research agenda for institutions, regulations and markets in transportation and infrastructure[1]

Jonathan L. Gifford

Institutions, regulations, and markets are an important part of the 'software' of transportation and infrastructure systems. They define roles and responsibilities for the delivery of the services that such systems provide.

The ownership, management, and regulation of infrastructure networks have traditionally been fairly independent from network to network. Industrial organization and public agency jurisdiction have tended to reflect the distinct physical networks, as have the associated professional and academic research disciplines. The field of facilities management has begun to span some of these traditional boundaries, but it has not emphasized networked infrastructure facilities.[2] The study of civil infrastructure systems (CIS) at the National Science Foundation, among other places, has focused on multiple infrastructure systems, but mostly those in the domain of civil engineering, with less emphasis on, for example, electric power and telecommunications.[3] Public utility economics provides some discussion of general principles, particularly for networks that are structured as public utilities.[4] But there has to date been relatively little focus on physical networks in a broader, more generalized, context.

Yet important changes are occurring in the institutional structure and regulation of infrastructure networks worldwide. Facility systems that were once assumed to be natural monopolies are being radically restructured. Vertically integrated public utilities in electric power, natural gas and telecommunications are being restructured to allow competition at the wholesale and retail level. Government monopolies in telecommunications, rail, and air traffic control are being privatized or 'corporatized'.

Along with this restructuring has come a blurring of the distinctions between the various infrastructure networks themselves. Natural gas companies are entering into the generation and transmission of electric power. Integrated freight companies are offering intermodal shipment services. Municipal public works departments are deploying fibre optic networks on public rights-of-way and selling use of it to wholesale and retail customers. Electric power transmission providers are exploring techniques for using power lines for both power transmission and communications.

Societal concerns and priorities are also shifting. In the developing world, increasing income often carries with it a sharp rise in the demand for the services that infrastructure networks provide, from clean water to private motor vehicles. Growing concern about the possibility that human activities are affecting the global climate, and about finite energy resources have heightened attention to sustainable transport and infrastructure systems.

The magnitude of these structural changes highlights the need for research to expand understanding of how institutional arrangements operate and the role and functioning of markets and regulation. This chapter presents a research agenda of key governance challenges for transportation and infrastructure networks. The agenda consists of eighteen topics, with a brief discussion of each.

Challenges

Security and safety

The security of the transportation system has been a matter of greatly heightened concern since the terrorist attacks of 2001. But transportation safety has long been a cardinal consideration in transportation system design and operation. Heightened attention to security, in conjunction with ongoing concern about safety, raises a number of important questions related to institutions, regulations, and markets. How and at what level should security be organized? How should resources devoted to security be coordinated with other resource requirements? Indeed, security and safety matters intersect with each of the remaining agenda items discussed below.

System level planning

The appropriate degree of system level planning for the transportation network is difficult to specify. Yet it is critical to improving the overall capability of the system to broaden choice and improve quality of life. On the one hand, strong system level planning may enable the achievement of system level changes that would otherwise be difficult to achieve. On the other, system level choices may suppress diversity and may lead to 'wrong' decisions being universally or widely applied.

In the US, system level planning has been an important function of central authority in some infrastructure networks, such as highways, air traffic control, and western water reclamation. In other networks, like traditional electric utilities, vertically integrated utilities plan their own facilities, working in cooperation with other utilities in their region, while state regulation of rates controls what capital investments are allowed into the rate base. Public officials always have the option of public inquiries and assessments in the event of network failures or excesses.

It is an article of faith for many that system level planning contributes positively to the long-term performance of a network, although it is difficult to substantiate that contribution empirically. To be sure, networks do not emerge spontaneously, suggesting that some level of planning is indicated. But the nature and extent of such planning, where to house it institutionally, and how to finance it is another matter.

The links and nodes of transportation networks more than many economic activities require significant capital investment and lead times to be placed into service. Major new facilities in some cases require lead times of one or two decades and billions of dollars.

The planning and development of such facilities has come to be dominated by two modes of analysis. Under private ownership and operation, analysis typically examines returns to the owner, subject to legal constraints on project impacts and regulatory restrictions on the ability to offer a particular service. Under public ownership, analysis typically examines general welfare using a cost-benefit framework, subject to constraints on budget and environmental impact, and implementation considerations.

The planning and development of such facilities becomes more difficult in the face of uncertainties about, for example, the demand for network services, technological innovation and obsolescence, and economic and regulatory conditions. The bundling of services that span several networks and the use of rights of way for multiple networks introduce a number of additional problems. The restructuring of network ownership and sources of capital often reveals sharp contrasts in the assumptions and treatment of uncertainty between public and private entities.

Governance

Infrastructure networks have traditionally been subject to a variety of governance structures, including national and sub-national public utility regulators. At the international level, networks have often been governed by treaties and conventions or by international commissions (for example, the International Civil Aviation Organization, ICAO). Striking the right balance between integration and autonomy is challenging, and research to examine the merits of alternative approaches utilized in Europe, the US, and elsewhere would be helpful.

Innovation

Technological and organizational innovations are potentially a powerful source of improvement in the performance of the transportation network. As information and communications technologies (ICT) continue to advance, the transportation network is likely to continue to make increasing use of

ICT for the delivery of its services. Some have labelled this 'convergence' of infrastructure networks. Research can help understand how institutions, regulations, and market structures can effectively foster innovation.

Reliability

The reliability of transportation is usually important to users. Reliability is also an important dimension of service quality in other infrastructure networks. But expectations about reliability vary considerably across networks, as do the consequences of failures. Some networks provide users choice about the level of reliability of services they acquire. 'Congestion pricing' or 'value pricing" in highway transport gives users an option, for a price, to avoid congestion. Electric power suppliers have begun to offer 'interruptible' service to users at a discount. Some forms of failure are unacceptable, however, such as midair collisions.

Growth and change in networks may give rise to intended or unintended changes in reliability. The maintenance of reliability in electric power networks under wholesale and retail wheeling of power raises a number of problems, for example. Multi-use infrastructure rights-of-way also introduce the problem of a failure in a single physical link causing failures in multiple networks, and of possible interference between different systems, such as electric power lines and telecommunications cable. The design of high reliability networks is also important for many network suppliers.

Research can help characterize reliability and shed light on institutional, regulatory and market arrangements for determining the correct level of reliability. Determining how much reliability is 'enough', and avoiding 'gold plating' – that is, providing more reliability than is efficient – are important areas for research.

Access to capital

Infrastructure networks have generally obtained capital from the capital markets and from government grants. US railroads, for example, were capitalized by large land grants from the national government. US electric power generation and transmission has traditionally used the capital markets, and municipal sewage treatment systems have relied on a combination of government grants and bond issues.

Many infrastructure networks have confronted a shortfall in traditional sources of capital. The US highway and airport systems, for example, have traditionally relied in part on dedicated excise taxes. But revenues from these sources have fallen short of overall capital requirements, leading to inquiries into alternative sources. European transport, by contrast, has not generally been supported by dedicated taxes.

Research on the merits of alternative sources of capital, both government and private, would be most useful. Another important issue is whether capital has been allocated efficiently across infrastructure networks. Because of the different sources of capital and the institutional arrangements for allocating capital, it may be useful to examine whether some networks have been over- or under-capitalized.

Valuation of networks

Closely related to access to capital is the valuation of transportation assets. In most cases, valuation of a specific facility poses problems, and traditional methods of valuation include replacement cost, historical cost, or net present value of future benefits, each of which presents its own problems. Valuation of a network is much more difficult, yet could be useful in determining the appropriate level of investment. Again, similar issues obtain in a variety of infrastructure networks.

Asset management

In the US, attention to asset management has been increasing in the highway sector, especially in state highway departments. The advent of new accounting requirements has been partially responsible.[5] Research on the institutional, regulatory and market aspects of asset management would include the identification of institutional barriers to adoption.

Equity

Changes to the transportation system have potentially enormous implications for equity. Again, this issue is also relevant in other infrastructure networks. Traditional governance often provided an umbrella for cross subsidies that may become difficult to maintain under deregulation or restructuring. Competition for local telephone service may strain the strong tradition of universal service in US telephony, for example. Another equity issue of considerable importance is the tension between local and non-local users. Who should bear the costs of interconnection with a regional or national network? Should the network be designed to optimize local use, subject to a requirement to accommodate non-local use? Or should it be optimized for non-local use with a requirement to accommodate local use? Or is some joint optimum possible?

Network operational control

The operational control of the transportation network is of course central to its efficiency and effectiveness. Different infrastructure networks employ different 'concepts of operation'. The use of networks by multiple autonomous or semi-autonomous users often requires some level of coordination and control to ensure safety, reliability, or efficiency. There is a very broad range of coordination and control strategies available, from aviation's 'see and avoid' policy for aircraft operating under visual flight rules, to telecommunications' 'token ring', to the command and control approaches of traditional electric power transmission and controlled air traffic. The evaluation of alternative coordination and control strategies is an area for research in institutions, regulations, and markets.

Competitiveness

The efficiency and effectiveness of transportation services can have important impacts on industrial competitiveness and economic vitality. To the extent the industrial organization, capital investment and delivery of services can adapt quickly to changing economic conditions and technological opportunities, the commercial and industrial users of infrastructure services may be able to reduce costs and improve product and service quality. The linkages between infrastructure and economic productivity and competitiveness have only begun to be explored in the context of distinct networks. Research on the nature and importance of these linkages at the level of multiple networks may provide useful insights for public policy.

Education and training

Education and training of the transportation workforce is a matter of increasing concern. Workforce demographic trends suggest a potential shortfall in the US, as well as a changing set of workforce characteristics. Ongoing initiatives in the European Union grow out of similar concerns about the capacity of traditional education and training institutions to deliver the quantity and type of workforce that is required for the ongoing development of the transportation system. Yet introducing change in education and training institutions is often challenging.[6]

Demand-side management

The conservation and environmental communities have often favoured demand-side management as an alternative to the construction of new infrastructure capacity. Demand-side management programmes have most often been instruments of regulation, however, and may not flourish in a deregulated environment. What should the scope of demand-side management be, and what are the most effective means for implementing programmes?

Forms of ownership

The ownership of transportation networks takes a variety of forms.

Highways are primarily owned and operated by state governments in the US, and occasionally toll authorities. Privatization of the motorway network recently occurred in Italy. Other infrastructure sectors also exhibit a range of arrangements. Electric utility networks have traditionally been owned either by investor-owned utilities, municipal utilities, or cooperatives. Telecommunications networks are primarily owned by investor-owned companies in the US, and until recently by government departments of post, telephone and telegraph (PTTs) abroad.

Restructuring of infrastructure networks may change the type of ownership of a network. Canada's air traffic control system is now owned by a private (or incorporated) entity that purchased it from the government of Canada. Research comparing and contrasting different forms of ownership could identify their respective advantages and disadvantages, and examples of shifts from one type of ownership to another.

Procurement

Traditional methods of procurement, especially in the public sector, have tended to emphasize lowest initial cost, often to the neglect of operation and maintenance considerations. Such approaches are problematic. Heightened rates of innovation and obsolescence suggest flexibility as a paramount consideration, which can be difficult to maintain under traditional procurement approaches. Research would be useful to identify and evaluate alternative procurement and project development approaches.

Spatial integration and interoperability

Transportation and infrastructure networks operate at a range of levels of spatial integration and interoperability. Air traffic control has a high degree of interoperability at a global level, even though airport operations (for example, security procedures) are highly variegated. The Internet also is also highly integrated at a global scale. Wastewater treatment systems, on the other hand, tend to be less integrated. Determining the appropriate level of interoperability and spatial integration for a particular network involves complex interactions between the technical difficulty of achieving interoperability, the latent demand for utilizing interoperable systems, and the institutional structure of network providers.[7]

Standards

Standards have traditionally played an important role in regulating and coordinating the technical compatibility and interoperability of network equipment and services. The standards development process can be cumbersome, however. Different nations observe sharply different roles for government in international standardization efforts. Research would be useful to evaluate the benefits of the degree of standardization, and the alternative institutional arrangements for achieving it.

Regulatory lag

Infrastructure networks are usually subject to some form of public regulation and governance. Restructuring is sometimes initiated or promoted by public authorities, as in the case of airline and trucking deregulation in the US. In other cases, however, the traditional governing institutions may resist surrendering any of their power or jurisdiction. Such regulatory lag may be operative in the US air traffic control system, for example, where the governing committees in Congress claim that air traffic control is an 'intrinsically public' function that cannot be privatized without sacrificing safety. A comparative study of the relationship between restructuring and governing institutions might shed light on the nature of political institutions, as well as suggest mechanisms by which public institutions might promote 'healthy' restructuring and resist 'unhealthy' restructuring.

Concluding remarks

Infrastructure systems and the societies that support and utilize them are evolving in important ways. While not exhaustive, this agenda of research subjects provides a foundation for extending understanding of the software of transportation and infrastructure networks. Research on institutions, regulation, and markets can support improved fidelity between society and its transportation and infrastructure systems.

Notes

1 A chapter based on the work reported here has been published (Gifford, 2004).
2 See, for example, Gifford, Uzarski and McNeil (1993).
3 Zimmerman and Sparrow (1997).
4 See, for example, Sichel and Alexander (1996).
5 The Government Accounting Standards Board has required that public entities either assign a value to their infrastructure and depreciate it annually, or adopt an asset management system that can demonstrate that their infrastructure is being maintained at a given level. Governmental Accounting Standards Board (1999).
6 See, for example, Sussman (1995). The European Union is currently exploring new education and training approaches. Fabrice Bardet, Ecole nationale des travaux publics de l'etat, personal communication with the author (17 March 2003).
7 Gifford (1996).

Bibliography

Gifford, J.L. (1996) E-Z pass: a case study of institutional and organization issues in technology standards development. *Transportation Research Record*, 1537, pp. 10–14.

Gifford, J.L. (2004) Policy perspectives, in Zimmerman, R. and Horna, T. (eds.) *Enabling Civil and Environmental Systems through Information Technology*. London: Routledge, pp. 57–71.

Gifford, J.L., Uzarski, D. and McNeil, S. (1993) Infrastructure Planning and Management, proceedings, New York: American Society of Civil Engineers.

Governmental Accounting Standards Board (1999) Basic Financial Statements and Management's Discussion and Analysis – for State and Local Governments. Statement No. 34, Governmental Accounting Standards Series, No. 171-A, Norwalk, CT, June 1999.

Sichel, W. and Alexander, D.L. (1996) *Networks, Infrastructure, and the New Task for Regulation*. Ann Arbor: University of Michigan Press.

Sussman, J. (1995) Educating the new transportation professional. *ITS Quarterly*, **3**, pp. 3–10.

Zimmerman, R. and Sparrow, R. (1997) Final Report Based on the Workshop on Integrated Research for Civil Infrastructure, 15–17 July 1996. Washington DC; New York University, Robert F. Wagner Graduate School of Public Service, Taub Urban Research Center, February 1997. Online. Available HTTP: <http://www.nyu.edu/urban/research/nsf-infra/report.html>.

Chapter 8

A comparison of work and nonwork travel: the US and Great Britain[1]

Genevieve Giuliano and Dhiraj Narayan

The relationship between transportation and land use continues to be of great interest to urban researchers across many disciplines. This relationship is also a public policy issue of growing importance. Automobile dependence is a major topic in sustainability discussions, and it is linked to the growth of dispersed, low-density patterns of urban development (e.g., Calthorpe, 1993; Newman and Kenworthy, 1998). This chapter explores the relationship between land-use patterns and individual mobility from a comparative international perspective. Building on previous work using individual travel diary data for the US and Great Britain, we present some preliminary results on work and nonwork travel patterns and their relationship with basic measures of urban form.

The dominance of the automobile in the US is explained in part by low-density development ('urban sprawl'), and a growing number of planners and policy-makers argue that land-use policies in the US must change, that higher density, mixed-use development, and expanded public transport be pursued as a means for reducing reliance on the automobile (e.g. Bernick and Cervero, 1997; Ewing, 1997; Katz, 1994). Others argue that transportation policy must change: the cost of auto travel should be increased via higher taxes and fees (e.g. Kain, 1999; Small, Winston and Evans, 1989).

However, comparison of travel and land-use trends over time show that automobile use is increasing throughout the world. Auto ownership continues to increase in European countries, despite far more restrictive land-use policy, better public transport, and higher costs of automobile travel, compared to the US. These trends suggest that larger structural and economic forces may be at work (Ingram and Liu, 1999). They generate questions about the respective roles of economic circumstances, land use, and public policies.

International comparative research

In previous work (Giuliano, 1999), we have argued that international comparative analysis of travel patterns is useful, because it allows comparisons across very different land-use and policy environments. It is well known that policy environments differ greatly across countries. Taxes on fuel and automobile purchases, subsidy support for public transport, parking availability and price have a direct impact on travel demand. Land-use regulation, housing policy, and even national tax policy have indirect impacts on travel demand.

Most international comparative research to date has been conducted at a high level of aggregation. For example, the various Newman and Kenworthy studies compare average metropolitan density with per capita fuel consumption (e.g., Newman and Kenworthy, 1998). Schafer and Victor (2000) collected travel diary data from twenty-six countries, but used only national averages in a test of the travel time budget theory. Land-use differences were not considered. Pucher and Lefevre (1996) examined travel patterns across the US and five European countries, noting land-use differences as one of the key explanatory factors, again at the national level.

Comparisons across national aggregates ignore within-country variations that might be important explanatory factors. For example, some countries are more urbanized than others, or have older population age profiles, and both these factors are known to affect travel behaviour. In addition, aggregate patterns are the outcomes of individual decisions regarding where, when, how, and with whom to conduct daily activities. Hence understanding differences in aggregate travel patterns requires understanding differences in disaggregate travel patterns.

An important reason for restricting international comparisons to aggregate analysis is the challenge of comparable household or individual data. Clarke and Kuipers-Linde (1994) restricted themselves to two regions, Los Angeles and the Randstad, to compare commuting patterns, and were able to compare only travel time and city-to-city flow patterns. They found that commute flows have lengthened and dispersed in both metropolitan regions, despite very different policy environments. These shifts are attributed to economic restructuring and the emergence of polycentric spatial form. More recently, Lleras *et al.* (2002) compared individual travel patterns across four countries using travel diary data. Because of data comparability problems, each country was modelled separately and with somewhat different variables. They found 'urbanization' measures to be (negatively) related to auto access.

Work and nonwork travel

The literature on work travel is extensive. Commuting behaviour has been examined in terms of residential and employment location choice (e.g. Simpson, 1992; Voith, 1991; Weisbrod, Lerman and Ben-Akiva, 1980); as an indicator of urban spatial structure (e.g. Clarke and Kupers-Linde, 1994; Giuliano and Small, 1993; Gordon, Kumar and Richardson, 1989); as the 'anchor' of daily activity patterns (e.g. Recker, McNally, and Root, 1986); and in terms of the determinants of mode choice, trip scheduling etc. (e.g. Ben-Akiva and Lerman, 1985; Small, 1992). International comparisons are typically descriptive, as explained above.

Nonwork travel includes trips for many purposes, from shopping for groceries, to visiting friends, to seeking medical care. Travel behaviour researchers have sought to categorize nonwork trips to capture the degree to which such travel is discretionary. Golob and McNally (1997) classified nonwork trips as maintenance and discretionary. Maintenance trips are those made in support of household maintenance (e.g. shopping, escorting children, conducting personal business). Discretionary travel includes social trips, which are more flexible in terms of regularity, scheduling, and frequency. All else equal, we expect more variability in nonwork travel, since individuals have more choices of where, when, and how to conduct such trips.

The differences in characteristics of work and nonwork travel are well known. Work trips are longer in both distance and time, are more likely to be made driving alone, and are more concentrated in time than nonwork trips. Nonwork trips are more price elastic, hence we observe reductions in nonwork travel as a response to higher fuel prices or increased transit fares. Nonwork trips are more likely made close to home, when appropriate destinations are available close to home (Ewing, Haliyur and Page, 1994; Hanson and Schwab, 1987; Kitamura, Mokhtarian, and Laidet, 1997). Nonwork trips are often chained with the work trip (Strathman and Dueker, 1995). These characteristics indicate economizing behaviour: people take advantage of the spatial and temporal flexibility of nonwork travel.

Comparing work and nonwork travel across different countries provides a unique opportunity to test whether differences in work travel are more or less pronounced than differences in nonwork travel. Comparing the US and Great Britain, we would expect greater differences in nonwork travel: the high price of private vehicle travel, together with higher density and more mixed settlement patterns, should provide both the incentive and the opportunity for less nonwork travel in Great Britain. In contrast, work travel is largely a function of the relative distributions of jobs and workers; hence, differences may be more apparent in mode rather than distance.

Research approach

In a previous paper (Giuliano and Narayan, 2003), we argued that in examining the role of land use, travel by all modes and all purposes should be considered, with the spatial range of travel (activity space) of particular interest. Our basic question is, what explains differences in work and nonwork travel patterns – particularly automobile use – between the US and the countries of Europe?

More specifically, what is the role of land-use characteristics? The literature shows that travel is a function of individual and household characteristics, household transportation resources (car availability, driver's licence), transportation prices and supply characteristics, and land use. If we assume that individuals are rational utility maximizers, it follows that similar people should have similar behaviour, all else equal. For example, household income or the individual's age should have a consistent relationship to travel across the two countries. However, cultural differences may promote differences. For example, if in Europe gender roles are more differentiated, we might find that women make a greater proportion of nonwork trips.

We specify a simple regression model of the following form:

$$Y = f(X, L, XR, LR, R)$$

where

Y = total daily travel (work or nonwork)
X = individual characteristics
L = land-use characteristics
R = country dummy variable.

Individual characteristics include age, sex, and household income. Land-use characteristics include metropolitan size and local population density. Differences in transportation supply and pricing will be reflected in the dummy variable. Use of interaction dummies allow for first order interaction effects. A key variable is car ownership. Car ownership depends on price as well as demand for travel, and hence is endogenous to daily mobility. Therefore a simple OLS regression model based on the equation above, with car ownership included on the right-hand side, will be biased. In order to avoid this problem we estimate a reduced form model, omitting car ownership variables. The effect of car ownership will be reflected in the income and employment variables. The model estimations are based on a random 50/50 sample of US and British adults drawn from the NPTS and NTS surveys.

Data

Although eventually we want to include several European countries in our research, the difficulties of generating comparable data sets constrained us to beginning with just one European country, Great Britain. We had access to travel diary data and to the government staff who managed the survey. We were therefore able to work through the many challenges of understanding the data and making the necessary changes to generate comparable data sets. From an analytical standpoint, Great Britain represents a reasonable representation of a 'European country', in that widespread car ownership occurred well after World War II, its central cities are dense, pedestrian oriented and well served by public transit, auto ownership and use costs are relatively high, and land-use controls are relatively strong. It is also important to note the large fundamental differences between the two countries in terms of population, size, and household income, as illustrated in Table 8.1.

Table 8.1 Basic statistics, US and UK

	US	GB
Population (2000 est)	275.5 million	59.5 million
Land area (km²)	9,158,960	241,590
Median household income (1999 ppp)	$33,900	$21,800

The NPTS and NTS

We use the US 1995 Nationwide Personal Travel Survey (NPTS) and the British 1995/97 National Transport Survey (NTS). Both are household-based surveys that elicit travel diary information from all members of the household.[2] The NPTS was conducted for the first time in 1969 to develop a database of basic travel information for the US. Households are selected via a complex stratified sampling method, and all members 5 years old or older of the selected households are interviewed. Information on household characteristics, individual characteristics, car ownership and use is collected. The 1995 NTPS included 42,000 households, of which half are from states or metro areas that paid to have their area over-sampled. Households were assigned a 24-hour 'travel day' and a 14-day 'travel period'. The survey data are weighted to account for sample design and selection probability, non-response bias, and non-coverage bias.[3]

The NTS is a series of household surveys designed to provide a national bank of personal travel information for Great Britain. The Ministry of Transport commissioned the first NTS in 1965. The NTS is based on a random sample of private households, and is limited to Great Britain (England, Wales, Scotland). In order to select the appropriate number of addresses, a stratified multi-stage random probability sample is used. Seven-day travel diaries are kept by each member of the household, with adults reporting for younger children and others unable to provide information on their own behalf. Data collected include information on: household, individuals, vehicles, long-distance journeys (including those made in the three weeks before the start of the seven day travel week), journeys made during the travel week, and stages of journeys made during the travel weeks. The NTS makes a special effort to include 'short walks', for example, walks trips of less than 1 mile. Respondents are asked to include these trips on Day 7 of the diary only. The NTS data are not weighted. The sample is presumed representative of the population based on the way the sample is chosen. The NTS is conducted on an ongoing basis; the '1995' survey was conducted from 1995 through early 1997. The NTS sample included 9,688 'fully co-operating' households in 1995/1997.[4]

In order to compare work and nonwork travel, all trip purposes are assigned as follows: work and work-related trips are work trips, and travel for all other purposes is defined as nonwork. Trips longer than 75 miles are deleted in order to restrict the analysis to intra-metropolitan travel. We use the Day 7 NTS data in order to include short walk trips. In order to make comparisons between work and nonwork travel as consistent as possible, we restrict our sample to persons 17 years or older. We eliminate all persons who did not travel on the survey day, as we are categorizing travel on the basis of trip purpose. It is important to note that by eliminating those who made no trips, we are reducing the variation between the two samples, as 21% of all GB persons made no trips on the survey day, compared to 14% for US persons. Thus differences in the *overall propensity to travel* are not part of this analysis.

Some important differences between US and Great Britain

There are some important differences in demographic, socio-economic, and residential location between the US and Great Britain. First, median household income is about one-third lower in Great Britain (see Table 8.1). Second, car ownership is much lower; in the US about two-thirds of all persons reside in households with as many cars as drivers, compared to just under one-half for Great Britain. Conversely, just 3% of US persons reside in households with no cars, compared to 23% for Great Britain. It bears noting that the 1995 fuel price per litre is $.90 for Great Britain and $.30 for the US, a consequence of starkly different fuel tax policies. Hence, relative to income, the price of automobile travel is far higher in Great Britain.

Third, the population distributions are quite different, as shown in Table 8.2. Over 40% of the British population lives outside of metropolitan areas,

Table 8.2 Place of residence by metropolitan size, percentage shares

	US	Great Britain
Not in Metro area of > 100k	14.4	40.6
100k – 250k	9.6	9.1
250k – 500k	6.4	24.8
500k – 1m	12.7	3.0
1m – 3m	18.8	10.7
> 3m	38.1	11.5

and the distribution is skewed toward smaller metro areas. The US distribution is just the opposite, with about 57% of the population living in metro areas of 1 million or more population. Fourth, the US population is more likely to live in low-density areas, while the British population is more likely to live in higher density areas. All of these differences (with the possible exception of the large proportion of non-metropolitan population) suggest lower rates of travel for Great Britain.

Results

It is useful to summarize our results of a US-Great Britain comparison of total travel before discussing differences in work and nonwork travel (Giuliano and Narayan, 2003). We then present some descriptive statistics, followed by the regression model results.

US – Great Britain comparisons of total travel

Our previous results on total travel indicated that three factors are important in explaining differences between the two countries. First, there is a large independent negative effect on both trips and daily travel distance for the British group, capturing the differences in transport prices and supply, as well as other country-specific factors that suppress travel and that were not directly incorporated in our models. Household income is the second key factor. The daily trip rate is relatively constant across income levels for GB, but increases with income for the US. For travel distance, the relationship is positive with income for both groups. One possible explanation is that the British have more options for substitution across modes (short non-motorized trips substitute for longer motorized trips when incomes are low).

Third, the relationship between density and travel is quite different between the two countries. The trip rate is lower for both low density and high density for the US, but not for Great Britain. If density is a surrogate for accessibility, the trip rate should increase with density. Density is negatively related to daily travel distance for both groups, but the relationship is far more pronounced for the US. Although this result suggests that density is even more influential in the US than in Great Britain (low density places in the US do not have the fine grain mix of local neighbourhood services, etc. that make shorter trips possible), we noted that high density may capture inner-city US characteristics (very low income, immigrant households, elderly households) that are associated with less travel.

Some comparisons

We begin with some simple comparisons. Table 8.3 shows the distribution of

Table 8.3 Trip distribution by persons, percent

Country	No trips	Work trip only	Nonwork trip only	Work and nonwork trip	Total persons
US	14.3	11.9	43.7	30.1	76,837
GB	21.0	15.5	46.0	17.6	17,754

persons by the types of trips made. As noted above, the British are far more likely to have made no trips, indicating lower overall propensity to travel. The table also shows that the British are less likely to make both work and nonwork trips on the travel survey day.

Table 8.4 gives total daily trip frequency, distance and time, for those who made a work or nonwork trip on the survey day. Turning first to work travel, the trip rate is slightly higher in the US, reflecting more work-related travel. In both the US and Great Britain, the median is two, as expected. Total daily work travel distance is far lower in Great Britain, while travel time is slightly higher, indicating greater use of slower modes by the British. Differences in nonwork travel are more pronounced: the British nonwork trip rate is 21% less than the US, and total distance is 43% lower. Again, nonwork travel time is slightly higher, indicating more use of slower modes. Cumulative distributions are shown in Figures 8.1 and 8.2 for work and nonwork travel distance respectively. Differences between the US and Great Britain are greater for nonwork travel.

Work trips account for 24% of all trips, 36% of all miles, and 33% of all travel time for the US. For Great Britain, the shares are 26% of all trips, 39% of all miles, and 30% of all travel time. Hence, the differences between work and nonwork travel are greater for Great Britain; nonwork trips are shorter in distance, but longer in time.

Table 8.5 gives mode shares for work and nonwork travel. Because of data limitations, we know whether the person drove or rode as a passenger in a

Table 8.4 Total daily trip frequency, distance, time, by purpose

	Trips		Distance		Time	
US	*Mean*	*Median*	*Mean*	*Median*	*Mean*	*Median*
Work	2.48	2.00	25.9	17.0	48.1	36.0
Nonwork	4.37	4.00	26.7	16.1	56.8	44.0
GB	*Mean*	*Median*	*Mean*	*Median*	*Mean*	*Median*
Work	2.36	2.00	18.4	10.0	51.5	40.0
Nonwork	3.47	3.00	15.2	7.6	60.1	46.0
Differences						
Work		−5%		−29%		+7%
Nonwork		−21%		−43%		+6%

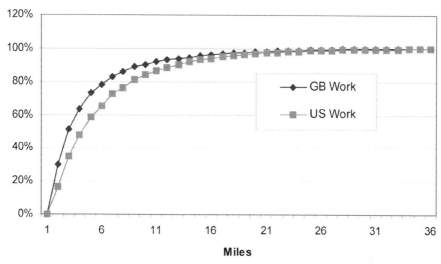

Figure 8.1 Work travel distance cumulative distribution

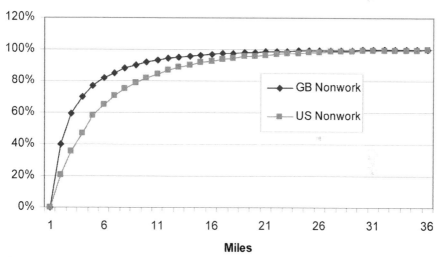

Figure 8.2 Nonwork travel distance distribution

privately owned vehicle, but not whether there were others in the vehicle in the case of driver trips. Hence, we cannot identify carpool trips. Work trips are overwhelmingly made in private vehicles in the US; all other modes account for less than 7%. However, nearly three-quarters of British work trips are also made in private vehicles. The difference from the US is 22 percentage points. The transit and walk/bike shares are orders of magnitude greater than the US: the British transit share is 3.4 times that of the US, and the walk/bike share is 6 times larger.

Table 8.5 Mode shares by trip purpose

	Work		Nonwork	
	US	GB	US	GB
POV driver	84.8	60.9	58.7	30.6
POV passenger	8.4	12.0	30.0	23.5
Total POV	93.2	72.9	88.7	54.1
Public transport	2.9	10.0	1.2	7.7
Walk/bike	2.7	16.2	7.1	36.8
Other	1.2	0.9	3.1	1.4

Nonwork trip mode shares are also quite different. The private vehicle accounts for 89% of all US nonwork trips, compared to 54% for Great Britain, a difference of about 35 percentage points. The biggest difference between work and nonwork in the US is the increase in passenger trips, an expected outcome. The modal nonwork mode for the British is walk/bike, accounting for 37% of all nonwork trips, and 5 times larger than the US walk/bike share. Transit carries about 1% of US nonwork trips, but nearly 8% for Great Britain. The differences in modal shares between the US and Great Britain are much greater than the differences in trip rate, distance, and travel time. Comparing work and nonwork, the greatest difference between the two countries is in private vehicle use. While there is little difference in the private vehicle share for work and nonwork trips in the US, there is a rather large difference in Great Britain. This is consistent with the generally lower rate of car ownership in Great Britain.

The travel patterns described here are consistent with greater demand elasticity for nonwork travel. The British make fewer nonwork trips, and are far more likely to make them via non-motorized modes than their US counterparts.

The role of household income and residential density

Our previous work indicated that household income and residential density are key factors in explaining differences in travel patterns between the US and Great Britain. Are these factors associated with greater differences in nonwork than work travel, as would be expected? Figures 8.3 and 8.4 illustrate the relationship for household income. The figures show that both work and nonwork travel increase with household income, as expected. For work travel, income seems to have more effect for Great Britain; at very high income, work travel approaches that of the US. A similar pattern is observed for nonwork travel, but note that US nonwork travel increases relatively little with income; even the lowest income persons travel about 25 miles per day for nonwork

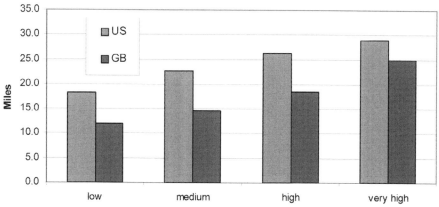

Figure 8.3 Household income vs. work travel distance

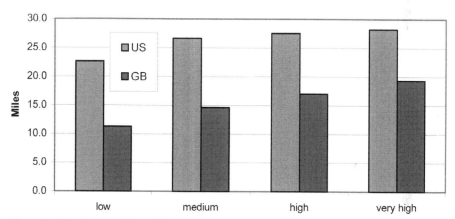

Figure 8.4 Density vs. work travel distance

purposes. The differences between the US and Great Britain are greater in every income category for nonwork travel, supporting our basic hypothesis.

Figures 8.5 and 8.6 provide similar data for residential density. As expected, travel distance decreases with increasing density for both work and nonwork travel. For both work and nonwork travel, differences between the two countries decline as density increases. As with household income, differences are greater for nonwork travel, again supporting our basis hypothesis. We turn now to the question of whether these relationships are observed after controlling for other relevant factors.

Regression results

We estimate separate models for work travel and nonwork travel. Because

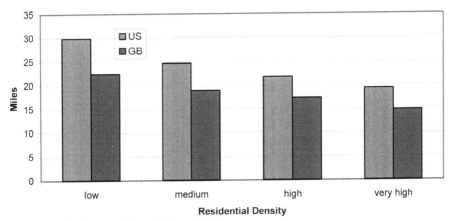

Figure 8.5 Density vs. work travel distance

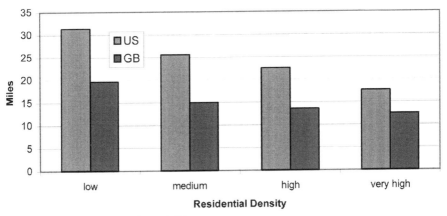

Figure 8.6 Density vs. nonwork travel distance

there is so little variation in trip making, we restrict this analysis to travel distance. We restrict the sample to persons 17 years or older in order to make the work and nonwork sample of travellers as similar as possible. As noted earlier, we include only those who made a work or nonwork trip on the travel day.

The regressions were performed as follows. From the original pooled data set, we drew a 50/50 US/GB random sample of persons who made at least one work trip, and another random sample of persons who made at least one nonwork trip. Hence, the work and nonwork samples are different from one another, but representative of the larger sample of persons in these travel categories. We estimated simple linear regressions. Demographic and socio-economic variables included sex, age, and household income.[5] We used two measures of urban form: metropolitan size and residential density.[6] We used a full set of interaction terms so that differences between the US and Great Britain can be compared for each independent variable.

Work travel distance

Table 8.6 gives results for work travel distance. Since all variables are in linear form, the magnitude of the coefficients can be interpreted directly. Results are reasonable. The constant term coefficient value is close to the sample mean, and the value of the GB constant coefficient is consistent with the GB mean value. Clearly there is a big difference in work travel distance, even when other factors are controlled. Turning to the socio-economic variable coefficients in the first column of results, most are significant, and all are of the expected sign. Females travel less work distance than males, and the elderly travel less distance than the 'middle' age groups.[7] Work travel distance increases with income, but there is a much bigger difference between the lowest and middle income categories than between the middle and high income categories. Among the GB group interaction terms for this set of variables, only high income has a differential larger effect (meaning that the range from lowest to highest income is greater for Great Britain, as shown in Figure 8.3).

Table 8.6 Dependent variable: work travel miles/day

Variable	Total sample		GB	
	B	S.E.	B	S.E.
Constant	**25.17**	1.44		
GB dummy			**-6.76**	2.72
Socio-economic				
Female	**-9.75**	0.71	-0.33	1.02
Age 17–34 yrs	-0.84	0.76	0.29	1.06
Age > 64 yrs	**-6.56**	1.94	2.22	3.31
HH inc – low quartile	**-3.33**	1.63	1.57	2.10
HH inc – 3rd quartile	**2.07**	0.98	1.64	1.34
HH inc – 4th quartile	**2.51**	1.02	**8.02**	1.42
Urban form				
Not in MSA	-1.37	1.42	3.58	2.56
MSA < 250K	0.05	1.57	1.18	2.79
MSA 250k – 500k	-3.14	1.80	2.55	2.85
MSA 1–3m	1.21	1.30	0.02	2.64
MSA > 3m	**6.51**	1.20	**-7.17**	2.61
Density < 1k/mile^2	**8.17**	0.90	**-5.75**	1.42
Density 4k–10k/mile^2	**-3.19**	1.05	1.35	1.48
Density > 10k/mile^2	**-6.98**	1.41	**4.17**	1.88
R^2 (adj)				0.10
N				10,000

Bold = sig. At p ≤ .01

Regarding the urban form variables, only the coefficient for metro areas of greater than 3 million population is significant. The GB interaction term is negative and of similar magnitude, indicating that work travel has no relationship to metropolitan size in Great Britain.

The most interesting results are those for residential density. The coefficients in the first column show a significant negative relationship of density and work distance travelled, consistent with many prior studies. The coefficients for the interaction terms are negative and significant for low density, not significant for medium density, and positive and significant for high density. The results suggest that the inverse relationship between work travel distance and density is much more pronounced for the US than for Great Britain (see Figure 8.5).

Nonwork Travel Distance

Table 8.7 gives results for nonwork travel distance. Again the value of the constant term is consistent with the sample mean, and the GB constant is large and negative, a result of the lower mean value and skewed distribution of nonwork travel distance (60% of British nonwork travel is less than 3 miles; see Figure 8.1). Independent effects of demographic and socio-economic factors are not significant, except for older age. The relationship

Table 8.7 Dependent variable: nonwork travel miles/day

	Total sample		GB	
Variable	B	S.E.	B	S.E.
Constant	**27.97**	1.59		
GB dummy			**−17.51**	2.85
Socio-economic				
Female	−0.69	0.71	−0.48	1.01
Age 17 – 34 yrs	1.63	0.81	−1.29	1.15
Age > 64 yrs	**−3.51**	1.18	1.30	1.59
HH inc – low quartile	−2.07	1.27	0.84	1.62
HH inc – 3rd quartile	0.24	0.98	**2.91**	1.39
HH inc – 4th quartile	1.54	1.02	**3.10**	1.50
Employed	**−4.36**	0.91	**4.51**	1.28
Urban Form				
Not in MSA	2.30	1.40	2.88	2.51
MSA < 250k	−2.08	1.52	**6.26**	2.72
MSA 250–500k	1.94	1.71	0.77	2.74
MSA 1–3m	0.74	1.28	2.55	2.57
MSA > 3m	0.74	1.19	1.75	2.56
Density < 1K/mile^2	**5.50**	0.88	−0.89	1.42
Density 4K – 10K/mile^2	**−3.11**	1.04	1.97	1.47
Density > 10K/mile^2	**−9.17**	1.38	**8.13**	1.86
R^2 (adj)	0.08			
N				10,000

Bold = sig. At p ≤ .01

with older age is expected and reflects the generally lower propensity to travel among older persons. The employment variable coefficient is negative, also as expected. Turning to the British interaction terms, household income has a positive effect on nonwork travel distance. This is probably due to differing levels of car ownership; low-income British households are less likely to own any cars, hence many more nonwork trips are made by non-motorized modes. The employment interaction term is positive and of the same magnitude as the independent effect coefficient. This may seem counter-intuitive, but upon checking the data, we found that among the British, employed people are indeed as likely to make as many nonwork trips as those adults who are not employed.

The urban form variable results are similar to those for work travel. Metropolitan size has no significant effect, while the relationship with residential density is highly significant and negative. One of the metropolitan size interaction coefficients is significant, contrary to expectations. The coefficient for high density is significant and positive, again suggesting that the relationship between nonwork travel and density is more attenuated in Great Britain than in the US.

The results for the GB group are somewhat surprising: we would expect that given the higher relative price of motorized travel, the British would be more inclined to economize and therefore make shorter trips in more accessible places. This should particularly be the case for nonwork travel, given its greater flexibility. There are two possible explanations for these results. First, the greater availability and higher quality of transit may provide a more uniform level of transport access across all levels of density. Second, mixed land-use patterns are widespread in Great Britain; consequently, population density may be a less useful proxy for urban form. That is, the higher price of travel promotes economizing everywhere, and land-use patterns make this economizing possible. We have seen that the differences in nonwork travel are greater than the distances in work travel, as expected – there is more economizing of nonwork travel in terms of trip frequency, mode, and distance travelled. In contrast, the extreme effect of low density for the US group may reflect highly dispersed land-use patterns that simply do not exist in Great Britain, even in low-density non-metropolitan areas.

Conclusions

We draw the following conclusions from our results. First, the differences between the US and Great Britain are greater for nonwork travel than for work travel, as expected. The independent negative effect on nonwork travel is greater for the British group. The group specific constant captures the differences in transport prices and supply, as well as other country-specific factors that suppress travel and that are not directly incorporated in our models. The greater flexibility of nonwork trips makes it possible to economize more for nonwork than work trips.

Second, demographic characteristics have consistent effects across groups for both work and nonwork travel, but the effect of high household income is greater for the British, we surmise due to higher rates of car ownership among high-income British households. These results indicate that observed differences between countries are in part explained by differences in population and income characteristics.

Third, the relationship between density and travel is quite different between the two countries. Density is negatively related to work and nonwork travel distance for both groups, but the relationship is far more pronounced for the US. As noted in our previous paper, if we could be certain that the density variable is not somehow picking up income-related population characteristics (elderly single person households, very low income minority and immigrant households) that are associated in the US with the inner city, we might conclude that density is even more influential in the US than in Great Britain, because low-density places in the US do not have the fine grain mix of local neighbourhood services, etc. that make shorter trips possible. However, we cannot rule out the possibility that effects of income-related population characteristics may indeed be playing a role here. If this were not the case, we would see greater similarities in the results for high density, because high-density places are more similar in levels of accessibility, transit availability, etc.

Policy implications

What do our results suggest for the role of policy in affecting travel behaviour? First, the higher relative price of owning and using automobiles is part of the explanation for less daily travel distance among the British. Differences in modal shares between work and nonwork travel are consistent with lower rates of household auto ownership: the auto is more often used for the journey to work, leaving other household members to use other modes for nonwork travel. The relationship between household income and nonwork travel distance among the British (in contrast to the US) is also consistent with lower rates of auto ownership. Moreover, it is worth noting that public transport prices are relatively high in Great Britain, due to privatization policies implemented in the mid-1980s. Hence long-distance commuting, by car or train, is economically feasible only for the highest income British households.

Second, we have both supporting and opposing evidence that land-use policies affect travel behaviour. On the one hand, residential density is a significant factor for both countries and for both work and nonwork travel. However, the relationship is more pronounced in the US, mainly because of the effect of low density. We would expect just the opposite; density effects should be *greater* when travel costs are high. But it is also possible that density is measuring two different things. Highly segmented, dispersed land-use patterns typical of American suburbs do not (yet) exist in Great Britain. Villages and small towns, as well as urban neighbourhoods, have commercial centres that serve the local population. Whether this integration of residential and commercial uses is the result of economic forces or deliberate policy is an open question, but certainly with high transport costs households are motivated to take advantage of local shops and services. In the US, conditions are just the opposite. The price of private vehicle travel is so low that highly segmented and dispersed land-use patterns are easily supported; only the lowest income segment of the US population faces price-related constraints on mobility.

Governments have many options for influencing travel demand, both directly and indirectly. The US and Great Britain have followed contrasting policy paths, particularly with respect to transport taxation and supply. Our results are consistent with these differences, but the interesting question is whether they will remain as per capita income increases in Great Britain. Historical data show trends of increasing auto ownership and use throughout the developed and developing world. Will higher incomes generate demand for larger houses and more consumer goods, resulting in more travel as households seek locations in lower cost suburbs and new towns? Will the shift to large-scale retailers result in a decline in neighbourhood services, as happened in the US, leading to longer nonwork trips? The answer depends on the policy environment – on the extent to which the public is willing to accept restrictive policies on automobiles in exchange for perceived benefits in quality of life and more liveable communities.

Notes

1   Support for this research from the US National Science Foundation, under grant number 0137029, Transportation and Land Use, A Comparative International Analysis, is gratefully acknowledged. All errors and omissions are the responsibility of the authors.
2   Specifically, all persons 5 years or older are included in NPTS; all persons of all ages are included in NTS.
3   The weighting is developed for households. The household weights are based on time of year, geographic region, race/ethnicity, and household size. Person weights are calculated from the household weight, adjusted for non-responding members of responding households. Trip weights are calculated based on the person weights. The weights are scaled to the total US 1995 population.
4   A fully cooperating household has completed all basic survey questions and each household member has completed the 7 day diary.
5   Life cycle variables work similarly to the age/sex variables, and hence are not included in the results presented here.

6 Residential density is measured at the Census Tract level for the US, and at the Postal Service Unit level for GB. The geographic size of CTs and PSAs are similar.
7 About 4% of those employed are 65 years or older.

Bibliography

Ben-Akiva, M. and Lerman, S. (1985) *Discrete Choice Analysis: Theory and Applications*. Cambridge, MA: The MIT Press.

Bernick, M. and Cervero, R. (1997) *Transit Villages in the 21st Century*. New York: McGraw-Hill.

Calthorpe, P. (1993) *The Next American Metropolis: Ecology, Community and the American Dream*. New York, NY: Princeton Architectural Press.

Clarke, W. and Kupers-Linde, M. (1994) Commuting in restructuring Urban regions. *Urban Studies*, 31, pp. 465–484.

Ewing, R. (1997) *Best Development Practices*. Chicago, IL: Planners Press.

Ewing, R., Haliyur, P. and Page, G. (1994) Getting around a traditional city, a suburban planned unit development, and everything in between. *Transportation Research Record*, 1466, pp. 53–62.

Giuliano, G. (1999) Land use and transportation: why we won't get there from here. *Transportation Research Circular*, 492, pp. 179–198.

Giuliano, G. (2002) Travel, location and race/ethnicity. *Transportation Research A*, 37, pp. 351–372.

Giuliano, G. and Narayan, D. (2003) Another look at travel patterns and urban form: The US and Great Britain. *Urban Studies*, 40(11), pp. 2295–2312.

Giuliano, G. and Small, K. (1993) Is the journey to work explained by urban structure? *Urban Studies*, 30, pp. 44–52.

Golob, T. and McNally, M. (1997) A model of activity participation and travel interactions between household heads. *Transportation Research B*, 31, pp. 177–194.

Gordon, P., Kumar, A. and Richardson, H. (1989) Congestion, changing metropolitan structure and city size in the United States. *International Regional Science Review*, 12, pp. 45–56.

Hanson, S. and Schwab, M. (1987) Accessibility and intraurban travel. *Environment and Planning A*, 19, pp. 735–748.

Ingram, G. and Liu, A. (1999) Determinants of motorization and road provision, in Gomez-Ibanez, J., Tye, W. and Winston, C. (eds.) *Essays in Transportation Economics and Policy*. Washington, DC: Brookings Institution.

Katz, P. (1994) *The New Urbanism: Toward an Architecture of Community*. New York, NY: McGraw-Hill.

Kain, J. (1999) The urban transportation problem: A reexamination and update, in Gomez-Ibanez, J., Tye, W. and Winston, C. (eds.) *Essays in Transportation Economics and Policy*. Washington, DC: Brookings Institution.

Kitamura, R., Mokhtarian, P. and Laidet, L. (1997) A micro-analysis of land use and travel in five neighborhoods in the San Francisco Bay Area. *Transportation*, 24, pp. 125–158.

Lleras, G., Simma, A., Ben-Akiva, M., Schafer, A., Auxhausen, K. and Furutani, T. (2002) Fundamental relationships specifying travel behavior – An international travel survey comparison. Paper presented at the TRB 2003 Annual Meeting, Washington, DC.

Newman, P. and Kenworthy, J. (1998) *Sustainability and Cities: Overcoming Automobile Dependence*. Washington, DC: Island Press.

Pucher, J. and Lefevre, C. (1996) *The Urban Transport Crisis – in Europe and North America.*, London: Macmillan Press.

Recker W., McNally, M. and Root, G. (1986) A model of complex activity behavior: Part I – Theoretical development. *Transportation Research A*, 20, pp. 307–318.

Schafer, A. and Victor, D. (2000) The future mobility of the world population. *Transportation Research A*, 34, pp. 171–205.

Simpson, W. (1992) *Urban Structure and the Labour Market: Analysis of Worker Mobility, Commuting and Unemployment in Cities*. Oxford: Oxford University Press.

Small, K. (1992) *Urban Transportation Economics*. Chur: Harwood Academic Publishers.

Small, K., Winston, C. and Evans, C. (1989) *Road Work: A New Highway Pricing and Investment Policy*. Washington, DC: Brookings Institution.

Strathman, J. and Dueker, K. (1995) Understanding trip chaining. *1990 NPTS Special Reports on Trips and Vehicle Attributes*. Report FHWA-PL-95-033. Washington, DC: US Department of Transportation, Federal Highway Administration.

Voith, R. (1991) Transportation, sorting and house values. *American Real Estate and Urban Economics Association*, **19**, pp. 117–137.

Weisbrod, G., Lerman, S. and Ben-Akiva, M. (1980) Tradeoffs in residential location decisions: transportation versus other factors. *Transportation Policy and Decision Making*, **1**, pp. 13–26.

Chapter 9

Institutional issues in on-street parking[1]

Edward Calthrop

It is often claimed that the average car is only driven for approximately 10% of the time – for the remainder, it is parked. On the basis of the transport economics literature, however, you might well be excused for thinking precisely the opposite. The bulk of the literature examines policies targeted at the use of the car: for example, congestion pricing scheme influencing the timing of a trip, or the route or mode chosen. Only a handful of papers consider the economics of parking, either as a direct policy objective or as a means to reducing urban congestion or air pollution.

This emphasis in the literature is also at odds with actual policy. Nearly every urban centre has an active parking policy. Typically such policies aim to reduce the search time required to find a vacant spot, which in a poorly regulated market can constitute a large fraction of total journey time. In addition, transport authorities often try to use the parking market as a means of tackling more general problems associated with car use such as road congestion and air pollution.

This chapter uses a formal model to identify the welfare impact of a revenue-neutral increase in an on-street parking fee. This allows us to define an efficient parking policy. It also gives a benchmark against which we can judge actual institutions: an efficient institutional structure can be defined, somewhat tautologically, as one that facilitates efficient pricing policy.

There may be many reasons why, in practice, institutions fail to set efficient prices. We focus on two examples, both of which stem from the *local* level of decision-making. This is clearly of practical relevance, as parking policy is mostly determined by local government, usually under the guise of a local transport authority (LTA).

The LTA faces strong incentives to maximize the welfare of local residents (or voters) only, and not to consider the impact of policy on commuters or tourists. This issue is formally examined in below (see page 135). As a result, pricing may be inefficient. In addition, the LTA may, in effect, compete with central government for urban transport tax revenues. As shown on page 137, by trying to maximize its own gain relative to the central administration, the LTA may face a strong incentive to set inefficient prices.

One caveat should be clear from the outset. The focus of this chapter is on pricing reforms within the on-street parking market. Though the message that emerges applies equally well to any variables under LTA control, we do not consider a large number of other pertinent parking issues, such as supply of space, regulation of the off-street market, information provision issues, or special parking needs (e.g. for large events, or for the disabled).

Model

A representative consumer derives utility from consumption of leisure, ℓ, a composite commodity, C and an aggregate quantity of transport trips. The aggregate quantity consists of trips across two modes (auto and rail), and, when travelling by car, two route choices (freeway F or back road B) and two parking markets (on-street X and off-street Y). All trips are assumed to take place in the peak-period.[2] Rather than examine all possible combinations, we consider a set j containing five markets, as shown in Table 9.1.

Table 9.1 Transport markets

j	Transport market
FX	Freeway, parking on-street
FY	Freeway, parking off-street
BX	Backroad, parking on-street
BY	Backroad, parking off-street
R	Rail

We assume a fixed transport infrastructure. Figure 9.1 shows the corresponding network graph.

Consumer utility is defined by

$$U = u(C,\ell,T_j) \tag{9.1}$$

where the number of trips of each type j is denoted by T_j. The time required to

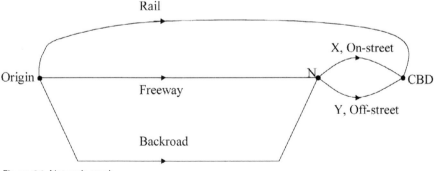

Figure 9.1 Network graph

complete a single trip is denoted by ϕ_j. Road use is assumed to be congestion-prone and hence travel time depends on the number of trips using the same infrastructure. Thus, we denote the time required to drive along the freeway and back road by $\phi_F(T_{FX} + T_{FY})$ and $\phi_B(T_{BX} + T_{BY})$ respectively, with $\phi'_F > 0$, $\phi'_B > 0$.

Similarly, on-street parking is assumed to require search time, which depends on the number of other drivers parking on street. Thus, we denote this search time by $\sigma(T_{FX} + T_{BX})$, with $\sigma' > 0$. Parking off-street, in contrast, is assumed to be congestion free, and thus the time required to park is constant (and, for ease, set equal to zero).

Thus, for road trips, we summarize:

$$\begin{aligned} \phi_{FY} &= \phi_F & \phi_{BY} &= \phi_B \\ \phi_{FX} &= \phi_F + \sigma & \phi_{BX} &= \phi_B + \sigma \end{aligned} \tag{9.2}$$

A rail trip is assumed to require a constant length of time,[3] ϕ_R. The consumer time constraint is given by:

$$L + \ell + \sum_j \phi_j T_j = \bar{L} \tag{9.3}$$

where $\bar{L}$ is the total time endowment.

The consumer money price of a trip is denoted by θ_j. A local transport authority (LTA) is assumed to be able to set a road toll on freeway[4] trips, τ, but not on back roads. In addition, the LTA can set the price of on-street parking, p_X, off-street parking, p_Y and the fare for rail, f. The producer price of a road trip, produced under constant returns to scale, is given by $\tilde{\theta}_r$ where $r \in \{F,B\}$. We summarize consumer prices by:

$$\begin{aligned} \theta_{FX} &= \tau + p_X + \tilde{\theta}_F & \theta_{FY} &= \tau + p_Y + \tilde{\theta}_F \\ \theta_{BX} &= p_X + \tilde{\theta}_B & \theta_{BY} &= p_Y + \tilde{\theta}_B \\ \theta_R &= f \end{aligned} \tag{9.4}$$

The consumer budget constraint is given by:

$$C + \sum_j \theta_j T_j = L + G \tag{9.5}$$

where G denotes a lump-sum transfer and units are adjusted such that the price of labour supply[5] and the composite good is equal to 1.

Production is under constant returns to scale, except for the rail sector, which produces under increasing economies of scale, with a fixed cost element, and a constant marginal cost, $\tilde{\theta}_R$. The fixed supply of on-street parking is provided at zero opportunity cost,[6] whilst off-street parking is provided at constant marginal cost, m_Y. The material balance condition for this economy is thus:

$$L = C + \sum_{j=FY,BY} (\tilde{\theta}_j + m_Y) T_j + \sum_{j=FX,BX,R} \tilde{\theta}_j T_j + F \tag{9.6}$$

The LTA budget constraint gives that:

$$
\begin{aligned}
G + F + \tilde{\theta}_R T_R + m_Y (T_{FY} + T_{BY}) = \\
\tau(T_{FX} + T_{FY}) + p_X(T_{FX} + T_{BX}) + p_Y(T_{FY} + T_{BY}) + f T_R
\end{aligned}
\tag{9.7}
$$

The representative consumer maximizes utility, expression (9.1), with respect to the quantities of the composite good, leisure and transport, subject to a budget constraint, (9.5) and time constraint, (9.3), taking the level of prices, the lump-sum transfer, time required to drive a kilometre and to search for a parking spot as parametric. Substituting the resulting demand functions into the utility function gives an indirect utility function:[7]

$$V(p_X, G, \phi_F, \phi_B, \sigma) \tag{9.8}$$

Given this model set-up, we are able to identify the welfare impact of a revenue-neutral increase in the price of on-street parking, in which the government maintains a balanced budget by recycling any additional revenues via the lump sum instrument, G. This welfare impact can be used to define an efficient parking policy.

Defining efficient LTA parking policy

As derived in Annex 1, the welfare impact of a revenue-neutral increase in the on-street parking fee can be written as the sum of five terms:

$$
\begin{aligned}
\frac{1}{\lambda} \frac{dV}{dp_X} = {} & (MEC_X - p_X)(-\left\{ \frac{dT_{FX}}{dp_X} + \frac{dT_{BX}}{dp_X} \right\}) + \\
& (p_Y - m_Y)\left\{ \frac{dT_{FY}}{dp_X} + \frac{dT_{BY}}{dp_X} \right\} + \\
& (MEC_F - \tau)(-\left\{ \frac{dT_{FX}}{dp_X} + \frac{dT_{FY}}{dp_X} \right\}) + \\
& MEC_B(-\left\{ \frac{dT_{BX}}{dp_X} + \frac{dT_{BY}}{dp_X} \right\}) + \\
& (f - \tilde{\theta}_R)\frac{dT_R}{dp_X}
\end{aligned}
\tag{9.9}
$$

where:

$$MEC_X = \frac{\mu}{\lambda}\sigma'\left(T_{FX} + T_{BX}\right) \qquad MEC_F = \frac{\mu}{\lambda}\phi_F'\left(T_{FX} + T_{FY}\right)$$

$$MEC_B = \frac{\mu}{\lambda}\phi_B'\left(T_{BX} + T_{BY}\right)$$

Each component can be examined in turn. The first term gives the welfare effect on the on-street parking market. It equals the general equilibrium change in demand for on-street parking[8] multiplied by the gap between marginal external search cost, MEC_X and the price. The marginal external search cost equals the utility loss (measured in income terms) to other on-street parkers from increasing the average time required to search for an on-street parking spot. If no other distortions are present, i.e. the subsequent four lines of equation (9.9) equal zero, then welfare increases until the point that the price of on-street parking equals MEC_X. This welfare message emerges from more detailed studies of the on-street parking market, including Arnott and Rowse (1999), Anderson and de Palma (2002), Calthrop and Proost (2003) and Vickrey (1959).

The remaining four terms relate to pre-existing distortions on *secondary* markets i.e. markets other than the on-street parking. As is well known, welfare assessment must take account of the extent to which a price reform exacerbates or alleviates distortions on other markets. The change in distortion on a secondary market takes the form of a distortive wedge, i.e. the difference between price and marginal social cost, multiplied by the resulting (general equilibrium) change in demand.

The second term in equation (9.9) takes account of pre-existing distortions on the off-street market. Increasing the on-street price induces some drivers to switch to the off-street market. If the off-street market is taxed, i.e. $p_Y > m_Y$, then the marginal benefit of off-street parking exceeds marginal social cost. Assuming that on- and off-street parking are substitutes (in total derivative terms), increasing the on-street fee alleviates the pre-existing distortion on the off-street market. Conversely, if the off-street market is subsidized, the distortion is exacerbated.

The third term accounts for distortions arising from congestion on the freeway. If congestion is underpriced, or not priced at all, the marginal social cost of freeway use is greater than the marginal benefit. To the extent that increasing the parking fee reduces freeway use, the presence of underpriced congestion will tend to increase the benefit of raising parking fees. The fourth term is entirely analogous, though relating to backstreet congestion. Recall that, by assumption, this cannot be charged for and hence the marginal social cost of back road use exceeds marginal benefit. Using parking fees to correct for under priced road congestion has been discussed by several authors, including Verhoef *et al.* (1995), Calthrop *et al.* (2000), Glazer and Niskanen (1992) and Arnott, de Palma and Lindsey (1991).

The final term refers to the rail market. Again, to the extent that rail travel is distorted (in practice, usually via an operating subsidy such that $f < \tilde{\theta}_r$), the welfare gain from reforming parking prices will need to account for induced effects on the distorted rail market.

Institutional barriers to efficient pricing

Efficient parking policy is summarized in equation (9.9). However, there are good reasons to suspect that the actual policy adopted by an LTA may be inefficient. In most countries, it is the LTA, and not central government, which sets the parking fee. But in so far as either the costs or the benefits of a policy change fall onto groups from outside the local area, this assignment of powers may give rise to inefficient pricing policies. Two examples seem reasonable: firstly, downtown spots are used by tourists and commuters as well as local residents. The LTA may rationally decide to ignore the consequences of policy changes on the welfare of non-residents, and instead attempt to extract rent from this group. This is an example of *tax-exporting (or horizontal tax competition)*, and is well-known phenomena in the tax competition literature (see, for example, Wellisch, 2000). We provide an example of this below.

A second example relates to central government. If central government sets taxes on transport markets, the LTA may perceive the transfer of revenue as a loss of local welfare. As a result, the LTA may use the tax instruments that are under its control to both correct for local externalities and reduce transfers to the central government. This phenomenon is usually referred to as *vertical tax competition*. An example is given below (see pages 136–138).

LTA as tax exporter

To focus on the central point,[9] we assume two representative consumers: a local resident, indexed by H (for home market) and a non-resident, such as a commuter or tourist, indexed by A (for abroad) with identical preferences given by equation (9.1). To simplify matters, we consider only a single aggregate transport market, an auto trip $T \equiv T_H + T_A$, subject to a parking tax, p_X. The results can be generalized to a number of transport markets in a straightforward manner. The time required to make a trip on this market is given by σ, which in turn depends on total demand: $\sigma(T)$.

Assuming that the LTA maximizes the revenue of local residents only, and redistributes all parking fee revenues to local residents, the welfare impact of a revenue-neutral increase in the parking fee is derived in Annex 2 as:

$$\frac{1}{\lambda}\frac{dW}{dp_X} = (MEC_H - p_X)(-\frac{dT}{dp_X}) + T_A \qquad (9.10)$$

where $MEC_X = (\mu/\lambda)T_H$. Before discussing this equation, we derive the full welfare impact of a price change, which would be considered by central government rather than the LTA:

$$\frac{1}{\lambda}\frac{dW}{dp_X} = (MEC - p_X)(-\frac{dT}{dp_X}) \qquad (9.11)$$

Equation (9.11) is just a simplified version of equation (9.9). The price of parking is raised until equal to the marginal external cost, defined in this case by $MEC = (\mu/\lambda)T$. In comparing equations (9.11) and (9.10), two distortions appear.

Firstly, the LTA ignores the benefit of the price reform on non-residents: it only considers MEC_H rather than MEC. This causes the LTA to set a price that is too low compared with the social optimum defined via (9.11). Secondly, the LTA considers the additional parking revenue gained from non-residents: the term T_A on the right-hand side of equation (9.10). This induces the LTA to set a price that is too high. In general, therefore, we cannot predict whether the price set by the LTA is higher or lower than the efficient level.

Imagine the extreme case in which local residents do not use the on-street parking market at all. All parking demand is from non-residents. In this case, equation (9.10) collapses to:

$$-p_X(-\frac{dT_A}{dp_X}) + T_A \qquad (9.12)$$

Increasing the parking fee increases welfare until rents from non-residents are maximized at

$$\varepsilon_A(p_X) = -1$$

which is just a standard profit maximizing condition (when marginal cost is equal to zero). The LTA acts as a profit-maximizer.[10] In practice, we would not expect that all on-street parking is used by non-residents, though in large cities such as London or New York, it is plausible that, at least at certain periods during the week, a majority of parkers are not local residents. Revenue-raising concerns, rather than social-welfare concerns, may play an important role in determining parking prices on these markets.

LTA competing with central government

The LTA is not the only tax-levying authority in a typical urban transport market. Rather, central government collects tax revenue from consumption of fuel, or vehicles themselves, or collects revenue from fine payments (speeding, illegal parking etc). The presence of such transfers to the central government may distort local government decision-making, as has been widely identified in the vertical tax competition literature – see Hoyt (2001).

This point can be demonstrated (in a somewhat simplified context) with the basic model above (see page 131). Matters are simplified by assuming that central government policy is fixed. We can then examine the reaction of the LTA to the level of the central government tax variable.[11] The simplest case to consider is where central government receives a fixed proportion, $1 - \rho$, of the on-street parking fee and where all secondary distortions are assumed away. Thus we can write the consumer indirect utility function as $V(\rho_X, G, \rho, \sigma)$. The budget constraint of the LTA reduces to $G = \rho \rho_X T_X$.[12] In such a set up, the local welfare impact of a revenue-neutral increase in parking fee is given by:

$$\frac{1}{\lambda} \frac{dV}{dp_X} = -(1 - \rho)T_X +$$

$$(MEC_X - \rho p_X)(-\frac{dT_X}{dp_X}) \tag{9.13}$$

where $T_X \equiv T_{FX} + T_{BX}$. Examine expression (9.13) in the two extreme cases: when the LTA retains all revenues, $\rho = 1$, and when central government retains all revenue, $\rho = 0$. For ease, these are summarized in equation (9.14):

$$\rho = 1: \quad MEC_X(-\frac{dT_X}{dp_X}) - p_X(-\frac{dT_X}{dp_X})$$

$$\rho = 0: \quad MEC_X(-\frac{dT_X}{dp_X}) - T_X \tag{9.14}$$

In either case, the benefit of raising the fee is given by the reduction in external costs.[13] However, the cost depends directly on which layer of government receives the revenue. If LTA receives the revenue (and can recycle this to consumers), the cost of the price increase is just the loss in consumer surplus, i.e. the price multiplied by the change in demand. However, if all revenues accrue to the central government, the cost is equal to the total increase in payment, i.e. demand.

It is clear that if the LTA does not receive the full revenue payment, ($\rho < 1$), it sets a sub-optimal price. In practice, where demand is relatively inelastic, we would expect[14] that the cost of raising the parking price is higher when $\rho = 0$ than $\rho = 1$ and hence the LTA sets a parking price that is too low when revenues are not returned to the local level.

We have illustrated this principle in the context of meter fee revenue. But in practice, this revenue usually accrues to the local level. However, this is not the case with parking fines. Calthrop (2001) investigates this issue. If the LTA does not retain fine revenues, it is shown that there is an unambiguous incentive to set the meter fee at too low a level: low fees encourage drivers to pay at the meter (rather than risk the fine) and thus keeps revenues within the local community. If the LTA can also set the level of costly enforcement, inspection probabilities may be set either too high or too low. When enforcement is relatively cheap, the LTA over-invests in enforcement, as a means of increasing the expected fine for illegally parking. The higher price of illegal parking encourages drivers to pay at the meter, and thus revenues are retained in the local community. In contrast, if enforcement is relatively expensive, the LTA may just set too low a level of enforcement. Low enforcement levels result in few illegally parked drivers being caught – and hence reduces the amount of fine revenue being transferred out of the local community.

Conclusions

We have defined efficient on-street parking pricing. The relevant factors to take into account when determining the price of on-street parking are determined in equation (9.9). Efficient parking policy needs to examine impacts both on the on-street parking market, such as a reduction in the time required to search for a vacant space, and all other distorted transport markets, most notably the effect on under-priced road congestion.

An efficient institutional structure is one that facilitates efficient pricing. Although there may be many reasons why, in practice, an LTA fails to implement efficient parking pricing, we highlight two reasons. Both stem from the fact that the LTA rationally accounts for the costs and benefits of policy reforms on its own residents (or voters). To the extent that costs or benefits fall onto other people (commuters or tourists, or, via central government transfers, other regions), the LTA has a clear incentive to pursue an inefficient policy. As such, price-setting powers are inefficiently allocated between different layers of government.

Several caveats need to be borne in mind when interpreting these results. Firstly, we defined efficient parking policy in rather reduced-form terms. More detailed micro-economic reasoning is required to define efficient parking policy. How do drivers determine their searching strategy? Can better information help reduce excessive search times? What is the relationship between general searching behaviour and road congestion? With such a small theoretical literature examining these questions, it is not surprising that many potentially important issues have been neglected. As a result, more work is required in determining what exactly an efficient pricing policy entails.

Secondly, we have suggested only one reason why institutions may fail to set efficient prices: competition between layers of government. Several others may be plausible, and a wide political economy literature[15] provides many ideas for further research, such as the role of special interest groups (for example, city centre businesses) in determining policy.

Thirdly, there is a clear lack of empirical work in this area. It is very hard to find even rudimentary data on actual urban parking policies. Casual observation suggests that some cities (for example, Amsterdam) set rather high parking prices, often justified on the grounds of tackling congestion. Applied empirical work could go some way to determining whether this seems to be the case (i.e. that prices more or less reflect marginal external congestion costs), or whether, as posited above (see page 135), the LTA is just extracting rent from tourists.

Finally, this chapter has stressed the inadequacies of local government decision-making. However, there may be good reasons why decentralized decision-making is beneficial, perhaps due to better information on local traffic conditions, or values of time. The examples of institutional failure given here should be seen as just that. An attempt at reforming institutions may need to account for several factors omitted from this chapter.

Notes

1 Pages 131–135 of this chapter are a revised draft of Chapter 1 of my doctoral dissertation, Calthrop (2001). I would like to thank all Committee members, particularly Piet Rietveld (Free University Amsterdam) and Stef Proost and Erik Schokkaert (Katholieke Universiteit Leuven) for useful comments on those sections. The paper as a whole has benefited from discussions with Bruno De Borger (UFSIA, Antwerp) and comments from an anonymous referee. Remaining errors are my own. The paper was funded by F.W.O. (Funding for Scientific Research - Flanders) contract number G.0220.01.

2 In Calthrop (2001), the model also allows for choice of time period: peak versus off-peak. Inclusion of the off-peak is only relevant to the extent that distortions are present. We implicitly assume here, as in Parry and Bento (2002*a*), that no distortions are present.

3 It is straightforward to allow for rail congestion – however, to simplify matters, we abstract from this.

4 As pointed out by a referee, the freeway need not be free!

5 To simplify matters, we assume that the labour market is not distorted. Incorporating such a distortion is conceptually straightforward (see Parry and Bento, 2002*b* or Calthrop *et al.*, 2003), but is not central to our discussion here.

6 This can be justified in the short-run: edge space to many roads cannot be used for any other purpose. Calthrop and Proost (2003) justify this assumption in more detail.

7 The indirect utility function is clearly defined over all prices in the model: however, we are interested in the case of increasing the price of on-street parking and recycling the revenues via the lump-sum instrument: all other prices remain constant, and hence, to reduce notation, we drop them.

8 Changes in demand in equation (9.9) are expressed wholly in terms of total derivatives. It is conceptually straightforward, if rather tedious, to decompose these expressions into partial derivatives and a feedback effect: see Calthrop *et al.*, 2003, for such an exercise. In this chapter, however, we prefer to simplify matters by retaining total derivatives.

9 As stressed by Wellisch (2000), however, the traditional tax-exporting results, such as those derived here, only hold if households have fixed residential location. We implicitly assume this,

which seems reasonable given the relatively small impacts of parking policy on total household welfare.

10 It is also worth noting that decisions may be made according to equation (9.12) rather than (9.11) if the LTA is a Leviathan: that is, maximising profit rather than social welfare. This is sometimes suggested to be the case (see, for example, Brennan and Buchanan (1980)).

11 This is the second-stage in a standard Stackelberg game, with the central government as leader and the LTA as follower. In principle, one could go on and solve for the Nash-equilibrium in space (ρ, ρ_x) for this game. If the central government is welfare maximising, the optimal level of ρ is clearly set to 1.

12 We have the stark assumption that central government spending does not affect the welfare of residents of the LTA region. This could be relaxed, but the basic mechanism discussed will hold as long as central government does not fully return the revenue to local residents. This, in general, seems likely given redistributional policy.

13 Though note, of course, that the marginal external cost depends on demand levels, which in turn depend on the value of ρ.

14 Strictly speaking, this is not proven by the conditions given in equation (9.14). Demand functions and external costs depend on ρ and thus a numerical model is required to show the relative magnitude of 'optimised' parking fees under different assumptions concerning ρ.

15 See Persson and Tabellini (2000) for a recent review of this literature.

16 Note that if revenues are distributed on the basis of contribution, transport demand and hence transfers are identical. It is identical to the case in which the LTA distributes total revenue equally between the groups.

Bibliography

Anderson, S.P. and de Palma, A. (2002) The Economics of On-Street Parking: Road Congestion and Driver Search. mimeo, November.

Arnott, R., de Palma, A. and Lindsey, R. (1991) A temporal and spatial equilibrium analysis of commuter parking. *Journal of Public Economics*, 45, pp. 301–335.

Arnott, R. and Rowse, J. (1999) Modeling parking. *Journal of Urban Economics*, 45, pp. 97–124.

Brennan, G. and Buchanan, J.M. (1980) *The Power to Tax: Analytical Foundations to a Fiscal Constitution*, Cambridge: Cambridge University Press.

Calthrop, E. (2001) Essays in Urban Transport Economics. Ph.D thesis 151, Katholieke Universiteit Leuven.

Calthrop, E., de Borger, B. and Proost, S. (2003) Tax reform for dirty intermediate goods: Theory and an application to the taxation of freight transport. CES Working Paper, Katholieke Universiteit Leuven.

Calthrop, E. and Proost, S. (2003) Regulating on-street parking. CES Working Paper, Katholieke Universiteit Leuven.

Calthrop, E. Proost, S. and van Dender, K. (2000) Parking policies and road pricing. *Urban Studies*, 37, pp. 63–76.

Glazer, A. and Niskanen, E. (1992) Parking fees and congestion. *Regional Science and Urban Economics*, 22, pp. 123–132.

Hoyt, W.H. (2001) Tax policy co-ordination, vertical externalities, and optimal taxation in a system of hierarchical governments. *Journal of Urban Economics*, 50, pp. 491–516.

Parry, I. and Bento, A. (2002a) Estimating the welfare effects of congestion taxes: the critical importance of other distortions within the transport system. *Journal of Urban Economics*, 51, pp. 339–366.

Parry, I. and Bento, A. (2002b) Revenue recycling and the welfare effects of road pricing. *Scandinavian Journal of Economics*, 103, pp. 645–671.

Persson, T. and Tabellini, G. (2000) *Political Economics: Explaining Economic Policy*. Cambridge, MA: MIT Press.

Verhoef, E., Nijkamp, P. and Rietveld, P. (1995) The economics of regulatory parking policies. *Transportation Research, Part A*, 29, pp. 141–156.

Vickrey, W. (1959) Statement to the Joint Committee on Washington DC Metropolitan Problems: Exhibit 53 – Economizing on Curb Parking Space – a suggestion for a new approach to parking meters. Reprinted in *Journal of Urban Economics*, 36, pp. 42–65.

Wellisch, D. (2000) *Theory of Public Finance in a Federal State*. Cambridge: Cambridge University Press.

Annex 1: Deriving expression (9.9)

Taking the total derivative of the indirect utility function, (9.8), gives:

$$\frac{dV}{dp_X} = \frac{\partial V}{\partial p_X} + \frac{\partial V}{\partial G}\frac{dG}{dp_X} + \frac{\partial V}{\partial \phi_F}\frac{d\phi_F}{dp_X} + \frac{\partial V}{\partial \phi_B}\frac{d\phi_B}{dp_X} + \frac{\partial V}{\partial \sigma}\frac{d\sigma}{dp_X} \tag{9.15}$$

Using Roy's rule and the definitions of the congestion function and search function, we know:

$$\frac{\partial V}{\partial p_X} = -\lambda(T_{FX} + T_{BX}) \qquad \frac{\partial V}{\partial G} = \lambda$$

$$\frac{\partial V}{\partial \phi_F} = -\mu(T_{FX} + T_{FY}) \qquad \frac{\partial V}{\partial \phi_B} = -\mu(T_{BX} + T_{BY}) \tag{9.16}$$

$$\frac{\partial V}{\partial \sigma} = -\mu(T_{FX} + T_{BX})$$

Also note that:

$$\frac{d\phi_F}{dp_X} = \phi_F'(\frac{dT_{FX}}{dp_X} + \frac{dT_{FY}}{dp_X}) \qquad \frac{d\phi_B}{dp_X} = \phi_B'(\frac{dT_{BX}}{dp_X} + \frac{dT_{BY}}{dp_X})$$

$$\frac{d\sigma}{dp_X} = \sigma'(\frac{dT_{FX}}{dp_X} + \frac{dT_{BX}}{dp_X}) \tag{9.17}$$

Finally, revenue-neutrality implies, via equation (9.7) that:

$$\frac{dG}{dp_X} = T_{FX} + T_{BX} + \tau(\frac{dT_{FX}}{dp_X} + \frac{dT_{FY}}{dp_X}) + p_X(\frac{dT_{FX}}{dp_X} + \frac{dT_{BX}}{dp_X}) +$$

$$(p_Y - m_Y)(\frac{dT_{FY}}{dp_X} + \frac{dT_{BY}}{dp_X}) + (f - \tilde{\theta}_R)\frac{dT_R}{dp_X} \tag{9.18}$$

Substituting equations (9.16), (9.17) and (9.18) into (9.15) gives expression (9.9).

Annex 2: Deriving expressions (9.10) and (9.11)

The time constraint for representative consumer i, where $i = H, A$, is given by $L_i + \ell_i + \sigma(T)T_i = \bar{L}$. The money budget constraint is given by $L_i + p_X T_i = L_i + G_i$. The LTA budget constraint is given by $\sum_{i=H,A} G_i = p_X T$, where further assumptions are made below concerning the distribution of tax revenue between the two groups. Substituting maximized consumer demand into the utility function gives the indirect utility function $L_i(p_X, \sigma, G_i)$ – clearly if the LTA transfer is equal between groups, indirect utility is identical between groups.

We consider two alternative cases: firstly, when the LTA maximizes an unweighted sum of the welfare of the representative resident and non-resident, and secondly, when the LTA maximizes the welfare of the local resident only.

Case 1 – Full welfare maximization

Let the objective function of the LTA be given by:

$$W = V_H + V_A \tag{9.19}$$

and let $G_i = p_X, T_i)^1$. Maximizing (9.19) with respect the price of transport gives:

$$\frac{dW}{dp_X} = \sum_{i=H,A} \left\{ \frac{\partial V_i}{\partial p_X} + \frac{\partial V_i}{\partial G_i}\frac{dG_i}{dp_X} + \frac{\partial V_i}{\partial \sigma}\frac{d\sigma}{dp_X} \right\}$$

Using an analogous procedure to Annex 1, we derive:

$$\frac{1}{\lambda}\frac{dW}{dp_X} = (MEC - p_X)(-\frac{dT}{dp_X}) \tag{9.20}$$

which is just equation (9.11).

Case 2 – Local welfare maximization

Let the objective function of the LTA be given by

$$W = V_H \tag{9.21}$$

and let $G_H = p_X, T$. Maximizing (9.21) with respect to p_X and using the same substitution procedure as above, gives:

$$\frac{1}{\lambda}\frac{dW}{dp_X} = (MEC_H - p_X)(-\frac{dT}{dp_X}) + T_A \tag{9.22}$$

Endnote

1   Note that if revenues are distributed on the basis of contribution, transport demand and hence transfers are identical. It is identical to the case in which the LTA distributes total revenue equally between the groups.

Chapter 10

Institutional issues in transatlantic aviation[1]

Aisling Reynolds-Feighan

The air transport industry is expanding rapidly and it is a driving force in the globalization of economic activity through its global air service networks. International organizations such as the WTO and ICAO, as well as trade blocks and economic unions such as NAFTA and the EU, are in the process of examining the regulatory framework necessary to enable competition on an enlarged international basis. While much research has been undertaken into issues such as airline competition, airport regulation, and pricing policies, there has been very little focus on the role of the institutions designing and managing the air transport industry in national and international contexts. The purpose of this chapter is to give an overview of the nature and role of institutions in aviation in Europe and the US and to explore potential research issues relating to institutional arrangements in the operation of the air transport sector. The chapter will investigate in a general way some of the institutional differences between Europe and the US and the evolution of institutions in the transatlantic market.

The chapter is structured as follows. The first section sets out the structure of the air transport industry in terms of its players, intermediaries, and institutions. The purpose of this exercise is to highlight the linkages and spheres of influence and to enable comparisons. The role of linked sectors in the economy, such as the defence sector, will be briefly discussed. The second section outlines key influences shaping the development of air transport in recent decades, highlighting the different institutional responses and approaches prevailing in the European and US markets. The impact of the events of 11 September 2001 on the aviation industry will be briefly outlined in order, first, to highlight differences in institutional arrangements between the US and Europe and, second, to emphasize the commonality of issues such as security, insurance liability etc, facing all jurisdictions and the benefits of co-operative research in analyzing these issues and examining feasible solutions.

The third section looks briefly at infrastructure and congestion in air transport and highlights some examples of the influences that the formal institutions in Europe and the US can have on the sector. Aviation is a capital-intensive industry that has been to the forefront in the development and adoption of new technologies. The role of institutions in fostering the development, exploitation, and adoption of new technologies is also considered briefly in this section. The motivating factors in research and development are explored and the instruments for achieving technological advancement will be briefly discussed. In the final section, several research questions capturing the role and influence of institutions will be framed for discussion and debate.

Institutions in air transport

Transatlantic scheduled airfreight and air passenger services began in 1939 with Pan American Airways' New York to Portugal (Azores and Lisbon) and Paris services. The institutional arrangements for the operation, maintenance and provision of international aviation evolved in the years following this service and gave rise to a complex, diverse and dynamic array of regulations and codes governing technical, legal, economic, financial and safety dimensions. From a national perspective, aviation has always been an instrument of economic, military and foreign policy. The establishment of the International Civil Aviation Organization (ICAO) as part of the United Nations emphasized the clear political role it would play in taking responsibility for the rules and regulations that would govern the development of international aviation (see Sochar, 1991).

National and international policy agendas have broadened over the 65 years since to take account of changing passenger/shipper and carrier demands, where conflicting economic, political, environmental, and technological objectives constrain or require complex short-run and long-run solutions. At the macro-level, globalization and economic integration among groups of nations require the creation of multi-lateral and flexible institutional arrangements facilitating greater freedom of movement for people and goods in a greatly increased activity space. At the micro-level, the closer integration of firm functions, and co-operation of groups of firms in the sourcing and distribution of intermediate and final goods and services requires broader frameworks for the construction and operation of international multimodal logistical networks. Understanding the nature of the institutions, their evolution (for example, do they lead or follow market forces?) and their influences on mobility and economic activity is of great significance to the academic community and to policy-makers, but as an area of research, these issues received relatively little attention to date. (Stough and Rietveld (1997) explore these challenges and issues in a general context.)

In this section of the chapter, the main players, intermediaries, and institutions in the air transport industry are set out in order to highlight the linkages and spheres of influence. The main components of air transport are the airports (nodes), air navigation and flow management systems (the way or paths), airlines, government or regulatory agencies, shippers and passengers. In Table 10.1, the nature of the relationships between the different groups of players is set out in a very simple manner in terms of whether direct or indirect interactions take place between the groups; examples of intermediaries for different pairs of players are given in the upper part of the cells in each case. The infrastructure and service providers interact directly with each other along with the government/regulatory agencies. Customers, whether shippers or passengers purchasing air transport services, tended to interact indirectly with suppliers prior to consuming the service. Recently, airlines have sought to sell directly to customers. The internet has facilitated direct selling of air passenger or integrated freight services. UPS, DHL and Federal Express have established extensive networks of pickup and distribution centres to facilitate direct interaction with shippers.

The intermediaries facilitate interactions between different groups by acting as agents. These intermediaries are not just travel agents or general sales agents, but also encompass trade associations and international bodies such as the International Air Transport Association (IATA). For example, airports interact with other airports directly (bilaterally or through associations such as the Airports Council International (ACI)) or indirectly through government agencies acting on their behalf through international organizations such as the International Civil Aviation Organization (ICAO). Governments interact indirectly with passengers, with airlines acting as intermediaries. The table can be applied to structure links between the different groups of players at national or international levels. At international scales, many new networks of intermediaries are spawned facilitating dialogue between different groups on a multilateral basis.

The institutions governing or supporting aviation can be divided into three main groups. These are:

♦   Institutions providing or funding aviation infrastructure and/or specifying design standards – these can include local, regional, state, national or international governments; intergovernmental institutions such as ICAO.

♦   Regulatory institutions – governing economic aspects; safety; border controls; labour/social policy; environmental aspects; international trade aspects of aviation.

♦   Related or supporting sectors and institutions: financial sector (funding/leveraging equipment and or infrastructure for airports, airlines; ATC/ATM); defence sector (funding R&D costs; product developments); the aerospace industry; other transportation sectors facilitating access to/from airports.

Table 10.1 Main players in aviation and nature of interactions, direct (D) or indirect (I)

	Infrastructure providers		Service providers	Customers		Government/ regulatory agencies
	Nodes: Airports	Way/Path: Air Nav/ ATC	Carriers: Airlines	Shippers: Firms	Passengers	Government
Airports	ACI; ICAO; Govt division D or I	ICAO; EURO-CONTROL D	ICAO; trade assoc. D	Airlines; trade assoc. I	Airlines; trade I	Regulator; Govt assoc division (e.g. FAA) D
ATC/ ATM	ACI; ICAO; Govt division D	ICAO; EURO-CONTROL D	ICAO; Govt division D	Airlines; trade assoc. I	Airlines; trade assoc. I	Govt division; EUROCONTROL D
Airlines	ICAO; trade assoc. D	ICAO; Govt division D	Airport user groups; IATA; ICAO; trade assoc. D	GSAs; Forwarders Ground Handlers D or I	Travel agents; trade assoc. D or I	Govt. division; DG TREN D
Firms	Airlines; trade assoc. I	Airlines; trade assoc. I	GSAs; Forwarders; Ground Handlers D	Forwarder; GSAs; B2B; 3PL D or I	Airlines D or I	Airlines; Govt division; trade assoc. I
Passengers	Airlines; trade assoc I	Airlines; trade assoc I	Travel agents; trade assoc. D	Airlines I	Airlines; Trade assoc. I	Airlines; Trade assoc I
Govt.	Regulator; Govt division (e.g. FAA) D	Govt division; EURO-CONTROL D	Govt. division; DG TREN D or I	Airlines; Govt division; Trade assoc. I	Airlines; Trade assoc. I	ICAO; Council of Ministers; Bilateral meetings D

Note: Main Intermediaries are: Travel agents; airlines; freight forwarders/consolidators/general sales agents (GSAs); international co-ordinating bodies or institutions; trade associations; (ACI is the Airports Council International; ICAO is the International Civil Aviation Organisation; FAA is the (US) Federal Aviation Administration; IATA is the International Air Transport Association)

In the arena of transatlantic aviation, national governments have negotiated bilateral agreements, beyond the limited multilateral framework established in 1944 and negotiated through the International Civil Aviation Organization (ICAO). Institutional structures in international aviation change at a slow pace and Table 10.1 demonstrates the complexity of the institutional relationships. The culture, objectives, and approaches to dealing with air transport issues will vary considerably from one jurisdiction to another. The institutions supporting the industry will reflect these differences. This can be seen in the EU, where the effort to liberalize the airline industry and bring harmonization and standardization to air traffic management has been a slow and very gradual process. Seeking a common set of rules for the operation of air transport in international markets may require common governance structures across jurisdictions. In the discussions in the remainder of the chapter, a small selection of topics will be presented to demonstrate some of the influences of institutions in international aviation.

Key influences shaping the recent development of transatlantic aviation

US air transport markets

US air transport markets are the largest in the world, whether measured by passenger or freight enplanements, movements, passenger-kilometres, or freight-kilometres. Americans fly more often and further on average than Europeans; the demographic, geographic, and economic characteristics of the country would justify a more prominent role for air transportation. Table 10.2 provides a comparison of modal share for the EU and US based on reported passenger-kilometres travelled in 1997. The US airline share is 2.21 times the European share, but the ratio between the two areas has declined steadily since the 1970s.

The US international traffic share increased significantly during the 1990s. International air passenger enplanements accounted for less than 5% of total enplanements for most of the 1980s. In 1999, international passenger enplanements accounted for 18% of total enplanements. The institutions governing the domestic industry changed significantly during the late-1970s with the deregulation of the air cargo (1977) and air passenger (1978) industries. The heavy economic regulation of air carriers was withdrawn, allowing the industry to rely to a much greater extent on market forces to determine fares, capacity, products (routes and service levels) and scale of operation (see, for example, Morrison and Winston, 1995). The US carriers had remained in private ownership throughout the regulated period of 1938–1978 and responded quickly to the new market environment. The domestic air transport market went through an initial period of rapid expansion as many new entrants began operating in the deregulated market. Figure 10.1

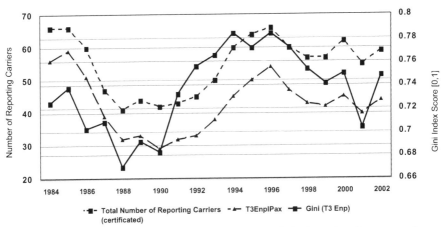

Figure 10. 1 Measures of the number of US air carriers and Gini Index for enplaned passenger shares, 1984–2002

shows the total number of reporting carriers (passenger and freight) operating in the domestic market between 1984 and 2002. These are based on the US Department of Transportation T3 database.[2] The 'T3 Enplaned Passenger' (T3EnplPax) trend shows the number of carriers operating air passenger services in the domestic market. The 'Gini T3Enp' trend shows the Gini index calculated for enplaned passenger market shares for these carriers over the same period. The number of carriers declined in the late 1980s due to financial failures, mergers, and takeovers in the industry. The Gini index declines as the number of carriers declines, showing a slightly less concentrated traffic distribution among the remaining carriers.

A second round of new entry occurred in the early and mid-1990s. Towards the end of the 1990s, the numbers declined again for similar reasons – consolidations, and financial failures. Many of the 1990s entrants were low-cost or low-fare carriers and most did not survive the decade (see Reynolds-Feighan, 2001). Regulatory policy in the US market during the 1990s was concerned with the impacts that increasing consolidation and domination of the large hub airports by the largest carriers (the 'majors') was having on the industry and on passenger fares. The concern was that the majors were charging significant hub premiums where they did not face competition from so-called 'low-cost' or 'low-fares' carriers (see US DOT, 1997). Growth in domestic markets during the 1990s was mostly driven by these low-cost carriers. Figure 10.2 shows the escalating average short haul fare (domestic, 1000-mile trip excluding taxes and not CPI-adjusted) through the 1990s, with a significant decline towards the end of the period. The successful expansion by Southwest Airlines during the 1990s played a significant role in growing domestic traffic and in placing downward pressure on airfares in

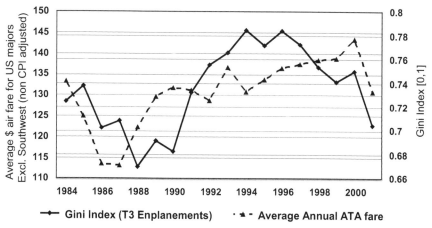

Figure 10.2 Average ATA short haul air fare in US domestic market and Gini Index, 1984–2002

markets where larger network carriers had not been challenged. The spatial distribution of carrier traffic is not an issue that has received much attention however, and this aspect will be developed later in the chapter.

The established network carriers were focused more on international markets. During the 1990s, the US Department of Transportation negotiated a large number of more liberal international air transport agreements (including 'open skies') with a host of European, Asian and other governments, including a multilateral 'open skies' agreement with Brunei Darussalam, Chile, New Zealand and Singapore in 2000. These agreements have quickly established new institutional arrangements for the development and growth of international air transport. As traffic volumes have continued to grow at pace, delays and congestion at the larger airports has been an issue of concern.

The US commercial airports system is funded substantially by the federal government through the Airports and Airways Trust Fund, which in turn is resourced by the federal budget, through passenger facility charges and en route charges. The airports are almost all in public ownership, though the privately owned airlines have a long tradition of owning and operating their own terminals at the larger airports. This relationship with airports evolved in the 1970s as a method for funding airport development and in many instances gave the airlines significant influence in the running of the airports. For example, the Majority-in-interest (MII) clauses in airline investment contracts at airports permitted the airlines in some cases to prevent other carriers or the airport authority itself from providing additional terminal space.

US air freight traffic has grown more rapidly than air passenger traffic and this trend is set to continue according to the main industry forecasts. The air freight industry has evolved most dramatically since deregulation to become a highly sophisticated and technology-intensive sector, integrating the transport function with inventory management, tracking and control from point of origin to point of destination. The growth of high-yield express freight has supported the development of specialist 'integrated carriers', a carrier group that has greatly increased its market share at the expense of the combination passenger/freight carriers. In the domestic and international environment, air cargo liberalization has preceded air passenger liberalization.

Table 10.2 Passenger transport market shares by mode: European Union compared to United States 1970–1997

Ratio of United States to European Union Market share	Auto	Bus	Railway	Airline
1970	1.23	0.22	0.09	3.18
1980	1.17	0.27	0.08	3.03
1990	1.09	0.35	0.09	2.58
1997	1.08	0.37	0.08	2.21

Note: Calculated from European Union and US Department of Transportation data, based upon passenger km/miles.

European air transport markets

The European air transport markets have traditionally been international in focus given the relatively small size of many of the countries on this continent. Thus the institutional arrangements for aviation have been based on international bilateral agreements negotiated between governments and focused around the sovereignty of each state's air space. These bilateral agreements tended to share capacity, revenues, and service frequencies, as well as limiting entry, typically, to one designated carrier for each state (this was usually the state-owned airline). Border formalities (customs clearance for freight; immigration/passport controls for passengers) were a basic characteristic of European air transport. Terrorist activities in the 1970s and 1980s gave rise to a significant and palpable security consciousness in the day-to-day provision of air transport services.

The legislative development of the Single European Market during the 1980s forced the negotiation of a liberalized internal European air transport market. This liberalization process was completed in 1997, with full cabotage granted to all European registered carriers. Since 1997, all European registered carriers *within the European market* have full and equal access to domestic and inter-state markets. They have complete pricing freedom and are now subject to the EU's competition policy.

However in negotiating external agreements, the nationality (ownership) of carriers is still of considerable importance as each member state negotiates reciprocal rights for access to airports within its territory for nationally registered carriers. Beginning with the Dutch government in 1992, the US negotiated 'open skies' agreements with twelve European member states during the 1990s and 2000s. These agreements liberalized access for US and the national carriers of the member state to any destinations within their respective territories, permitted fifth freedom rights[3] and in the case of cargo carriers, permitted more liberal operating conditions for other modes of transport beyond the airport gateway. The agreements have also granted antitrust immunity for certain carrier alliances. The European Court of Justice ruling in November 2002 found eight member states' 'open skies' air service agreements with the US to be illegal.[4] EU Transport Ministers in June 2003 granted the European Commission the right to negotiate a common agreement with the US on behalf of all member states. These negotiations began in late 2003, with agreement not expected before 2005 at the earliest. The European Commission has indicated elsewhere that it is keen to promote consolidation in the European airline industry (European Commission, 2001).

Passenger air transport is the fastest growing mode of transport in the EU. The modal split in terms of passenger-kilometres is given in Table 10.3 below. It is noted that air transport has increased its share to 5.4% in 1999, with rail accounting for just over 6%. European investment in high-speed rail has allowed some substitution of rail for short-haul air transport services, particularly in the UK and French markets; this trend will continue given the policy stance in the European Commission's White Paper on Transport, published in 2001 (European Commission, 2001). Driven by environmental concerns, the White Paper is concerned with the promotion of 'cleaner' modes of transport. A large number of measures will be implemented in the next 8 years that will have the effect of raising user costs in air and road transport.

Environmental policies have also played a significant role in shaping investment strategies for the Trans European Networks (TENs) of rail and air

Table 10.3 Modal split in EU15 (percentage of passenger-kilometres by mode of transport)

	Passenger cars	Buses and coaches	Tram and Metro	Railway	Air
1970	74.0	12.6	1.8	10.1	1.5
1980	76.2	11.6	1.4	8.4	2.5
1990	79.1	9.2	1.2	6.7	3.9
1995	79.5	8.7	1.1	6.1	4.6
1996	79.3	8.8	1.1	6.2	4.7
1997	79.3	8.6	1.1	6.1	4.9
1998	79.1	8.7	1.1	6.0	5.2
1999	79.0	8.4	1.1	6.1	5.4

transport infrastructure. Environmental concerns and appeals have delayed the planning process across Europe. The provision of the fifth terminal at London's Heathrow Airport illustrates the long delays that can be experienced between the initial planning and eventual provision of increased elements of airport capacity. Table 10.4 illustrates the range and intensity of noise restrictions that European and US airports have introduced since the mid-1990s. The growth in environmental restrictions contributes to congestion. The build solution to growing congestion is in turn being delayed by environmental policies. So other solutions are being sought simultaneously, such as technological developments that permit tighter separation of aircraft in the vicinity of airports. Increasingly in Europe, it is the international or intergovernmental institutions that play the key role in regulating the safety parameters for flight operations.

Impacts of terrorist attacks of September 11

The events of September 11 in New York and Washington have had and will continue to have significant and long-lasting impacts on air transport in the US and globally. Apart from the dramatic declines in traffic in the US and elsewhere in the immediate aftermath, key industry forecasts have revised downwards the long-run growth rates for both the air passenger and air freight sectors. The US federal government paid substantial subsidies to the airlines in the immediate aftermath of the attack. Issues of security and insurance

Table 10.4 Selected noise restrictions adopted by EU 15 Member States and US, April 2002

	Curfews	Operating quotas	Stage2/ Chapter 2 restrictions	Noise charges	APU restrictions	Noise budget	Noise abatement programmes
Austria	5		4	3	2		3
Belgium	2	2	2	3		1	3
Denmark	2	2	2		4	1	4
Finland							2
France	10	1	7	14	7		13
Germany	23	2	17	25	3	1	18
Ireland							1
Italy	9		6	11	5		8
Luxembourg	1		1	1			1
Netherlands	3		2	2	1	1	1
Norway	2		2	2	3		3
Portugal	1				2		2
Spain	4	1	2		2		2
Sweden	7	1	4	7	5	1	7
UK	26	12	16	10	13		31
USA	75	13	4	4	11	5	186

Note: Figures indicate the number of airports applying each restriction

liability will have a longer-term impact on the costs and operational aspects of domestic and international air transport. The fact that the US air transport system was heavily focused on domestic transport in the passenger sector gave rise to a less formal experience for travellers there compared with European travellers. The need now to secure all modes of transport will change that experience permanently and increase transaction costs for shippers as well as generalized travel costs for passengers.

The training of staff to deal with security threats is a costly and slow process: profiling suspects, screening of passengers and baggage on a routine basis requires an extensive education process as well as the provision of costly infrastructure. Transportation systems will be designed with increased emphasis on security and the assessment of vulnerability to attacks – a mind shift that is already evident in US government transportation institutions. Some evidence of how these costs will affect mobility and transportation choice may be gathered from European experiences of the last 20 years. The Lockerbie air crash over Scotland in the early 1990s resulted in significant changes in security arrangements for passenger and freight services in the UK and elsewhere. For example, all international passengers were required to fly with their baggage. The working assumption was that the aircraft was secure if baggage and passenger were tied to the same flight. This assumption must now be revised.

For many companies who had come to rely on 'just-in-time' inventory management practices, the September 11 events exposed their vulnerability to economic and social disruption. Firms responded by building up stocks of components to cushion themselves from the costs of delays in the supply of raw materials and parts. The long-run implications for supply-chain management practices and the role of institutions in facilitating these practices must be monitored.

For air cargo, the UK authorities initially required airfreight to be held for 24 hours prior to lift. This facilitated 'air truckers' who could move freight travelling under airway bill from airport bond to airport bond since the 24-hour wait began once the freight was checked at any airport bonded warehouse. New security screening equipment capable of x-raying full palettes was installed at the largest airports, as this reduced the pre-flight wait period. Clearly, these types of developments favour concentration of air freight at a limited number of centres and will encourage the continued separation of freight and passenger services in air transportation. Several European carriers have withdrawn from intra-European air cargo services and focused instead on long-haul air freight from the larger EU hub airports (e.g. British Airways).

Research on the economics of security in transportation, and the institutional requirements and responses will benefit all policy-makers involved in international aviation. The interrelationships between military and foreign policy on one hand, and economic and aviation policy on the other requires an interdisciplinary approach.

Infrastructure, technology, sustainability and growth in aviation

Aviation is a technology-intensive industry. Development of new aircraft, navigational and flow management systems, security and tracking systems etc requires substantial research and development capabilities, and the capacity to develop markets for the new products. Institutions have an important role to play in leading the research agenda by setting new design or performance standards and also by encouraging uptake of new technologies/equipment through regulations or directives. The US defence budget has for many years funded the development of new technology or technical knowledge that has been utilized subsequently for commercial purposes.

Environmental concerns in both Europe and the US led to the non-addition and gradual banning of so-called 'chapter 2' or 'stage 2' aircraft during the 1990s. This process encouraged the airlines to upgrade their fleets with new aircraft developed by Boeing and Airbus and meeting more stringent noise, emissions, and fuel consumption requirements. The airports have gradually imposed more stringent noise management requirements, increasing the costs to carriers for operating at certain times of the day and operating particular types of equipment. These regulations are more restrictive on cargo carriers, since these carriers tend to operate night-time services and have tended to use older aircraft, because of their lower utilization rates. Institutional specification of performance and design standards can lead the R&D process and can influence the direction of change in transport. Sustainable transport technologies develop in an institutional context. The key point however is that these influences prevail in the *long run* – institution-led shifts to new technologies take a long time to implement.

Congestion delays have been worsening in both Europe and the US in the last 5 years, as the air traffic control and management systems struggle to cater for the increased demand. Congestion delay patterns are highly seasonal, peaking in periods of high demand and poor weather conditions. A number of factors needs to be considered in this context. The pressure on carriers to provide increased frequency of service, the demands of customers for direct service, and the rapid growth in regional jets to fill these needs are acting to compound the congestion problems. New guidance and air navigation systems have helped to optimize traffic flows, and in Europe, to harmonize and reduce separation minima, thereby facilitating an increased number of hourly movements. Approaching the capacity and congestion problem from a 'systems perspective' may require new incentives to encourage carriers to transfer at less congested facilities. The development and deployment of the Airbus A380, on one hand, and regional jets, on the other, may require institution-led allocations of scarce airport resources. Pricing to reallocate traffic and build capacity outside of the largest cities will require more of a role for international institutions, but would also require harmonization of financial, operational, and regulatory environments in the participating states.

Research issues

Several issues have been raised throughout this chapter exploring the role and impacts of institutions in the development and growth of international aviation. Clearly there are many institutions involved in aviation and their influences and implications cannot be addressed comprehensively in a short chapter. The issues selected in this section focus on spatial aspects of aviation and thus can be summarized:

1 Comprehensive, consistent and reliable data are required for analysis of international aviation and its many institutions.

2 An understanding of the spatial distribution of traffic is required: the links between firm behaviour, industry structure and organization, and the spatial manifestation of transport production decisions at national, regional and local levels need to be clearly set out, so that institutional roles and influences can be isolated and comprehended.

3 The full costs of accessibility (including external costs and opportunity costs) need to be appraised so that the regional implications of the 'efficiency-accessibility' trade-off can be traced.

4 The role of institutions in initiating and influencing the development of new technologies that in turn permit improved use of existing infrastructure and facilities needs to be explored. In this context, the extent to which binding regulations/directives may create markets for products nationally and internationally needs to be researched. Since the economic objectives interact with political and in some cases military goals, an interdisciplinary approach to these issues is needed.

5 Do new institutions need to be developed to deal with multi-modal transport networks and to facilitate international transport by combined modes?

The forecast for the continued growth of air passenger and freight traffic though dampened by the events of 11 September 2001 in the US still suggest annual growth rates of 2–4% per annum. Where and how this growth will be facilitated is a crucial question. The spatial distribution of air traffic in the US has become gradually more concentrated on the larger centres since deregulation in the late 1970s. Air traffic volumes are closely related to population distributions in the national urban system. However, there is significantly greater variation in the traffic volumes of the very large population centres in the US *and* among the smaller centres than there is in the medium-sized communities (i.e. medium-sized communities record a higher correlation between population and air traffic volumes than either larger or smaller centres). The relationship between spatial concentration of traffic and industry (or market) concentration needs to be understood, as does the role of local and state institutions in influencing these trends.

The European industry has experienced an increase in the total number of carriers since it began significant liberalization in 1993. The trend towards consolidation among the long-established 'national carriers' has not been observed however. Member states *have* resolved to refrain from giving state aid to their national carriers. The resistance on the part of the member states to European Commission negotiation of external agreements has been overcome since the ruling of the European Court of Justice in 2002 on the legality of the 'open skies' agreements with the US. The resistance to a common external policy is understandable as national governments are seeking to protect 'national interests'; consolidation in Europe will mean fewer large carriers and traffic concentration at a limited number of airports as a result, particularly long-haul traffic. International traffic through an airport confers employment benefits and, in particular, empirical evidence would suggest that such traffic plays an important role in attracting and maintaining 'new economy' employment (Guiliano and Small 1999; Button *et al.*, 1999). Not surprisingly, national institutions seek to protect and consolidate any advantages or market share they currently hold.

The European-wide data on aviation are very poor. European carriers operating between the US and Europe provide the US Department of Transportation with monthly traffic data on a route-by-route basis, by aircraft type. ICAO publishes international 'traffic by flight stage' based on traffic statistics reported by carriers flying 'international routes'. Public policy research without these data is likely to lead to vague and inefficient outcomes. International comparisons are very difficult without sufficient comparable data. Co-operation in the specification of data needs and of reporting requirements would be an important contribution to air transport research in Europe and the US.

Notes

1   The author wishes to acknowledge the very helpful comments on earlier drafts of this chapter by

David Krause, Juan Carlos Martín Hernández participants at the STELLA Group 5 Workshop and an anonymous referee. All remaining errors are the authors.

2   See U.S. Department of Transportation, Airport Activity Statistics of the Certificated Route Air Carriers, Washington D.C, 1984 to 2002.

3   Fifth freedom rights refer to the right to pick up and drop off passengers and freight in countries other than the parties to a bilateral agreement.

4   European Court of Justice, Judgment 2002-11-05 (C-466/98) Commission v Royaume Uni; European Court of Justice, Opinion 2002-01-31 (C-466/98) Commission v Royaume-Uni

Bibliography

Button, K., Lall, S., Stough, R.R. and Trice, M. (1999) High-technology employment and hub airports. *Journal of Air Transport Management*, 5, pp. 53–59.

European Commission (2001) *European Transport Policy for 2010: Time to Decide*. DG TREN. Brussels: European Commission.

Giuliano, G. and Small, K.A. (1999) The determinants of growth of employment subcenters. *Journal of Transport Geography*, 7, pp. 189–201.

Morrison, S. and Winston, C. (1995) *The Evolution of the Airline Industry*. Washington D.C.: The Brookings Institution.

Reynolds-Feighan, A.J. (2001) Traffic distribution in low-cost and full-service carrier networks in the US air transportation market. *Journal of Air Transport Management*, 7, **pp.** 265–275.

Sochar, E. (1991) *The Politics of International Aviation*. London: Macmillan.

Stough, R.R. and Rietveld, P. (1997) Institutional issues in transport systems. *Journal of Transport Geography*, 5, pp. 207–214.

US DOT (1997) *The Low Cost Airline Service Revolution*. Washington, DC: US Department of Transportation. Online. Available http: <http://ostpxweb.dot.gov/aviation/domav/lcs.pdf>

Chapter 11

Evolution of transport institutions that facilitate international trade[1]

T. R. Lakshmanan and William P. Anderson

While international trade and the movement of economic activities across national borders have been increasing for a century or more, recent growth has been remarkable. In the 1990s, trade in goods and services grew twice as fast as global GDP. In an affluent economy such as US, trade has grown three times as fast as GDP since 1980, and the share of trade attributable to the developing countries has climbed from 23% to 29% in the 1990s (World Bank, 2000).

The common explanation for this explosive growth in trade emphasizes the creation of new incentives for trade expansion that have been embodied in new trade institutions. Indeed, institutions (such as the General Agreement on Tariffs and Trade (GATT), World Trade Organization (WTO), etc.) have succeeded in lowering tariffs and a variety of other barriers to cross-border trade. Consequently, the scale, composition, and spatial reach of international goods trade have vastly increased. It is in this context that there has been a surge in the formation of regional trading blocks (such as NAFTA, EU, Mercosur, etc). Each trade bloc represents a cluster of neighbouring countries, which link their economies and seek to create dynamic comparative advantages in terms of the global economy.

While the contribution of GATT and WTO to the lowering of trade barriers and promoting trade is widely noted, the role of two other factors – *technological changes* and *institutional reforms in the transport sector* – in the explosion of international trade appears to be less widely recognized.

Technological change in the transport sector has arrived in two forms. First, transport innovations (jet aircraft, containers, the interstate system, the 'megaship') have sharply improved the quality of service, and lowered the costs of international transportation. Second, the performance of transport vehicles and infrastructure is greatly increased by developments in the *complementary* information technologies. Information technologies (IT – representing a confluence of computer and communication technologies) are improving the responsiveness and efficiency of vehicles and their operators, and making possible other innovations by transforming both the technologies of transport and communications and the technologies of products and processes.

The notion that recent developments in these *enabling and space-shrinking technologies of* transportation and communication are fundamentally transforming the space-time relationships between all parts of the world is widely acknowledged. These technologies make possible the management and coordination of a globally distributed set of diverse economic activities. They permit increasing division of labour in the production processes as the component activities are further disaggregated and spatially reallocated. This partition of production processes (or the slicing the 'production value chain') across national borders results in different stages of production being carried out in different countries. For example, raw materials and components come from two different countries, with assembly in a third, and marketing from yet other countries in response to consumer signals from around the world. Parts and components are 'sourced' internationally (a process likely to be expanded with growing Internet use) accounting for a $800 billion trade (World Bank, 2000); and the whole process is globally coordinated.

However, in spite of the trade regime reforms and transport technology changes (which have removed institutional and physical barriers to trade), a variety of non-tariff barriers to free trade remain. *A major class of such non-tariff barriers derive from the institutions governing transport,* which embody a variety of incentives appropriate to an earlier era of restricted cross-border trade and regulated services. Even as the tariff and other barriers have fallen under the impetus of free trade areas (FTAs), trade within an FTA is still not completely 'free', in the sense that cross-border movement of goods is no more costly than the movement of the same goods over the same distance within a country. Such institutional characteristics, inherited from the era of closed trade regimes, act as non-tariff barriers hindering free cross-border goods flows.

As trading regimes have become progressively more open, the traditional transport institutions governing international goods flows have been required to reinvent themselves in order to service the emerging global economy. The aim of this reinvention effort is to change the economic incentives in a way that minimize the consequent costs of cross-border goods flow. As a consequence, there has been a recent spurt of *reform of the transport institutions governing international trade.*

A transport governance system, or a trade and transport facilitation system, is a combination of two major cross-border goods flow facilitation components, which jointly influence the speed, ease, and costs of cross-border freight flows. The first component of this trade and transport facilitation system reduces the prevalent physical barriers to transport and cross-border transit by appropriate *physical infrastructure.* This includes transport infrastructure and facilities, and communication infrastructure that complements transport infrastructure. The second major component can be termed as *non-physical infrastructure or transport institutions.* Transport institutions embody knowledge and competencies about how to transport and communicate in specific legal, economic, financial, and governance frameworks in various parts of the world, and how such frameworks may be changed (under rapidly evolving technical and economic conditions) to facilitate improved transport and trade facilitation.

Such *institutional and organizational capabilities* applied to the cross-border goods traffic embrace:

♦   the economic institutions governing transport (economic regulation, privatization of transport assets, etc.);
♦   rules governing cross-border physical flows (customs and other border inspections, rules for size and weight of vehicles, etc.);
♦   mechanisms for financial coordination across economies scattered over the globe; and
♦   business logistical practices.

This chapter on transport institutions that facilitate international trade has three objectives. First, it aims to characterize the cross-border transport governance system, that has evolved in support of international trade expansion. It identifies the various elements of this transport governance system and the role of each in facilitating efficient cross-border goods flow.

The second objective of this chapter is to highlight the on-going process of reform and reinvention of transport institutions governing trade. It highlights the socioeconomic context in which these reforms became possible and the outcomes. Such an organizational and institutional reform has appeared in the last two decades particularly in North America, Europe, and Japan in many guises. For example *(a)* in the form of business logistics innovations that squeeze out time and cost delays from the goods supply chain; *(b)* in the form of new mechanisms that improve financial coordination; *(c)* in the form of reinvented economic institutions and policies governing the transport sector; and *(d)* in the form of reformed cross-border practices (inspections, harmonization of vehicle and driver standards) governing the cross-border physical goods flow. Items *(a)* and *(b)* are autonomous organizational market innovative responses to new opportunities thrown up by transport and IT technologies by firms in the logistical and financial sectors (Chatterjee, 2001; Lakshmanan and Anderson, 2002; Lakshmanan *et al.*, 2001). This chapter focuses in particular on the last two items where the public sector is the actor in those transport institutional changes.

Third, the chapter describes the uneven development of the transport institutional reform movement in different world regions and the consequent variations in competitive advantage these institutional reforms confer on these regions. One purpose of this comparison is to identify lessons that can be gained from the experience of the North American and European FTAs and which may help developing countries as they upgrade their transport and trade systems.

Institutions of transport governance

A transport governance system refers here to the specific economic, financial, legal, and political frameworks that define the environment or the conditions under which goods can be transported across national borders. The frameworks relate to regulations governing transport services, rules of cabotage, privatization of infrastructure, banking practices and payment systems, the nature of customs and other goods inspection, the harmonization of vehicle standards, and trade practices. These institutional frameworks have evolved to facilitate trade in the affluent industrialized countries, with transport becoming increasingly faster, more flexible and (with jet transport, fast container ships, container handling practices, and intermodal systems) more predictable within a narrow time range. Transport and information industries are being privatized, and deregulated. New logistical innovations such as just-in-time and quick-response are reengineering business systems, as well as production and commodity flow systems. Containers and cargoes are continually tracked around the world by automatic identification devices and are continually 'visible' in transit to shippers and carriers. The traditional slow and tedious paper trail that accompanies goods to secure clearances across borders from customs, revenue agencies and financial intermediaries is being replaced by electronic data interchange (EDI) and e-commerce. Customs agencies, finance ministries, and regulators are beginning to reinvent their practices in this new environment.

As compared to these state-of-the-art systems in North America, Japan, and Europe, the prevalent transport and trade facilitation systems in free trade areas (FTAs) located in developing countries such as Mercosur (the free trade agreement between Argentina, Brazil, Paraguay and Uruguay) and the South Asian Region are deficient in terms of supporting physical infrastructure, and in terms of the institutions necessary for the efficiency and speed of domestic and cross-border transportation of goods, and the harmonization and simplification of processing the information (that accompanies the goods) across a border. The greater the gap between the state-of-the-art transport and trade facilitation (TTF) systems and the system available in a particular FTA, the greater the penalty the specific regional trading bloc will pay in terms of foregone trade and economic growth.

This efficiency penalty of an inadequate transport and transit facilitation system in Mercosur or any other regional trading bloc can be experienced in several ways. International agencies estimate that the costs of the current antiquated types of trade administration and the failure to adopt IT-supported trade facilitation and the downstream effects of those systems account for 7% of the value of the goods (Schware and Kimberley, 1995).

If existing and emerging FTAs in developing countries such as Mercosur, or in South Asia, or in South Africa have substandard transport and trade facilitation (TTF) systems, they cannot participate effectively in the global production networks. As noted earlier, the increasing division of labour in the global economy leads to a partition of the production 'value chain' among production locales that are spatially distributed in many countries. One-third of world trade in the mid-1990s occurred within such global production networks (World Bank, 2000).

Manufacturing industries continue to be reallocated in these networks from industrial countries to developing regions such as Mercosur, trade expansion is likely not only in goods but also in services (which are becoming increasingly tradable). Third, unimproved transport and transit systems can reduce trade in Mercosur and thereby restrict the realization of the benefits of globalization, such as increasing the markets for exports, the acquisition of new technology, and the favourable effect of competition on the efficiency of domestic producers.

The long-term benefits of a superior transport and trade facilitation system lie, beyond the cost reduction and trade expansion benefits noted above, in the potential for cross-border integration of manufacturing and service activities and the potential for exploiting the economies of scope and scale in the larger Mercosur market. The latter developments lead in time to self-sustaining economic expansion. While such developments take time, they can set in motion a sequence of cumulative processes that lead from falling costs from output increases to incentives for the creation of spatial agglomerations of production (cities), on to rising output and profits, in turn attracting more production to these cities.

The components of an advanced transport governance system

As noted above, an advanced transport governance system oriented to trade facilitation (Table 11.1) reduces the barriers to transport and cross-border transit through the use of *knowledge and competencies applied* to the transport vehicles and infrastructure. Such knowledge and competencies are embodied in the reformed institutions and private organizations. These institutions and organizations incorporate knowledge about how to transport and communicate in the specific legal, economic, financial, and governance frameworks, which are operative in different countries. Further, these institutions and organizations are learning systems that develop adaptive knowledge relating to how such frameworks may be changed over time to facilitate continual improvement of transport and trade.

Table 11.1 Components of a transport governance system facilitating trade

Transport institutions
(Knowledge and competencies in transport and trade facilitation)
1. Overall governance of transport and trade facilitation
2. Systems of governance of physical flows
Market organizations
1. Business logistical systems
2. Financial coordination systems

1   Overall governance of transport and trade facilitation. This defines the economic, institutional, legal, and administrative frameworks within which cross-border transport activities are carried out. Examples of recent reforms of these frameworks in order to promote trade include: deregulation of transport services in North America and Europe; progressive removal of cabotage restrictions and other residual economic regulations; privatization of transport infrastructures, etc.

2   Systems of governance of physical flows. Goods moving from one side of a national border to the other are normally subject to a variety of processes governed by a multiplicity of rules. Examples of such rules pertain to the size and weight of vehicles permitted in freight across borders, customs inspection practices, forms of other border inspection relating to agricultural products, drugs, etc. To promote seamless intermodal freight flows across borders, knowledge and competencies related to such governance systems (that vary across borders) and ways of reforming them are crucial.

3   Business logistical systems. Business capabilities are enhanced by new logistical systems that offer fast, reliable, and low-cost service. Logistical systems represent an integrated analysis and active management of a production firm's overall supply chain, from the spatially far-flung sources of inputs to delivery of finished products (Chatterjee, 2001). These systems can also provide competitive advantage by slashing costs (minimum inventory), quickening market feedback, and expanding market reach.

4   Financial coordination systems. Since money is exchanged for the transfer of property rights to the goods at the time of goods delivery, financial coordination across different economies in a vast global economy is crucial. Financial instruments help pool and diversify risk. Financial

coordination is improved by trade-friendly banking practices and new payment systems. Risk-reduction innovations can reduce the costs of linking the shipper and the customer. Organizational innovations can create efficient entities for marketing and distribution in the rapidly evolving marketplace.

The rest of this chapter will focus on this process of reform of transport governance. Specifically, the chapter concentrates on two components (listed below) of the transport and trade facilitation that require *considerable institutional reform* by public sector agents:

- overall governance of transport and trade facilitation; and
- governance of physical flows.

This chapter illustrates the importance of a transport governance system by case studies of recent developments in NAFTA, European Union, and Mercosur. An alternative approach is a more formal analysis of the effects of institutional reforms on the promotion of cross-country goods flow. Indeed, such a formal model of the influence of institutional reforms on the volume of bilateral trade flows in the international economy has been developed (Groot *et al.*, 2003). This model demonstrates the positive contribution that institutional improvements make in promoting cross-border goods movement.

Reform of overall governance of transport systems

The reform of the elaborate and divergent economic regulations governing transport in the different countries that make up an FTA is often a prerequisite for the promotion of a seamless cross-border freight flow among these countries. This derives from the fact that in affluent countries the transport sector was regulated to varying degrees for much of the twentieth century. In North America, processes of transport deregulation and privatization have played complementary roles with trade liberalization to promote transport integration. After all the economic regulatory reform that has occurred in Canada, Mexico, and the US, there is still remnant economic regulation in the form of cabotage rules that hinder efficient transborder operations. As noted below, more recently Europe has witnessed similar deregulation and privatization processes. We also discuss the progress towards these goals in FTAs in developing countries, such as Mercosur.

The North American experience

The public policy regimes in transport in North America have included a high level of economic regulation for nearly a century. This derived from the fact that transportation carriers, which are integrated with fixed facilities and vehicles and enjoy network economies, were able to engage in monopoly pricing, market segmentation pricing and similar actions that seriously disadvantaged shippers and communities.

Since 1887, the US instituted economic regulation of railroads that allowed the Interstate Commerce Commission (ICC) to assure a normal rate of return for railroads' assets while balancing the advantages of shippers and equity of service to communities. To this end ICC engaged in elaborate control of investment, pricing, and operations in the railroad industry by specifying the conditions of entry, exit, the creation of complex rate structure, and even rules of operations – without the ability to compute costs effectively. During the 1930s, similar economic regulation was extended to motor carriers and airlines. Canadian carriers have also been subject to economic regulation, though more lightly than in the US and predominantly at the provincial level. Mexico also regulated through the award of transport concessions, the grant of route capacity and freight rate structures.

The adverse effects of such intrusive regulation became very evident by the 1970s in the poor financial performance of US railroads and high truck rates in the LTL (less than truckload) sector. Economic analyses have shown that the price and entry regulations introduce inefficiency by creating a vicious cycle of artificially high prices, high service quality competition and the resultant losses due to raised costs (Douglas and Miller, 1974). Three sets of such regulatory distortions have proved costly. First, in both road and rail, rates were set above marginal costs – costing the economy $1 billion annually (Winston, 1985). Second, the entry and exit regulations cost the carriers dearly. The prohibition on railroads on exiting from poorly performing lines leading to annual production cost inefficiencies of $2.5 billions (Winston, 1985). Third, restrictions such as disallowing backhauls, designation of routes, etc. led to X-inefficiency costs of several billion dollars (Winston *et al.*, 1990), hindering productivity growth, technical change, and service quality.

In addition to these economic arguments, the political resistance to change was weakened by division of viewpoints on deregulation among the (weak and strong) airlines. The resulting drive for deregulation led in short order to regulatory reform of airlines (1978), railroads (1980), and motor carriers (1980) first in the US. Entry conditions were eased, freedom to price was promoted, reliance on the market and competition was encouraged. Canada followed suit through the *National Transportation Act (NTA, 1987)*, the *Shipping Conferences Exemption Act (SCEA)*, and the *Motor Vehicle Transport Act* together with the amendments to other legislation such as the *Railway Act*.

Transport deregulation came to Mexico in the late 1980s, as the government restructured the economic institutions and promoted domestic investment-friendly policies. Liberalization of the motor carrier industry occurred in 1989, permitting greater pricing freedom, opening the transport market to private carriers, and allowing Maquiladora operators to use their own fleets to move goods to and from the US.

Major changes occurred in the US in the conduct, performance, and structure of airlines, trucking and railroads after deregulation. More competition among all modal carriers, lower prices, wider set of service offerings, and new entry into most geographic and product markets (Figures 11.1 and 11.2). Carriers have been able to rationalize their networks, improve the efficiency of their operations, and set rates in line with competitive market conditions. There was a significant change in the cost structure of the railroad industry following deregulation with productivity growing at well over 2% a year (Bereskin, 1996).

Several studies have shown that average airfares (in constant dollars) have fallen since 1978 and competition stays rigorous on most city-pair routes, though concentration has gone up in the industry (US GAO, 1990; NRC, 1991). US domestic airfares adjusted for distance have been consistently lower in the last two decades than in Europe, Asia, or the world.

Shippers, confronting technological change and globalization, have begun to coordinate their production activities more effectively with their transportation services, and this has resulted in productivity gains. The

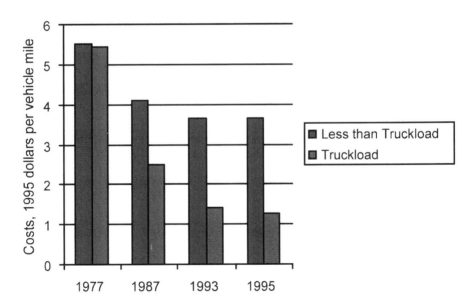

Figure 11.1 Operating costs of less than truckload and truckload carriers, 1977–1995, in 1995 dollars per vehicle mile

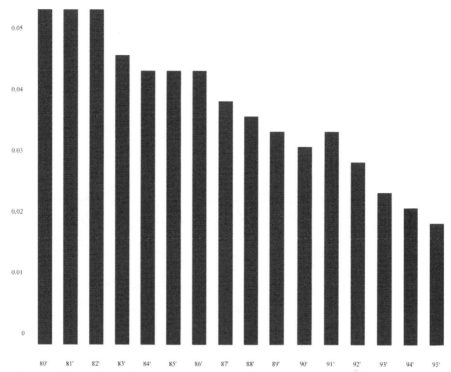

Figure 11.2 Railroad operating costs per revenue ton-mile, 1980–1995, in 1995 dollars

experience in Canada since 1987 has been broadly similar, with competitive pressures lowering rates in international air traffic, railroads, and trucking (Figure 11.4). Trucking deregulation in Mexico in 1989 increased competition and lowered rates by 29% (Strah, 1995). It also promoted expansion of intercity routes and the vehicle fleet.

Cabotage. Cabotage refers to the ability of foreign vehicles and labour to transport goods within a country. The cabotage rules and regulations, instituted by customs and immigration departments are typically symmetric. Such rules involve the use of labour and equipment of one country in the other. For example, foreign drivers cannot carry domestic freight and the use of foreign equipment is restricted to domestic movements that are incidental to international movements. The existence of these cabotage-rule barriers increases the cost of transborder transport. Railroads are less affected by cabotage restrictions, though they too incur additional costs because of the need to change crews at the border.

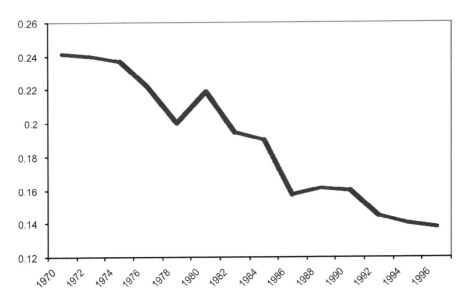

Figure 11.3 Average revenue per passenger-mile for domestic airlines, adjusted for inflation

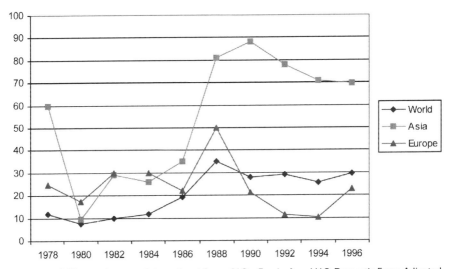

Figure 11.4 Difference between International Fares (U.S. - Foreign) and U.S. Domestic Fares Adjusted for Distance, selected years, 1978–1996.

Another major remaining cabotage barrier is the existing US restrictions on trade in domestic water transportation. In the large, multi-coastal US economy, foreign participation in its intercoastal trade is restricted by the 1920 Jones Act. The Jones Act (justified by the need to secure a sufficient merchant marine capacity for US defence needs) reserves the shipping cabotage traffic

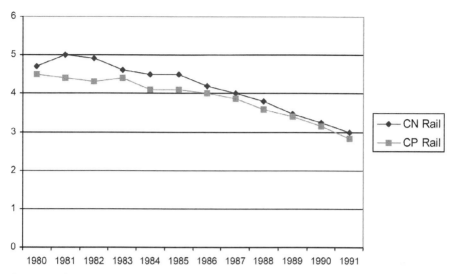

Figure 11.5 Canadian railroad costs in 1980–1991 (in 1986 cents per revenue ton-mile)

to US built and registered ships that are predominantly owned and crewed by US nationals. The US maritime carriers and other stakeholders have excluded these provisions from the GATT and NAFTA. The Jones Act permits domestic shippers to levy rates substantially above comparable world prices, effecting thereby a massive transfer from US users of water transport to US maritime carriers. This amounts to a welfare cost around $3 billion in 1989 according to a recent analysis of the Jones Act (Francois *et al.*, 1996).

Aviation is an important component of foreign trade, for example accounting for $355 billion or 27% of US trade in 1995, 60% of which is hauled in US carriers (US GAO, 1996). The rapid growth in international air freight services reflects the emergence of global systems of producing and distributing goods, together with 'just-in-time' inventory and supply chain management systems. Such services are handicapped by the bilateral international aviation agreements that specify traffic rights, including the routes, the number of flights on each route and the number of airlines that can fly them. Such restrictions on transborder airline traffic have recently been relaxed by the US negotiations on 'open skies' agreements with many European countries such as Germany and the Netherlands. In 1995, the US and Canada signed the Open Skies Agreement, under which carriers in each country were given full access to destinations in the other, procedures for international fare approval were streamlined, and gates at some of the busiest US airports were dedicated to Canadian flights. The agreement extended both to passenger and all-cargo air services. The agreement with Mexico (1991) is not 'open' but liberalized to include open routes, no capacity restrictions, freedom to transfer cargo for 'onward flights', and operational flexibility but restricted in the number of airlines allowed to operate (one on any city-pair segment), and double approval pricing.

As both production and transportation firms in all three countries rationalize their operations across the NAFTA region, the transport non-tariff barriers noted in this section cause inefficiencies and generate the political demand for their relaxation. The direct effect of these barriers would be higher costs, and the longer term indirect effect would be less competitive and efficient activities in the logistics industry and the consequent loss of productivity in the NAFTA region.

The European experience

Creating an integrated transportation system within the EU area requires progress on three interrelated objectives: interoperability, free market access, and interconnection. Interoperability refers to the harmonization of technical standards for infrastructure elements ranging from rail gauge to air traffic control systems as well as rules applying to service providers such as truck size and weight restrictions. Free market access refers to the removal of restrictions that prevent providers of transportation services based in one member state from operating in another. Interconnection refers to the problem of linking up national infrastructure networks. The relatively sparse connections among these networks are partly due to the fact that many borders coincide with physical barriers such as mountains, rivers, and seas. It also reflects the fact that national networks have been developed primarily to meet the domestic needs of member states.

The reasons for slow progress in achieving these objectives are varied, but most relate to the traditional mandate of national governments in transportation policy and their unwillingness to transfer authorities to the EU. For example, nearly all national governments were owners of major transportation suppliers, including railways and airlines, and therefore had interests in preserving their local monopoly powers. Furthermore, transportation policy is frequently used as a means of pursuing national economic goals. The role of sub-national and even local governments in transportation complicates the process of harmonization further. Thus, the member states had some interest in preserving the *status quo* of policy fragmentation.

By the 1980s, groups representing consumers of transportation services who were increasingly frustrated with high costs and poor quality began to bring both political and judicial pressure for the EU to take action. In 1985, the European Court of Justice (ECJ) ruled that the European Commission had failed to act appropriately to implement the Common Transport Policy required under the Treaty of Rome. This ruling related specifically to opening up national transportation markets to suppliers from other member states, but it marked a major turning point after which the Commission and Parliament became more active in all aspects of transportation policy.

Between 1987 and 1992, major new legislation was enacted regarding air, marine, road, rail, and inland water transportation. This legislation dealt mostly with issues of market access and interoperability, as well as common work rules for transportation employees. In the 1990s, however, the Commission began to focus more on issues of interconnection. For example, a 1993 White Paper on growth, competitiveness, and employment emphasized the transformations in production systems, methods of organizing work, and consumption patterns that were already being adopted in North America and Asia. Economic fragmentation and adherence to traditional practices made it difficult for European businesses to manage complex value chains and spawn small innovative firms, placing the EU in a weak competitive position *vis-à-vis* other major production regions.

Repeating a goal that had already been enshrined in the 1992 Treaty on European Union, the White Paper called for the development of integrated and complementary information, transportation, and energy Trans-European Networks (TENs). This led to the announcement in 1994 of a major infrastructure programme specifically geared to filling gaps in the existing European transportation networks.

Rules of market access for transportation services have been contentious from the inception of the EU. The final language of the Treaty of Rome left considerable room for interpretation. For example, while the Treaty committed the member states to a Common Transport Policy, it did not call for a common market in transportation. Also, specific reference was made only to road, rail, and inland waterways, leaving the impression that air and sea transport were excluded from EU control. Furthermore, competition (anti-trust) rules contained language excluding transportation.

Air transportation is an especially interesting case. Until the 1980s, all member states had ownership interests in national flagship airlines. These airlines had long been considered instruments of national economic policy and influential public sector unions dominated their labour forces. Furthermore, national airlines were a matter of prestige for most states. Thus, despite the fact that most of them lost money, member states were loath to allow competition that might threaten the viability of national flagship carriers.

Regulation on inter-country service was handled via bilateral arrangements whereby the two national governments designated carriers, defined timetables, set fares, and divided the revenues (O'Reilly and Stone Sweet, 1998). For the most part, independent carriers were closed out of these routes. Also, foreign carriers were given access only to major national airports, with service to regional airports limited to national carriers.

Impetus for change came primarily from business groups, who argued that the poor quality and high cost of air travel within the EU was a major barrier to economic integration and global competitiveness. They had a sympathetic ear in the European Commission, whose 1979 attempt to institute a programme of airline liberalization had been thwarted by the member states. By the middle of the 1980s, they also had the support of two member governments (the United Kingdom and the Netherlands) that had begun their own deregulation initiatives.

An example of the objections of member states is provided by Greece, which argued that economic, regional development, and security priorities depended upon year round service between the mainland and the Greek islands. If independent operators were allowed into this market, they would offer services only during the lucrative summer tourist season, leaving the unprofitable months to the national carrier.

A key event in the breakdown of the old system came when the French government prosecuted some independent airlines offering domestic services below the regulated fares. A French court referred the case to the ECJ, which found that although air travel was protected from some elements of competition policy, it was not completely immune and that the European Commission had some authority regarding airline practices.

In the aftermath of this decision the Commission attempted for the second time to reform air travel. It did not propose a wholesale American-style deregulation, but rather that national regulation regarding inter-country flights be removed in favour of a EU regulatory regime. Under a new set of rules (1987), many of the old restrictions remained, but avenues for greater competition were created including:

♦   permission for carriers to offer restricted services with fares discounted below the reference rate approved by the two member states;

♦   a requirement that each state permit more than one airline from another state access to its airports (although not necessarily more than one to the same airport);

♦   under some restrictions, permission for carriers to offer services to a regional airport in another country; and

♦   under carefully controlled circumstances, permission for an airline from one country to provide services between two other countries.

Note that an airline in one country still cannot offer services between two points within another country (cabotage) (O'Reilly and Stone Sweet, 1998).

The result of this transformation is a more competitive and efficient environment, but not a fully deregulated one. This environment led to a restructuring of the industry, including the emergence of cut-rate carriers and a number of international alliances. The result has been greater choice and lower fares for EU air travellers (McCormick, 1999).

In those areas of transportation services where governments have been less involved in the supply side, much greater strides have been made toward achieving a true common market. Transportation of freight by road (trucking) is a good example. Under 1992 regulations, any operator with a 'community authorization' has unlimited access to the market for freight movement between member states. This includes both trips beginning or ending in the state where the carrier is based and trips between any other two states.

The liberal community market access rules also extend to cabotage. Starting in 1990, any carrier with a 'community cabotage authorization' can carry goods within any state in the EU 15. These authorizations were issued under an increasing quota system until 1998, when all quotas were scheduled to be removed. Complementary rules with respect to licensing of and work rules for drivers and other employees are also in place.

There are provisions to protect national trucking industries from extreme damage from foreign competitors with either community or community cabotage authorization. If a significant number of domestic firms are found to be in danger of severe financial damage, a crisis period is declared during which market access is restricted. The restrictions are imposed for six months, renewable once (EU DG Transport, 1999).

Mercosur region

Transport service liberalization and deregulation arrived in the 1990s in the Mercosur countries. They were propelled by the inability of publicly offered transport services in these countries to improve operational efficiency and services, to arrest cost increases, to attract new investment, to achieve quality maintenance, and to lower public subsidies. Transport industries were privatized to varying degrees in Mercosur countries. Argentina was one of the leaders of privatization programmes in the early 1990s, when the government sold off various public enterprises, including the Aerolineas Argentinas (one of the largest airlines in Latin America), railroads, and important turnpikes. Brazilian railways were privatized more recently and need to catch up with their Argentine counterparts (Zinn, 1999).

The transport privatization efforts in Argentina, together with Chile and Mexico, went further than most Latin American countries in liberalizing various parts of the transport sector. Unlike the power and telecommunications sectors which were sold outright, Argentina granted transport concessions of 10 to 30 years, with ownership and control of assets returning to the government at the end of the concession. The concession dealt with the problems that motivated privatization without limiting government's future options or flexibility. While these efforts in rail, road, and ports and waterways are described in detail in Lakshmanan *et al.* (2001), a few summary comments are in order.

A major consequence of rail privatization was savings in railroad subsidies (which averaged US\$ 1.4 billions annually in the 1980s and now reduced to US\$ 0.1 billions/year and intended only for commuter railroads and subways). These savings derived from a combination of increased labour productivity and abandonment of lightly used (inter-city passenger) services and lines. Ridership was increasing in urban commuter rail (45%) and subway (18%). The freight volume reached the 1980s levels, but some of the freight lines had difficulties stemming from the intense competition from truck services which were helped by geography and public policy. The condition of the privatized highways has improved significantly and the cost of maintenance was off the government budget. However, there is no direct evidence that the cost of road maintenance is lower for the private sector (Gomez-Ibanez, 1997). Road usage has also climbed, partly due to road improvements, but mainly from economic recovery.

The mix of privatization and deregulation in ports and waterways sharply reduced port charges and barge and ocean shipping tariffs. Shipping costs for containers from Argentina to Northern Europe fell between 30% and 70% (1991 and 1993) for grain and bulk shipments, and savings of 10% materialized. The savings largely derived from labour productivity, with employment at the ports of Buenos Aires falling from 8000 to 2500. The concession for the Atlantic Ocean-Santa Fe waterway was expected to offer considerable savings from cheaper maintenance of the channel, but also with an additional requirement to have a deeper channel depth north of Buenos Aires (Gomez-Ibanez, 1997).

Reform of governance system for physical flows

The NAFTA experience

In addition to economic regulation, cross-border transportation is subject to a host of technical regulations and standards. These include:

- size and weight regulations for trucks;
- size, weight and other technical standards for locomotives and other railroad stock;
- age, language, licensing and health regulations for vehicle operators;
- conventions for road signs and traffic signals;

♦ procedures for ensuring vehicle safety;

♦ procedures of transportation of hazardous goods.

Technical regulation of goods flow

In all of these cases, somewhat different regulations, standards, and procedures have evolved over many years in the three NAFTA partners, increasing the cost of moving goods across borders. This is a form of non-tariff barrier.

Inconsistencies in truck size and weight regulations are a good example. These regulations are imposed for two reasons. The first is that excessively large vehicles will not operate effectively in mixed traffic streams, resulting in congestion, delays, and accidents. The second is that oversized vehicles result in accelerated wear and damage to road infrastructure, and may result in the failure of bridges.

Truck size and weight regulations can be complex. For example, not only the gross weight of the truck, but also the weight per axle, the way the weight is distributed to the front and back axles, and the distance between the axles, may be included in the regulations. Truck length regulations may be defined on overall length, on the length of tractor and trailer independently, or even on the length of the trailer beyond the back-most axle.

Unfortunately, there are some significant inconsistencies between these regulations in the three NAFTA partners. Even on the most basic dimension – gross truck weight – there is no consistency. As Table 11.2 indicates, the United States limits all trucks to a gross weight of 36,288 kg (80,000 lb). Both Mexico and Canada allow higher weights for all categories of trucks and increase the weight limit for trucks with more than the standard five axles. This inconsistency is due mainly to conservative assumptions by US officials about the maximum weight that can be supported by bridges.

To make matters worse, different regulations may apply in different places. For example, Canadian regulations are set at the provincial level, and despite recent efforts at standardization, some variation remains across provinces. There are also some state level variations in the United States and different regulations apply on different parts of the highway network (this is especially true for regulations applying to trucks hauling more than one trailer).

Table 11.2 Maximum gross vehicle weights in the NAFTA countries (in kg)

Truck type	US	Canada*	Mexico
Tractor – semitrailer (5 axles)	36,288	39,500 – 41,500	44,000
Tractor – semitrailer (6 axles)	36,288	46,500 – 53,000	48,500
Double trailer (6 axles)	36,288	47,600 – 43,500	47,500

Note: * range of provincial regulations

These inconsistencies have the potential to add significantly to the cost of cross-border transportation. For example, it is already the case that some Canadian trucking firms must maintain separate fleets of trucks for shipments into the US and for domestic shipments (Prentice and Wilson, 1998). Also, given these inconsistencies, each country must take measures that trucks entering their territory are not in violation of its rules. This implies border inspections, which add to the cost of border operations and may contribute to costly border delays.

Recognizing the potential problems arising from inconsistencies in the technical regulation of transportation, a provision of NAFTA established the Land Transportation Standards Subcommittee with responsibility for harmonizing all the categories of technical regulation listed above. To date, significant progress has been made in the regulation of vehicle operators and in harmonization of road signs and signals. The issue of safety compliance, especially with reference to Mexican trucks coming into the US, still presents problems.

Border crossing areas may be subject to long delays. Canada and the US have traded large volumes of goods for a number of decades, and in the process both governments have worked cooperatively to develop relatively efficient border crossing routines. The border crossings along the US–Mexican frontier are plagued by long delays and many Mexican trucks must be sent back due to violations of various US regulations.

Large volumes of freight movement at the US–Mexican border are a more recent development, so there has been less time to work out the problems. Also, the issues of illegal immigration and transport of drugs in commercial vehicles is a major concern. Finally, the Mexican truck fleet is in a relatively poor state and Mexican carriers and drivers are not well informed on US regulations, so many trucks fail inspection.

The situation along the Mexican border has presented a major impediment to full implementation of NAFTA provisions. NAFTA specifies a timetable for providing full freedom of truck movement across the US–Mexico border. Initially, Mexican trucks were only allowed to operate in a relatively small commercial zone extending only a few miles into the territory of the four states that border Mexico (Mexican goods bound for destinations outside this zone must be transferred to American trucks). The NAFTA December 1995 deadline for Mexican trucks to be allowed to make deliveries throughout the territories of the border states and US trucks to have similar access to Mexican border states was not implemented till 2001.

There is considerable potential for new information and communication technologies that come under the general heading of Intelligent Transportation Systems (ITS) to speed border crossings by eliminating much of the need for paper handling, remotely reading truck identification and cargo information, and conducting certain basic checks on weight, length, height, and width while the truck is in motion. Also, electronic databases can be used to identify trucks and drivers with previous violation histories so that inspection efforts can be concentrated on them.

The European experience

Achieving interoperability in European transportation systems involves two related tasks. The first is to see that all new infrastructures incorporate a common set of design standards. The second is to ensure that equipment and employees operating on existing infrastructure meet a common set of technology and safety standards. The programme for achieving interoperability in high-speed train (HST) networks is an example of the first task.

Because most ongoing HST projects receive some support under the TEN (Trans European Network) programme, the EU is well-placed to ensure consistency of technical standards. However, under the 'new approach' to interoperability the goal is to establish only those common standards that are necessary to achieve a smooth interface between systems, rather than stifle innovation by insisting on a full set of common specifications. A body known as the European Association for Interoperability is charged with proposing an appropriate set of technical specifications for interoperability (TSI). This body is made up of representatives from railways and related industries, rather than officials from either the Commission or member state governments. The TSI are submitted to the Commission, which approves them after consultation with an expert committee (European Commission Directorate General for Transport, 1999, doc. 1.1.2).

Adopting and enforcing a common set of road vehicle weight and dimension standards is a precondition for interoperability. A new set of standards was adopted in 1996 to apply to vehicles operating throughout the EU. These include the maximum length, height, and weight for different categories of trucks, including 'road trains' that can be as long as 18.75 metres and weigh up to 44 metric tonnes (European Commission Directorate General for Transport, 1999, doc. 2.13.1).

Given the complex nature of these regulations, checks at borders to ensure that incoming trucks meet regulations can be time consuming. Given the high level of harmonization of EU standards, however, it has been determined that such checks are no longer necessary. Since all EU trucks must conform to common standards, there is no reason to treat domestic and foreign trucks any differently. Thus foreign trucks can be subjected to the same spot-checking procedures that are used for domestic trucks, and authorizations for cabotage etc. can be checked at the same time. Border checks for control of both authorization and size and weight rules were eliminated at the end of

1989 (European Commission Directorate General for Transport, 1999, doc. 2.11.1).

Concluding remarks

The increasing openness of trade regimes in recent decades reflects a convergence of institutional thinking. First is the progressive lowering of tariffs and trade barriers with the help of a new international institutional architecture of GATT, WTO, and various trade rounds. Second, technological changes in the transport and communication sectors are making possible vast movements of commodities at ever lower costs. The third factor, the scope of this chapter, is the quickening reform of the transport governance system, or the transport institutions governing international trade.

Finally a conundrum: for students of sustainable development, the enthusiasm for transport institutional reform and the increase in the world movement of goods in this chapter may be a cause for concern. The argument can be that the increasing division of labour and the global organization of the production system, made possible by transport changes, can lead to major increases in the ton-miles of goods flow and the consequent growth of energy use and environmental emission. Perhaps, but not necessarily so.

Several forces are at play here with conflicting impacts and outcomes. First, there is a broad dematerialization process accompanying the new knowledge – intensive production system. The material and energy intensities of production processes are dropping. Physical flows per unit $ of Gross Domestic Product are dropping. Second, on the one hand, physical technologies are reducing energy use per unit of work. Recent improvements in vehicle technologies (e.g. ocean shipping) are creating scale economy effects, and sharply reduced energy/ton mile of goods movement. On the other hand, improvements in the transport organizational technologies are creating new logistical processes (for example, just-in-time, time-definite, world delivery) for moving knowledge-intensive goods. These logistical processes involved the use of faster transport modes (typically more energy intensive). The net effect of these interactive technological, economic, and organization processes cannot be theoretically known *a priori*. It is an empirical question.

For the sustainable transport development policy-maker, the focus meanwhile can be on designing economic and other incentives which will promote energy savings in the variety of production and transport processes described here.

Note

1 The authors gratefully acknowledge partial financial support from the World Bank in the preparation of this paper.

Bibliography

Amjadi, A. and Winters, L.A. (1997) Transport Costs and Natural Integration in Mercosur. World Bank Policy Research Working Paper 1742, Washington DC.

Bereskin, C.G. (1996) Econometric estimation of the effects of deregulation on railway productivity growth. *Transportation Journal*, 35, pp. 34–43.

Borenstein, S. (1992) The evolution of airline competition. *Journal of Economic Perspectives*, 6, pp. 45–73.

Brown, W.M. and Anderson, W.P. (1999a) The influence of industrial and spatial structure on Canada – US regional trade. *Growth and Change*, 30, pp. 23–47.

Brown, W.M. and Anderson, W.P. (1999b) The Potential for Economic Integration Among Canadian and American Regions. Department of Geography, McMaster University, Hamilton, Ontario, Canada.

Button, K. (1993) The future of European transport, in Thord, R. (ed.) *The Future of Transportation and Communication: Visions and Perspectives from Europe, Japan, and the USA*. Berlin: Springer-Verlag.

Chatterjee (2001) Transportation, Logistics Value and Supply Chains. Research report. Bureau of Transportation Statistics, USDOT.

Chow, G. (1997) North American trucking policy, in Oum, T.H. *et al.* (eds) *Transport Economics*. Amsterdam: Harwood Academic Publishers, pp. 591–624.

Chow, G. and McRae, J.J. (1989) Non tariff barriers and the structure of US-Canadian (transborder) trucking industry. *Transportation Journal*, 30, pp. 4–21.

Douglas, G.W. and Miller, J.C. III (1974) Quality competition, industry equilibrium and efficiency in the price-constrained airline market. *The American Economic Review*, 64, pp. 657–669.

European Commission (1993) *Growth, Competitiveness, and Employment: The Challenges and Ways Forward into the 21st Century*. White Paper. Luxembourg: Office for Official Publications of the European Com-munities.

European Commission (no date) *The Common Transport Policy Sustainable Mobility: Perspectives for the Future*. Commission Communication to the Council, European Parliament, Economic and Social Committee and Committee of the Regions. Luxembourg: Office for Official Publications of the European Communities.

European Commission Directorate General for Transport (1999) *Guide to the Transportation Acquis*. Luxembourg: Office for Official Publications of the European Communities.

Federal Highway Administration (1998) *North American Initiatives*. Wash-ington DC: US Department of Transportation.

Francois, J.F., Arce, H.M., Reinert, K.A. and Flynn, J.E. (1996) Commercial policy and the domestic carrying trade. *Canadian Journal of Economics*, 81, pp. 181–19.

Gomez-Ibanez, Jose A. (1997) Privatizing Transport in Argentina. Kennedy School of Government Case Program, Harvard University.

Groot, H.L.F., Linders, G.-J., Rietveld, P. and Subramanian, U. (2003) *The Institutional*

Determinants of Bilateral Trade Flows. Sponsored study. Washington, DC: World Bank.

Helliwell, J.F. (1996) Do national borders matter for Quebec trade? *Canadian Journal of Economics*, **24**, pp. 507–522.

Kinnock, N. (1995) The Private Sector's Role in Development of TENS. Speech by Director General Transport to the European Investment Bank Conference, Amsterdam, May 18.

Krugman, P.R. (1979) Increasing returns, monopolistic competition, and international trade. *American Economic Review*, **70**, pp. 950–959.

Lakshmanan, T.R. and Anderson, W.P. (1999) Trade and Transport Inte-gration: Lessons from the North American Experience. Paper presented at the World Bank/ESCAP Workshop on Transport and Trade Facilitation, Bangkok, April.

Lakshmanan, T.R. and Anderson, W.P. (2002) Transportation Infrastructure, Freight Services Sector, and Economic Growth. White Paper prepared for the US Department of Transportation, Washington, DC.

Lakshmanan, T.R., Subramanian, U., Anderson, W. and Lautier, F. (2001) Integration of Transport and Trade Facilitation, Selected Regional Case Studies. Washington. DC: World Bank.

McCallum, J. (1995) National borders matter: US–Canada regional trade patterns. *American Economic Review*, **85**, pp. 615–623.

McCormick, J. (1999) *Understanding the European Union.* New York: St. Martins Press.

Meyer, J.R. *et al.* (1959) *The Economics of Competition in the Transportation Industries.* Cambridge: Harvard University Press.

Montufar, J. (1996) Trucking and Size and Weight Regulations in the Mid-Continent Corridor. MSc Thesis, Department of Civil and Geological Engineering, University of Manitoba, Winnipeg.

Morrison, S.A. and Winston, C. (1999) Regulatory reform of US intercity transportation, in Gomez-Ibanez, J., Tye, W. and Winston, C. (eds.) *Essays in Transportation Economics and Policy: A Handbook in Honor of John R. Meyer.* Washington, DC: Brookings Institution.

NRC (National Research Council) Transportation Research Board (1991) *Winds of Change: Domestic Air Transport Since Deregulation*, Special Report 230. Washington. DC: NRC.

National Transportation Act Review Commission (Canada) (1993) *Competition in Transportation Policy Legislation in Review*, Vols. I & II. Ottawa: Minister of Supply in Services.

North American Free Trade Agreement Land Transportation Standards Subcommittee (1997) Vehicle Weights and Dimensions, Harmonization of Vehicle Weight and Dimensions. Regulations within the NAFTA Partnership. Working Group 2. October.

OECD (1998) Implications of the Mercosur Agreement for Cereal and Livestock Product Markets and Trade. Directorate for Food and Agriculture, AGR/CA (98)4 Final, Geneva.

Ohlin, B. (1933) *Interregional and International Trade.* Cambridge: Harvard University Press.

O'Reilly, D. and Stone Sweet, A. (1998) The liberalization and European reregulation of air transport, in Sandholtz, W. and Stone Sweet, A. (eds.) *European Integration and Supranational Governance.* Oxford: Oxford University Press.

Prentice, Barry, E. and Wilson, William W. (1998) Future transportation developments in the U.S./Canada/Mexico grain-livestock subsector under NAFTA and WTO, in Lyons, R. M. A., Knutson, Ronald D. and Meilke, Karl (eds.) *Economic Harmonization in the Canadian/U.S./Mexico Grain–Livestock Subsector.* Proceedings of the Fourth Agricultural and Food Policy Systems Workshop, December. Winnipeg, MB: Friesen Printers.

Schware, Robert and Kimberly, Paul (1995) Information Technology and National Trade Facilitation. Technical Paper 316. World Bank, Washington, DC.

Sowinski, L.L. (2000) Is there a perfect logisticsproduct in the market? *World Trade,* February, pp. 32–36.

Strah, T.M. (1995) Mexican truckers set off alarms. *Transport Topics,* March 13, p. 7.

Subramanian, U. (1999) South Asian Transport: Issues and Options. Paper presented at the World Bank/ ESCAP Regional Technical Workshop on Transport and Transit Facilitation, Bangkok, April.

Transport Canada (1998) *Transportation in Canada 1997: Annual Report.* Ottawa: Minister of Public Works and Government Services.

US Department of Transportation (1997) *Comprehensive Truck Size and Weight Study.* Vol. II, *Issues and Background.* Washington, DC: US Department of Transportation.

US General Accounting Office (1990) Report on Fares and Reduced Com-petition at Concentrated Airports. GAO/RCED–90–102. Washington DC: US GAO.

US General Accounting Office (US GAO) (1996) *Commercial Trucking: Safety and Infrastructure Issues under the North American Free Trade Agreement.* GAO/ RCED–96–61. Washington DC: US GAO.

US General Accounting Office (1997a) *Commercial Trucking: Safety Concerns About Mexican Trucks Remain Even as Inspection Activity Increases.* GAO/RCED–97–68. Washington, DC: US GAO.

US General Accounting Office (1997b) *Commercial Passenger Vehicles: Safety Inspection of Commercial Buses and Vans Entering the United States from Mexico.* GAO/RCED–97–194. Washington, DC: US GAO.

Von Klaudy, S. (1999a) Southern Africa Transport Corridor. World Bank/ ESCAP Regional Technical Workshop on Transport and Trade Facilitation, April 1999.

Von Klaudy, S. (1999b) *Topical Note: Maputo Corridor.* Washington DC: World Bank.

Winston, C. (1985) Conceptual developments in the economics of trans-portation: an interpretive survey. *Journal of Economic Literature,* **23**. p. 83

Winston, C., Corsi, T. and Grimm, C. (1990) *The Economic Effects of Surface Freight Deregulation.* Washington, DC: Brookings Institution.

World Bank (1995) Improving African Transport Corridors. Operations Evaluation Department, Precis Number 84. World Bank, Washington, DC.

World Bank (2000) *Entering the Twenty-First Century.* World Development Report 1999–2000. New York: Oxford University Press.

Yeats, A. (1997) Does Mercosur's Trade Performance Raise Concerns About the Effects of Regional Trade Arrangements? Policy Research Working Paper 1729, World Bank, Washington, DC.

Zinn, W. (1999) Supply Chain Efficiency in a Trade Bloc Environment: Three Cases in Mercosur. Manuscript, University of Miami.

Chapter 12

Impact of border regime institutions on transport network development in Central and Eastern Europe

Tomasz Komornicki

The influence exerted by the various kinds of institution on the development and use of transport infrastructure appears at all the levels of spatial organization, from the smallest self-governmental units up to the supra-national structures. A particular concentration of this impact takes place at the interfaces of the political organisms constituted by the state borders. This is associated both with the filtering function of borders (national borders have a negative impact on the intensity of spatial interaction; see Chapter 1) and with the necessity of international co-operation in realization of the transport-related projects. In Europe more than fifty overland border segments (excluding the internal boundaries within the Schengen Area) characterized by different border inspection regimes still exist. That is why the existence of boundaries and of the institutions connected with boundaries still influences the mobility of persons and goods, and the development of the European transport infrastructure. In North America there are only two land borders and two border regimes, thus the impact is much more limited there. In addition, the European borders are frequently the focus of conflicts between transport and the natural environment. In Poland, for example, there are twenty-three national parks, nine of which are directly adjacent to the state borders, and a further six are close to the borders. The environment is threatened by the border congestion.

The purpose of this chapter is to show the transformations associated with the changes in border functions in Central Europe and the influence exerted by border institutions on the development of transport. The object of analysis is to investigate the direct influence of border institutions' actions on the development of international transport links, where the interactions between neighbouring regions are weak (Rietveld, 2001). However, a strong reverse feedback exists between the development of international transport links and the intensity of social and economic interactions.

The analysis was carried out primarily in Poland prior to the country's membership of the EU, but the majority of the problems are typical of the countries that have just joined the European Union (EU). The common issue for all of these countries (except for the Czech Republic) is the presence of the eastern boundary of the EU and the future establishment of the eastern boundary of the Schengen area.

Functions of the borders

Borders serve three fundamental and broadly conceived functions (beside their basic role as the boundaries of state sovereignty): military (providing a barrier to military aggression from abroad); economic (constituting a barrier to the free flow of goods); and social (as a barrier to the free movement of people). As recently as in the nineteenth century it was still the first of these functions that predominated. The significance of all three functions began to change rapidly. The military functions gradually became concentrated along the borders between different alliances. After the Second World War, this concentration took on the extreme form of the 'Iron Curtain', which at the same time implied a significant enhancement of the economic and social functions of the borders along which it ran. In Western Europe, economic integration resulted in the lifting of customs barriers and a reduction in controls over goods and vehicles crossing them. The progressive strengthening of the social functions of political boundaries was a result of two basic factors. In totalitarian countries, there was a fear that citizens would make contact with the outside world, and that they would emigrate *en masse* to it. Equally, the democratic countries were afraid of mass immigration from poorer states.

It is possible to identify several basic phases to the functional changes along Europe's state borders (Doliwa-Klepacki, 1996; Komornicki, 1999):

- Phase I. Maintenance of the significance of the military function of borders, with simultaneous development of the economic and social functions – a situation that currently applies once more in the area of the former Yugoslavia.

- Phase II. The decline of the military function with the maintenance of well-developed economic functions (customs) and social functions (restrictions on exits via passports and on entries via visas) – a situation which now hardly occurs along any European border.

- Phase III. With this phase, the economic and social functions of borders are steadily limited. There is a liberalization of foreign trade and passport policy, with simultaneous retention of visa-mediated movements of people, and full border controls over individuals and goods (for example, to this day at the Norwegian–Russian border). The transition to phase III may be associated with the onset of economic integration.

- Phase IV. The trade in goods undergoes further liberalization (usually as a consequence of economic integration). Non-visa travel is introduced, though border controls over people and goods are retained (as along the Polish–German border until May 2004).

- Phase V. There is a full liberalization of the trade in goods (lifting of the majority of customs duties and fees at borders). Visa-free travel gives way to full freedom of movement, the taking-up of work and changes in place of residence. Border controls over people and goods are simplified and minimised (as at present along the French–Swiss border).

- Phase VI. The elimination of all border controls, thereby permitting the crossing of borders at any point (as in the case of the Schengen group of countries or between Belgium–France from 1991).

In the last 40 years, there has been a gradual change in the spatial extent of areas with borders at the different stages of the above functional changes. An ever greater part of Europe has come to be embraced by ever more advanced phases, with an associated increase in the permeability of borders.

The degree of openness (and thus the permeability and the functions) of borders in Central and Eastern Europe has changed fundamentally in the last 15 years, as has the intensity of the traffic crossing them. This has been a result of: (1) the fall of the communist system, as the main and most fundamental factor; (2) changes in the economic and visa policies towards Central European countries in Western Europe; (3) a different level of economic development and different rates to the systemic transformations in the different countries of the region; and (4) the expansion of the EU15 to the EU25.

The criterion of the role played by the border institutions can be used to produce a typology of the state borders in Europe:

1   The internal boundaries within the Schengen area (like the French–German border), with an actual absence of border inspections.

2   The few guarded internal borders of the European Union (between the Schengen area and the countries which do not belong to it, like the United Kingdom), and the boundaries between, on the one hand, the Union, and Switzerland and Norway on the other.

3   The boundaries between the European Union and those countries joining the EU in 2004, like the Polish–German border.

4   The boundaries between the new member countries themselves, as, in particular, the Polish–Czech border.

In all of these, there is a tendency towards liberalization.

5   The boundaries between the new member countries and the third countries (the future borders of the European Union, for example the Polish–Ukrainian border).

6   The few direct boundaries between the European Union (EU15) and the third countries, (the Finnish–Russian border).

7   The boundaries between the third countries (the Ukrainian–Russian border).

In these last three cases, there is still some regulation and limited liberalization.

Since May 2004, with the accession of the 10 new states to the EU, there will be a significant increase of the number and total length of the border segments between the EU and the third countries. The outer boundary of the EU25 is now with Russia, Belarus, Ukraine, Romania (until this country ultimately joins the EU), Serbia and Croatia will cross the entire Continent, from the Baltic Sea to the Adriatic. There will be a polarization of the border regimes in Europe, between the practically non-existent borders within the EU, and the highly formalized borders at the outside limits of the EU.

Border as the institutional space barrier

Boundaries in Central and Eastern Europe function in definite geographic, historical-political, and economic environments. These kinds of environments find their reflection in the existence of various sorts of barriers (Figure 12.1), which together exist as the formalized spatial barrier (Boggs, 1940). In the literature, four kinds of broadly understood barriers in the trade sector are differentiated: institutional, technical, social, and network barriers (Giaoutzi and Nijkamp, 1994). In reference to the transport sector the cost, language, physical and cultural barriers are also distinguished (Salomon and Tsairi, 1994; Giaoutzi and Stratigea, 1995). In many cases the existence of a barrier of one kind implies the emergence of barriers of other types. The analysis of mutual interactions between various kinds of barriers confirms the particular significance of the infrastructural barrier (as the one which focuses other constraints to border permeability) and the institutional barrier.

The institutional barriers in freight traffic result from the existence of: (1) export and import custom tariffs; (2) various kinds of fees similar to custom tariffs (border taxes, excise taxes, compensation fees); (3) prohibitions on import or export of certain goods; (4) concession or licensing systems for import of some goods; (5) the phyto-sanitary and veterinary limitations; (6) transit guarantee procedures; (7) the licensing systems in carrying out the international cargo transport activities; (8) road traffic regulations applying to truck transport. These limitations result in particular border procedures expressed through the: (1) preparation of appropriate documents, starting with the certificates of origin and ending with SAD (single administrative

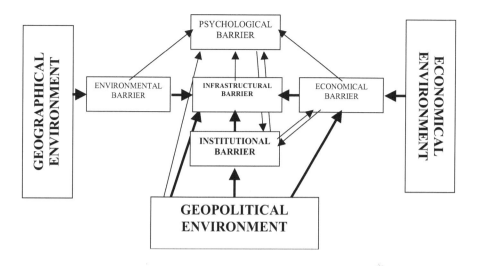

Relations:

 strong

→ others

Figure 12.1 Boundaries as spatial barriers

document) forms; (2) being subject to customs clearance (perhaps inside the country); (3) being subject to border control; and (4) being subject to transit procedures.

Before 2004 Polish custom tariffs listed more than 14,000 items. Along with the abandonment of the centrally planned economy, tariff policy also underwent a change. Later it concentrated on import limitations, and its main tasks were constituted by the protection of its own market and securing budgetary revenues. The tariffs themselves and the existence of a (custom-free) import quota resulted, partly from the international agreements signed by Polish authorities. Included here are (1) the association agreement with the European Union of December 1991; (2) the CEFTA (Central European Free Trade Area) agreement; (3) the bilateral free trade agreements (e.g. between Poland and Lithuania).

The barriers to the movement of persons result from: (1) limitations to the citizens' right to leave their own territory (passports, border passes etc.); (2) limitations to the right of entering the territory of a given country (visas, vouchers, financial guarantees, etc.); (3) functioning of the previously mentioned limitations to cargo traffic (customs and possibly also sanitary controls of persons); (4) limitations to the forms of traffic admitted on particular border crossings; (5) principles of road traffic of passenger cars and buses; and (6) insurance regulations. These limitations entail: (1) passport control of persons; (2) customs clearance of persons; (3) vehicle control; (4) in some cases also sanitary or health control of persons.

The 1990s brought a breakthrough in the visa policies with respect to the citizens of Poland and other Central European countries. Agreements abolishing the need to have visas were signed with almost all countries of Europe (except Bosnia-Herzegovina, Albania, Serbia and Turkey; Figure 12.2), and with some countries from the former Soviet Union (Lithuania, Latvia, Estonia, Moldova and Ukraine), as well as some non-European countries. In the case of the remaining countries of the former USSR, the old agreement concluded between the Polish People's Republic and the Soviet Union in 1979 is still valid. This agreement guarantees visa-free entry for the participants of group excursions, for the bearers of certified personal invitations, accommodation vouchers for the stay, or appropriate stamps in the passport. The possibility of crossing the border on the basis of vouchers gave the opportunity for virtually unlimited traffic between Poland and its eastern neighbours. The use of forged vouchers (for 2–10 US$) was common, with the trade often being conducted at the border crossing. Poland has now introduced normal visa traffic with these countries (2003).

In Central Europe, a significant barrier is the carriers' tariff policies in public transport. This is connected to the continuing strong position of national carriers, which are interested in maintaining their monopoly of power (Lakshmanan and Anderson, this volume). This phenomenon takes place not only in the aviation sector (where international regulatory agreements often limit the supply of international services; Rietveld, 2001), but also in rail transport. The cost of a railway ticket from Warsaw to Berlin, for example, is approximately 10 Euros higher than the sum of the prices of tickets from both

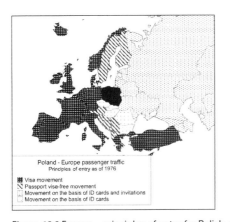
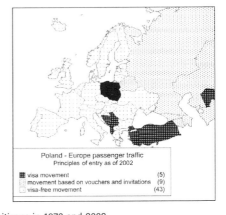

Figure 12.2 Europe – principles of entry for Polish citizens in 1976 and 2002

of the capitals to the border. Polish State Railways has not been able to lead an active tariff policy despite a systematic loss of the international transport market.

In the 1990s, an important institutional factor was the changing regulations in vehicle insurance. Over time, an increasing number of Polish insurance companies issued free of charge (together with their insurance policies) 'green cards' guaranteeing insurance against civil liabilities in most of the European countries. At the same time, countries of the former USSR neighbouring with Poland (including Lithuania) do not belong to the 'green card' system. This situation forces drivers to buy an additional insurance policy costing approximately 20 Euros (sometimes just for a trip lasting no more than a few hours). In addition, most Polish insurance companies introduced clauses in the Auto Casco policies exempting insurance companies from liabilities in the case of theft of vehicles on the territory of the former USSR. Formal institutions superimpose themselves on the interaction of broadly understood informal institutions (including norms of behaviour, personal experiences of officers, their satisfaction in doing their job, as well as stereotypes in reference to some groups of foreigners). The increased border traffic together with a limited state budget lead to a shortage of staff in some border regime institutions, even though this is a key employer in the near border regions. This impacts negatively on the possibility of improving the organization of work.

Two somewhat conflicting tendencies were present in the 1990s. The 'strong' barriers limiting the free flow of people, vehicles and goods (especially in the direction to and from Western Europe) were liberalized, as foreign trade and a common transport policy (as well as in passport and visas) were encouraged. However, other institutional barriers emerged, including large state carriers and insurance companies, as well as informal institutions. Although some barriers have disappeared, national (or even company) self-interest has created new barriers (Nijkamp, 1995).

Border transport infrastructure

Two basic factors affect the degree of infrastructure-related penetrability of borders (Komornicki, 1995): (1) the existence of infrastructure of purely transport character (roads and railroads crossing the border, seaports and airports); and (2) the degree of use of this infrastructure reflected through the functioning of the generally accessible road border crossings, as well as regular railroad, ferry and air connections. The first element derives from the course of the border as set against the natural conditions, and from the historical past (the time a given border has existed). The second element is connected with the political and economic constraints prevailing before 1989, the stipulations of the international agreements, as well as the speed of realization of the current investment projects.

The availability of the direct transport infrastructure (element 1) is measured by the length of the border (in km) per one hard surface road (table 12.1) and per one railroad line crossing the border. In Poland as a whole, one hard surface road crosses the state border every 23 km on the average. The densest network of transboundary roads occurs along the boundary with the Kaliningrad district of the Russian Federation. There is one hard surface road per 12 km on this particular border. The boundary with the Kaliningrad district (established in 1945) cuts through the economic organism of Eastern Prussia, which existed for several centuries. The situation along the border with the Czech Republic is also good (one road per 14 km of the boundary), and is not so bad along the border with Germany (24 km). The poorest border accessibility by road is observed along the border with Slovakia (one road per 40 km of the boundary line), which is primarily due to the fact that the border goes along the Carpathian mountains, and along the border with Ukraine (one road per 47 km).

The degree of use of the infrastructure described above is measured by the percentages of roads on which there exist any (or only generally accessible) border crossings, and by the percentages of railways on which such border crossings are located, or railways on which passenger trains routinely run. The degree of use of this infrastructure increased considerably (1989–2002). For all the land boundaries of Poland, the percentage of transboundary hard surface roads passing through the generally accessible border crossings increased from 30% to 48% (1993–1997). The highest level of use of the transboundary road network is observed on the Polish–German border. Border crossings are found there on 90% of the existing relevant hard surface roads (yet only 68% in 1993). The degree of use of the road infrastructure is the lowest along the border with the Kalinigrad district (only 24% for all border crossings and 18% for the generally accessible ones). The degree of infrastructure use is somewhat higher for the rail network (the average for all the boundaries is 75%). The vast majority of the rail network is used for freight transport. Passenger trains run across the border over exactly half of the transboundary lines (22 out of 44).

Cross-border traffic of people, goods and vehicles

The increase in the level of border passenger traffic in the 1990s was without precedence in the history of Poland (Figure 12.3). While there were a total of 59 million individual crossings of all the borders (1989), the figure was 84 million (1990), and 157million in 1992 (a 2.5 times increase in three years). In subsequent years, the rate of increase in the traffic slowed, but was still more than 10% each year. By 1999, the number of individual crossings

Table 12.1 Border related infrastructure and border traffic in Poland

Category	1990	2001	Increase 1990=100
Number of hard surface roads crossing the border	131	134	102
Number of rail track crossing the border	44	44	100
Number of generally accessible road border crossing	32	69	216
Number of rail border crossing with passenger traffic	15	23	153
Passenger car border traffic in thousand	11,740	55,299	471
HGV border traffic in thousand	1,077	5,441	505

of the border in both directions exceeded 285 million, of which Poles were involved in 33% of that traffic. By 2001 the traffic declined, mainly because of the Russian crisis, price equalization between Poland and Germany, and less intensity of informal trade on the Eastern and Western border. In 2003 Polish borders were crossed by 178.7 million people.

There was also a major change in the modal structure of cross-border traffic in Poland. In 1980, only just over half of all crossings took place by road (including on foot). One-fifth of those crossing at that time made use of railways and just over 4% went by air. At the same time, as much as 18% of all crossings were without passports (minor border traffic, army traffic etc.). From the late 1980s onwards, there was a steady rise in the role of road traffic at the expense of rail and air. By 1996, the share taken by road traffic had exceeded 94%, while those taken by air and rail were only 1.1% and 3.1% respectively (the only part of the border along which rail crossings remained

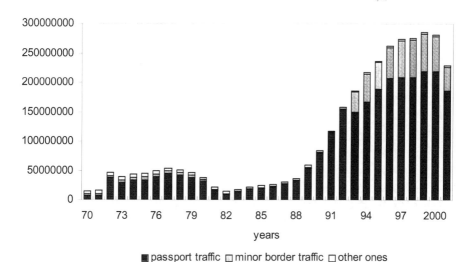

Figure 12.3 Passenger traffic at Poland's borders in the years 1970–2001

of greater significance was that between Poland and Belarus). At the end of the 1990s, the role of sea and air crossings was higher again (mainly because of Polish citizens' ferry and charter air holiday departures). However, the significance of rail passenger border traffic was still decreasing (in 1999 it accounted for only 2.4% of total border traffic).

The decline of international railway transport was primarily due to: (1) a substantial increase in the price; (2) major competition from the developing international coach transport; (3) rapid growth of car ownership both in Poland and in the countries of the former Soviet Union; and (4) polarization of the rich and poor travelling abroad on public transport (the 'rich' choosing air transport, while the 'poor' opted for the cheap and uncomfortable bus trip).

In 1990–1991, most traffic growth was along the German and eastern borders. In 1993–1994, the German border was again predominant (Komornicki, 1999), followed by those with the Czech Republic and Russia. In 1995–1996 the biggest increase took place along the Czech, Slovak, Ukrainian, and Russian borders. The greatest streams of cross-border passenger traffic are focused on the borders with Germany and the Czech Republic (with the two together accounting for 80% of the traffic in terms of numbers of people and 85% in terms of numbers of cars). In 1997–2000, the share of passenger trans-border traffic increased with all Eastern neighbours (except Lithuania).

A separate issue is the increase in the level of border traffic involving heavy goods vehicles (HGV). While 295,000 HGVs crossed all of Poland's borders taken together in 1980, the figure for 1990 was 1.1 million, and that for 2003 was 6,2 million. This growth in HGV traffic has taken place virtually uninterruptedly along all the borders. The traffic through the Polish–German border dominates (more than 50%). This share decreased up to 1997 by almost 15% compared with 1993, mainly to the advantage of Polish–Belarusian, Polish–Lithuanian and Polish–Russian borders (Figure 12.4). This was evidence for the increasing significance of the transit transport between Western Europe and Russia and the Baltic States. At the end of 1990s, the HGV border traffic growth was still continuing on the western and southern border, on the sea border and on the border with Lithuania, but had halted on the border with Russia and Ukraine. The traffic with Belarus significantly decreased in this period. The Polish–Belarussian main custom post at Kukuryki (on the Berlin–Moscow transport corridor) was no longer the Eastern border crossing most overcrowded by HGV traffic. This position was taken by the Polish–Lithuania custom post at Budzisko on the 'Via Baltica' transport corridor (595,000 HGVs in 2003). The future dimension of Eastern border traffic is not clear. The main factors affecting the situation are: (1) the present and future trade agreements between EU and Russia; (2) economic

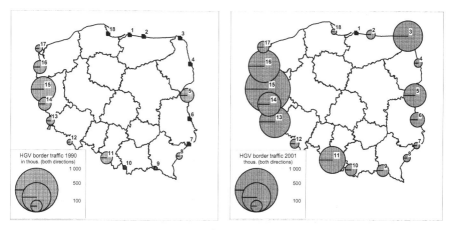

Note: Corridors: 1. Gdansk–Kaliningrad, 2. Warsaw–Kaliningrad, 3. Warsaw–Tallinn, 4. Warsaw–Hrodna, 5. Warsaw–Moscow, 6. Warsaw–Kiev, 7. Warsaw–Lviv, 8. Kraków–Kiev, 9. Rzeszów–Miskolc, 10. Kraków–Budapest, 11. Warsaw–Vienna, 12. Wroclaw–Praha, 13. Wroclaw–Frankfurt, 14. Wroclaw–Berlin, 15. Warsaw–Berlin, 16. Szczecin–Berlin, 17. Szczecin/Swinoujscie–seaports, 18. Gdansk/Gdynia–seaports.

Figure 12.4 Heavy goods vehicles border traffic in Poland by main transport corridors (1990 and 2001)

development of Lithuania, Latvia and Estonia; (3) possible competition from Baltic ferries.

The impact of border regime institutions

The influence of the border regime on the development of transport can be considered from three perspectives:

- the development of the cross-border transport infrastructure;
- the directions and the modal structure of the international traffic of persons and goods;
- border congestion.

During the 1990s, there was a lack of new cross border transport infrastructure being built. The only exceptions were the Vienna–Budapest motorway and the modernization of the railway line Warsaw–Berlin. This situation largely reflects the funding situation. Border crossing projects have often been implemented with the help of the pre-accession funds of the European Union (PHARE). Some have also obtained support from the respective border-adjacent self-governmental units. However, the major infrastructural undertakings also required substantial input from the central budget and/or private capital.

Considerable significance should also be assigned to the frequent divergence of the investment plans in neighbouring countries, and the political will. An example of this is provided by the reconstruction of the old German motorway from Gdańsk to Kaliningrad. It was carried out on the Russian side in the mid-1990s, while on the Polish side it is still under consideration, because the majority of politicians treat this undertaking as competition for the promoted Via Baltica route (Warsaw–Tallinn). Another good illustration is Polish–Slovak truck traffic, which still travels within the confines of the Tatra Mountains National Park. The Slovak side has refused to move it to the neighbouring border crossing, because trucks would then pass close to the governmental recreational centre.

The gradual differentiation of the border regimes in Central Europe caused the spatial shift of the cross-border flows of goods and people. And thus, for instance, the strengthening economic ties between the Baltic States and the European Union brought a rapid increase of the transit traffic through Poland. Despite the enormous difference in the economic potentials between the Baltic States and Russia (to the disadvantage of the former), the cross-border commodity traffic is today greater along the route Tallinn–Warsaw–Berlin than over the axis Moscow–Warsaw–Berlin. A good example of a bilateral agreement is provided by the transport connections between Warsaw and Vilnius. The shortest and the best equipped route between these two cities, both in terms of railways and of road transport, passes through the town of Grodna and the territory of Belarus. This route was used by Polish–Lithuanian traffic over several centuries, until the beginning of the 1990s. Today it has entirely lost its significance, due exclusively the institutional factors. All the railway and coach lines from Poland to Lithuania go through the direct border crossings. In spite of the longer distance (by more than 100 km), the travel time is shorter in view of the much less complicated and single border procedure.

One of the factors influencing the modal structure of the cross-border traffic is the traffic form allowed at the individual border crossings. Thus, at almost all border crossings between Poland and the countries of the former Soviet Union, crossing on foot is forbidden. This resulted in the establishment of a large number of short-distance international public (railway and coach) transport lines (Komornicki, 1996). Additionally, the Polish Customs Office has forced the transport operators to provide two buses or trains at border stations (in order to prevent alcohol being smuggled across the border). The regular train from the Polish town of Terespol to the Belarusian Brest has nowadays to cover only the bridge on the river Bug and a distance of 2 km. The journey takes five minutes, while the customs procedure takes place at the station and often requires waiting for several hours.

The most pronounced sign of spatial barriers is constituted by the queues at the border crossings. They result from two types of barrier: the institutional barrier plays the dominant role. With the help of officers from the Headquarters of the Border Guards information was gathered in 1992 on the queues of vehicles at the Polish borders (Komornicki, 1994). The annual average of the waiting time exceeded 1 hour (for at least one category of vehicles) on 14 border crossings. The longest waiting time for trucks entering Poland was noted on 18 December in Kuźnica Białostocka (160 hours). The worst situation that occurred on the western border took place in Świecko on 4 November (60 hours of waiting time for leaving the country). The waiting times of 26 hours for entry occurred on the southern border in Cieszyn and Kudowa.

The infrastructure barrier results from lack of investment. Projects implemented in the years 1992–1997 brought very limited improvement in terms of the queues at the borders, as increases in supply were countered by further increase in demand. Investment was not accompanied by improvement in the functioning of border services (especially of those in the CIS countries). The situation with respect to the queues of trucks at the German border is virtually unchanged in spite of the apparently largest concentration of various kinds of projects on both sides of this border, while waiting times for freight traffic increased quite markedly at the southern border.

Queues of lorries occurred at the borders within the European Union as well. According to the study carried out in 1988 in the framework of the programme 'Cost of NonEurope' (encompassing Belgium, France, The Netherlands, the then West Germany, United Kingdom and Italy) the average delay of transport related to existence of internal boundaries ranged between 1.44 hours in case of trips from Belgium to The Netherlands and 7.6 hours in the case of transport from France to Italy (CEC, 1988). In the framework of the same study, it was estimated that the total cost of delays caused by clearance (in traffic between the six countries mentioned) amounted to 780 million ECU.

The Polish Central Customs Office estimated that the average cost of waiting in the border queue in 1999 was 50 DM (Deutsche Marks) (Kitowski, 2000). This estimate, however, included only the cost of the car and the work time of the driver. No costs associated with the delays in supplies and other external factors were taken into account. In the same year the average waiting time in Świecko on the Polish–German border (the Warsaw–Berlin corridor) was 4.7 hours for those leaving Poland and 5.2 hours for the ones entering it. Considering that the border was crossed in these two directions by 336,000 and 378,000 trucks a year respectively, the total annual cost of border congestion at just this one border crossing can be estimated at roughly 180 million DM.

In addition, border congestion brings about local environmental hazards, resulting, in particular, from the increased emissions of exhaust gases (in winter, trucks often do not have their engines turned off), the accumulation of waste along the roads near the border, and the excessive noise in the border localities. There are also social costs associated with the phenomenon including decreased road safety, the spread of prostitution in the regions of the biggest border crossings, and the increase of petty and organized crime (robberies of the waiting trucks).

Conclusions

In the period before 1989, the limitations to the cross-border flow of people and goods in Central Europe were first of all the effect of institutional factors. Most of these limitations were rapidly removed (1989–1991). In conditions of a quick increase of the traffic of persons, vehicles, and goods, infrastructure became the primary barrier existing at the borders. After a few years, however, new border crossings and customs facilities were built, satisfying in general terms the demand that had arisen. Consequently, the significance of the institutional factors increased again. The limitations resulting from the regulations in force in the neighbouring countries have been further amplified by the influence of the European institutions.

Integration with the EU means that new significance has to be attached to the eastern border of the EU. This has a direct influence on the development of transport and on the general economic situation of the future 'European' border regions. Their peripheral position may even be aggravated as a result of further integration inside the enlarged Union (Nijkamp 1995).

The ways towards a more balanced development of the cross-border transport in Central Europe include, first of all:

♦   the development of the cross-border inter-modal transport (supported or even enforced by the institutional factors);
♦   the ending of border congestion by simplification of the formalities and/ or their physical removal away from the border;
♦   construction of roads bypassing the towns located close to the border;
♦   reduction of international railway tariffs.

The influence exerted by the institutions on the sustainable development of the cross-border transport in Central Europe includes issues relating to the delay in the development of transport infrastructure, the cost of the existence of political boundaries borne by the enterprises, transport operators, and consumers, as well as the external ones, including those affecting the natural environment, the scenarios for the development of transport infrastructure relating to the new eastern boundary of the EU, liberalization within Europe, and the opportunities for the development of intermodal transport under the conditions of the post-socialist economies and the reduction in all forms of barriers.

Bibliography

Belgium-France-Germany-Luxembourg-Netherlands (1991) Schengen Agreement on the Gradual Abolition of Checks at Their Common Borders and the Convention Applying the Agreement. International Legal Materials, No. 143, 146, 147, Brussels

Boggs, S.W. (1940) *International Boundaries: A Study of Boundary Functions and Problems.* New York: Columbia University Press.

Commission of the European Communities (1988) *The 'Cost of Non-Europe': Border-related Controls and Administrative Formalities. An Illustration in the Road Haulage Sector,* Vol. 4. Brussels-Luxembourg: Ernst and Whinney.

Doliwa-Klepacki, Z.M. (1996) *Europejska integracja gospodarcza (European economic integration).* Temida 2, Bialystok, (in Polish).

Giaoutzi, M. and Nijkamp, P. (1994) Barriers and missing networks in European infrastructure inland waterways and coastal transport, in Nijkamp, P. (ed.) *New Borders and Old Barriers in Spatial Development.* Aldershot: Avebury.

Giaoutzi, M. and Stratigea, A. (1995) Barriers in network performance in border areas, in Coccossis, H. and Nijkamp, P. (eds.) *Overcoming Isolation.* Berlin: Springer-Verlag.

Kitowski, J. (2000) Czas oczekiwania na odprawę pojazdów samochodowych na drogowych przejsciach granicznych w drugiej połowie 1999 roku (Waiting time for clearence of car vehicles at border road crossings in the second half of 1999), in Kitowski, J. and Lijewski, T. (eds.) *Prace Komisji Geografii Komunikacji,* No VI, Warszawa-Rzeszów, pp. 27–52 (in Polish).

Komornicki, T. (1994) Przepustowość polskich drogowych przejść granicznych na podstawie analizy czasów oczekiwania na odprawę w 1992 roku (Permeability of Polish border crossings based on custom clearance waiting time in 1992), in Eberhardt, P. and K. Miros, K. (eds.) *Podstawy rozwoju zachodnich i wschodnich obszarów przygranicznych Polski,* Bulletin no. 5, IGiPZ PAN, Warszawa, pp. 85–102, (in Polish).

Komornicki, T. (1995) Transgraniczna infrastruktura transportowa Polski (Trans-border transport infrastructure of Poland). Przegląd Geograficzny, T.LXVII, z.1-2, Warszawa, pp. 45–53, (in Polish).

Komornicki, T. (1996) Bus connections between Poland and other European countries. *Transport Reviews,* **16**, pp. 99–108.

Komornicki, T. (1999) Granice Polski. Analiza zmian przenikalności w latach 1990–1996 (Polish borders. Analysis of permeability 1990–1996). *Geopolitical Studies,* vol. 5, IGiPZ PAN, Warszawa, (in Polish).

Lakshmanan, T.R. and Anderson, W.P. (2002) Evolution of Transport Institutions that Facilitate International Trade. Paper presented at STELLA Focus Group 5 meeting, Brussels.

Nijkamp, P. (1995) Borders and barriers in the new Europe: impediments and potentials of new network configurations, in Coccossis, H. and Nijkamp, P. (eds.) *Overcoming Isolation.* Berlin: Springer-Verlag.

Rietveld, P. (2001) Obstacles to openness of border regions in Europe, in van Geenhuizen, M. and Ratti, R. (eds.) *Gaining Advantage from Open Borders. An active space approach to regional development.* Aldershot: Ashgate Publishing, pp. 79–96.

Rietveld, P. and Stough, R.R. (2002) Institutions, Regulations and Sustainable Tansport; A Cross National Perspective. Paper presented at the STELLA kick-off meeting, Amsterdam.

Salomon, T. and Tsairi, B. (1994) Barriers and communication technologies in a global society, in Nijkmap, P. (ed.) *New Borders and Old Barriers in Spatial Development.* Aldershot: Avebury.

Chapter 13

A conceptual framework for analyzing policy-maker's and industry roles and perspectives in the context of sustainable goods transportation

Lars Sjöstedt

Some 10 years ago, the head of the logistics department of one of the largest multinational companies in Europe was scheduled to deliver the final presentation at a transport research conference. Much to the surprise of his audience, he deviated from the title in the programme and instead delivered a very critical speech directed at the profession of logistics, which he accused of naivety in handling sustainability issues. The main thrust of his message was captured in the following sentence: 'We must stop cross trading bottled drinking water across the oceans!'.

This simple sentence illustrates several things. To achieve sustainability in the transport of goods, it is not sufficient to look at the way a shipment is transported, which already can be expanded into a wide range of issues. We must also ask between which origins and destinations it makes sense to transport a product from a sustainability point of view and, at the end, whether a product should be transported at all, or if a better way of designing the supply chain should be looked for.

But the context in which the sentence was phrased also illustrates the frustration a logistics manager may feel. She or he is well placed to see the potential for significant improvements of sustainability, but because of the large number of stakeholders involved, both within and outside her or his own company, she or he seldom has the executive power to realize more than a fraction of this potential.

The wide understanding of sustainable transport as reflected in the sentence above is compatible with the definition given by Rietveld and Stough in this book: 'Sustainable transport is the maintenance of mobility and accessibility at some socially predetermined level and perhaps subject to selected social and environmental constraints, for example, maintaining predetermined levels of environmental residuals'. The central question that will be addressed in this chapter is to what extent we can expect the main stakeholders in logistics and goods transportation, including public policy-makers to provide the informal and formal institutions that promote sustainable transport in spite of the differences that exist, both in terms of professional perspectives and scientific methodology in the disciplines involved. A first step towards understanding the difficulties involved is briefly to describe these differences. This is attempted in the second section (see page below).

Establishing the necessary institutions would be facilitated, if some kind of joint conceptual framework could be identified. Therefore, a specific objective of this chapter is to present a very general conceptual model that may serve this purpose. A brief history of the development of this model is given in the third section (see page 203). A specific use of the model is to identify common elements and differences in logistics and transportation and demonstrate the complementarities of these concepts; this is done in the fourth section (see page 207).

The latter part of last century is often perceived as a period when economic development was largely driven by rapid changes in transport technology as such, and in the production systems that deliver the systems and conveyances used for transport. Presently this rapid change has declined and instead information and communications technologies (ICT) have taken the major roles as agents of change. ICT have considerable impact on transport services in two ways: they change the character of the demand for transport; and they change the ways transport services are composed, marketed, and produced rather than the basic technologies of the different conveyances. These services increasingly constitute logistics packages, where the pure transport is just one component. Another consequence of modern ICT is that they greatly reduce costs and increase speed of transactions while almost eliminating the frictions previously induced by the spatial factor. Some of these development trends are discussed in the fifth section (see page 209).

One of the impacts of the material and work flow orientation in industry is radical changes in the way business is performed, which in turn have strong impacts on logistics and transportation. This is briefly treated in the sixth (see page 215).

While all these changes certainly make the transport sustainability issue even more complex, they may simultaneously show ways of dealing with such issues. In the concluding section some approaches are discussed that may be needed if climate changes provoke far-reaching regulations on transport sustainability.

Background

The different origins of transportation and logistics

Today the word logistics is painted as a trademark on an increasing number of trucks on our highways. It gives the impression that transportation and logistics are almost non-distinguishable. But this is a false picture. It takes a

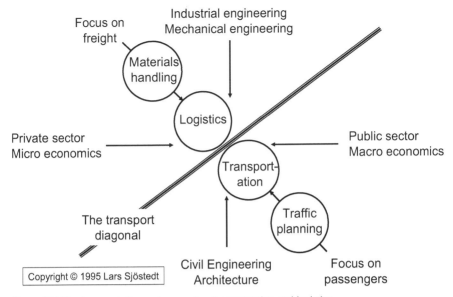

Figure 13.1 The transport diagonal separating transportation and logistics

long time to shape professions and disciplines and the roots of transportation and logistics are very different. This is illustrated in Figure 13.1.

In post World War II development, scientific efforts in transportation and logistics largely originated in operations analysis as researchers and planners migrated from the military to the civilian sector. But the foci were very different; transportation researchers primarily took an interest in providing infrastructure for the quickly expanding traffic on highway, with emphasis on traffic theory and traffic forecasting methodologies, while logistics researchers concentrated on the administrative routines and technology required to improve the flow of materials through a production facility from its warehouse for purchased materials through its manufacturing operations to its stock-rooms for finished goods. Here emphasis was on materials handling and production economics; external goods transportation was still something that was called upon *ad hoc* when needed.

These early developments can still be traced in the structure of our universities. Most academically trained people have their background in at most one of the two sides of the transport diagonal in Figure 13.1. Courses taught in civil engineering and architecture at technical universities mostly dwell on transport with emphasis on passenger transport and the public sector of our society, while courses in mechanical and industrial engineering give priority to logistics and emphasize goods transportation and the private sector of our society. This reflects that logistics and transportation grew out of materials handling and traffic planning, respectively, and thus as academic subjects used to be vastly separated.

In business schools the transport diagonal is less visible, although it could be argued that passenger transportation and the public sector tends to be closer to a macroeconomic perspective, while logistics and the private sector are closer to a microeconomic perspective.

The transport diagonal is now slowly disappearing as supply chain managers and traffic planners realize that they share the ultimate goal of facilitating accessibility and mobility without impairing sustainability. This is the end result of a long process over several decades of successive broadening of their interests, respectively. Already in the 1970s traffic planners moved from an interest to provide infrastructure capacity, i.e. cater for traffic, to an interest in understanding the needs and providing the means to move from specific origins to specific destinations, i.e. cater for transport. At the time organizations and research bodies in many countries switched from using the word traffic in their names to the word transport or transportation. The next step is reflected by the more recent launching of concepts such as mobility management, which confirms the reorientation of traffic planning from operational issues towards administrative and strategic issues. At the same time interest in goods transportation, which used to be the poor relation in transportation research, has increased substantially.

Since this broadening of interests is closely related to progress in the use of ICT, the equivalent process in logistics will be treated below (see page 209).

Some lessons from the series of OECD studies on global logistics

The main role of traffic planners is to advise public policy-makers and to carry out the preparatory work needed to suggest new institutions and regulations in the field of transportation both at the national and community levels. As a supranational organization, the OECD early identified the need to increase knowledge in the public sector of their member countries about logistics development, especially as a consequence and facilitator of global trade. As a result two consecutive projects were initiated and finished in the 1990s as part of the OECD Road Transport Research Program (OECD, 1992 and OECD, 1996). A dominant finding was that logistics practices already then were well developed by most large multinational companies and applied in a rather similar fashion in many countries. Thus, no significant barriers seem to prevent the introduction of advanced logistics by technology transfer to an environment with no or little experience in the field. Another observation is that while logistics practices seem to be rather similar among large companies in a specific industrial sector, they differ a lot among different industrial sectors. The main explanation is the large differences from a logistics point of view in handling, at one end of the spectrum homogeneous raw materials with a value density that counts in dollars per ton, and at the other end of the spectrum high-tech specialized customer made components with a value density measured in dollars per microgram. This may also explain why the knowledge level about logistics at the public policy level varies greatly among different nations and among different administrations within the same country.

Thus, logistics competence outside universities seemed to be a result of activities of multinational companies, and was almost totally lacking as a domain of public policy. A notable exception was Singapore, the only country that at the time had a national logistics plan. A showcase that logistics competence can be developed very fast in the public domain is Taiwan, which in less than 10 years has developed a role as a logistics hub for global trade that offers Hong Kong and Singapore serious competition.

The OECD studies noted that few attempts had been made to compare in a rigorous way the different perspectives on goods-related transport policy that for historical reasons have developed in Europe, North America and elsewhere. One reason, of course, is that this is not an easy task. As a result of the fast globalization process in trade and tourism, there is a need for an improved understanding of these differences as a basis for harmonizing procedures and elimination of barriers. In addition a new need has arisen: the growing role of logistics in smoothing global trade flows has created a need to provide and harmonize public and industrial logistics policies at all levels, i.e. locally as well as nationally and internationally.

These observations prompted OECD to launch a third project with the goal of comparing logistics development in the Asian-Pacific, European, and North-American regions. The Trilateral Logistics (TRILOG) project started in 1996 but soon ran into difficulties. These were partly administrative and financial but in the end methodological. The main problem was the absence of relevant data. Because few governments had felt the need to establish national logistics policies, there had been no systematic collection of data to support the formulation of such policies. Thus, when the final plenary report (OECD, 2002) was compiled, its focus had shifted to looking at common elements rather than for differences among the regions. This is also reflected by its title: 'Transport Logistics: Shared Solutions to Common Challenges'.

As part of the TRILOG study, an attempt was made to find useful indicators of the performance of supply chains. The results were meagre, primarily because of a lack of data. The supply chain seems to fall half way between the traditional macro-level on which national statistics in all countries are based, and the traditional micro-level on which annual reports from individual companies are based. This dilemma is illustrated in Figure

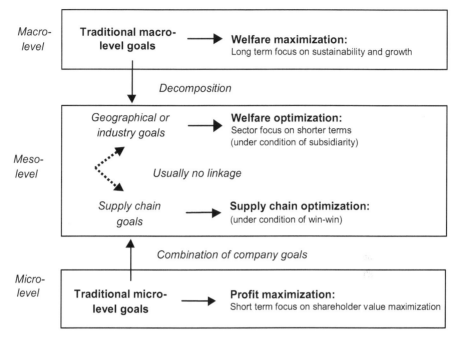

Figure 13.2 Illustration of the shortcomings in trying to bridge the gap between the macro and micro.

13.2. Traditionally macro-level goals are aimed at maximizing welfare while micro-level goals reflect the ambition of industry to maximize profits. To a certain extent the indicators formed to measure welfare and profits can be extended to industrial sectors and supply chains, respectively, but there is still a poor understanding of methods and data needs to handle the meso-level and establish links between short-term welfare optimization in different industrial sectors and supply chain optimization under conditions of win-win.

The conceptual model

An early conceptual systems model that was presented in Manheim (1979) is shown in Figure 13.3. It sees the traffic flows and the service levels offered in traffic as a short-term equilibrium resulting from interaction between the activity and the transportation systems. There are two feedback loops that change the long-term equilibrium. The most visible of these is the explicit intervention by traffic planners that result in changes to the transportation system. The less visible feedback is caused by reactions to the service levels offered in the form of decisions that influence the activity system, such as relocations of homes and industrial facilities, changes of purchasing habits etc. The use of this model was to organize and explain the contents of a textbook on transportation systems analysis.

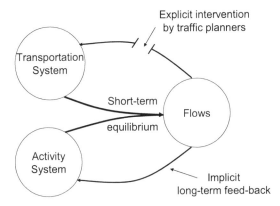

Figure 13.3 The traffic flow pattern equilibrium as a result of the interaction between the activity system and the transportation system.

Manheim's model inspired the model shown in Figure 13.4. This model identifies the most important actors and stakeholders influencing a transportation system and their immediate connection to one of the three major components of the system. In the model, the transportation system is broken down into two subsystems: the traffic system, which is seen as an interaction between vehicles and the infrastructure; and the transport system,

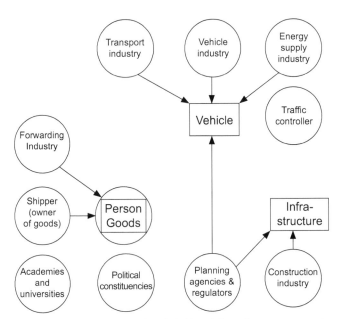

Figure 13.4 The most important actors and stakeholders influencing a transportation system and their immediate connection.

which is seen as an interaction between persons or goods and the vehicles. The interaction between persons or goods and infrastructure is seen as part of the activity system. For reasons of simplicity, the interactions are not shown in Figure 13.4.

The new model was developed as a tool to organize the programme at a convocation of the Council of Academies of Engineering and Technological Sciences with the theme: 'Sustainable Engineering; the Challenge of Developing Transportation for Society'. The programme was organized around 13 issues. For each issue a version of the conceptual model was constructed, where only those actors that were directly affected by the particular issue were shown together with a graphic illustration of their relationship to the three components and subsystems of the model. The issue-specific models were used to help choosing speakers and structure the discussion for each issue. The model is presented here for the purpose of underlining the importance of identifying and bringing together those stakeholders, whose actions influence the sustainability of specific transportation systems. The proceedings of the convocation are published in SATW (1994) and the specific use of the model in Sjöstedt (1994).

The final version of the model incorporates facilities as a fourth structural component. This was proposed by Professor Tony Ridley of the University of London as a way to obtain a structural similarity between the model and a classic four-stage traffic forecasting model. The basic version of this model is shown in Figure 13.5. It is identical to the version first published in EuroCASE (1996) except that accessibility has been changed to accession.

It has been attempted to make the model very robust in terms of exactly defining its elements and subsystems. An early set of definitions is given in Sjöstedt (1997). The formal definitions are excluded here and only some important observations are made.

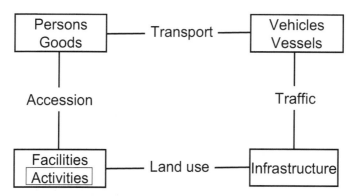

Figure 13.5 Generic conceptual model linking land use, accession, transport and traffic

The spatial dimension is in its entirety contained in the concept of infrastructure. This means that at the level of resolution of the model a facility is represented by a single point in space. The address of this point relative to some kind of fixed coordinate system is part of the infrastructure. To understand this convention it is useful to refer to a taxi driver. She or he is requested by the passenger to know the address of a specific facility, but not necessarily what is going on inside. From this it is clear that, for example, roads and railways, which in normal language are also facilities, in the model language are not facilities but parts of infrastructure. The opposite also occurs: for example, shopping malls or terminal buildings, which normally are seen as parts of infrastructure, are in the model language treated as facilities as long as they, with the resolution of the model, are represented by a single point. If the resolution increases, they may either be in their entirety seen as parts of infrastructure or split into several facilities, connected by pieces of infrastructure.

The reason for this care in definitions is to guard the generic qualities of the model. It should be possible to move from the conceptual model to, for example, a simulation model without having to change any definitions. But this also gives rise to problems of terminology, since it is difficult to find words that can be used without conflicting with their established and usually much broader common meaning.

For the same reason it is important to restrict the definitions of the finality of the subsystems to their core functions. Thus, transport is the administration of the change of address including the boarding (loading) and deboarding (unloading) of vehicles and vessels, unless these operations are separately modelled. Traffic is the movement and manoeuvring of vehicles and vessels relative to the fixed coordinate system, normally on some kind of dedicated infrastructure. This means that the entire trajectory of a vessel belongs to infrastructure, which again may violate normal conventions. Pedestrian traffic, which is often forgotten in transportation statistics, should strictly speaking be seen just as movement and guidance of pairs of legs.

A remark: this way of splitting transportation makes it easy to see the difficulties in diverting transport demand away from the use of private cars. A driver of a private car performs three functions; she or he transports herself or himself, supplies the transport capacity, and manoeuvres the vehicle. This is obviously highly rational.

Land use is defined as allocation of land to specific activities or to infrastructure and the creation of specific facilities or transportation infrastructure. Accession is chosen instead of the more common accessibility. It refers to all action that aims at improving accessibility including options, such as advance booking of transport capacity in space and time

Activities, finally, are restricted to those activities that take place in a facility. Transport and traffic, which are explicitly modelled, are with the language of the model not seen as activities.

In order to show the generic character of the model, its applicability both to passenger and goods transportation has been retained above. From now on only goods transportation will be treated, which somewhat alleviates the terminology problem. The reader interested in seeing the application of the modelling approach to public transportation is referred to Franzén (1999).

The duality of logistics and goods transportation

Logistics and goods transportation are complementary

The subsystems in Figure 13.5 are controlled by a large number of humans, who act according to the specific role they are performing. In this chapter, the term actor is used to signify anyone influencing the structure or performance of the systems. Actors behave differently not only because of their different roles, but also as a result of personal values, educational background, professional experience, etc. This also influences how they perceive a system. It can be seen, for example, as a technical, exogenously controllable system, as a system endogenously controlled by actors with greatly varying vested interests, as a market for business transactions between independent actors, and a system subjected to analysis and planning activities in preparation for implementing structural changes through investments or political measures. The resulting different perspectives have been discussed in Sjöstedt (1994) and EuroCASE (1996).

Historically, transportation has been seen as a technical system organized around a specific traffic mode. This system competes in different markets for its passengers and or freight customers. In Figure 13.6, the conceptual model has been redrawn to fit this particular perspective.

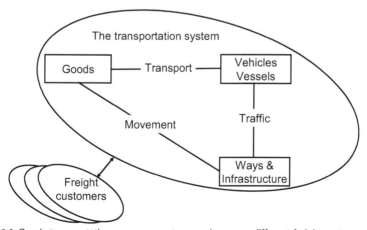

Figure 13.6 Goods transportation seen as a system serving many different freight customers.

Similarly, the logistics system has been seen as the flow of materials to, through, and from a specific production facility, where specific products are being manufactured. Originally, transport was seen as an indirect cost, an unwanted evil on top of the direct costs associated with manufacturing a specific line of products at that particular facility. Whenever transport was needed, it was bought in the transport market from any of a large number of transport providers with or without the mediation of a forwarder. Applying this perspective to the conceptual model results in the modified version shown in Figure 13.7.

In summary a large number of stand-alone production systems were served by a number of stand-alone transportation companies. Transport was organized around the individual shipment, which was purchased in the market whenever needed or carried out by the use of in-house transport resources. This dominant practice prevailed until the 1970s.

Logistics and goods transportation are becoming integrated

Since the early 1980s, with the launch of the just-in-time (JIT) principle, production facilities could no longer be seen as independent. Suppliers, manufacturers, and customers were interfaced, and the need to internalize external transport within the scope of joint production plans arose. Transport is now seen as one of the activities in a value-added chain, where in principle each link should add maximum value at minimum cost. From a logistics point of view the value-added chain is equivalent to a supply chain. As products become more complex, supply chain lengths increase and become more complex, and every manufacturing unit is part of an increasing number of chains supplying a web of enormous complexity.

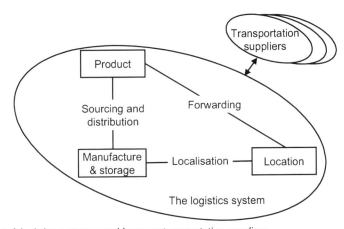

Figure 13.7 A logistics system served by many transportation suppliers.

Goods transportation systems are going through a similar interfacing process, although the rate of change is considerably slower than for logistics systems in large multinational companies. Here the pressure is both on integrating traffic modes into seamless intermodal systems and expanding the geographical scope of goods transportation into global systems that with minimum friction interface with regional, national, and local transportation systems.

The two types of systems need further integration. The pressure from industry to achieve this is great, and the potential benefit is also great. But for political reasons, environmental concerns, and a range of other factors, this integration will take a long time. Figure 13.8 illustrates the two systems, their closeness, and their complementary character.

The impact of rapid progress in ICT on logistics and goods transportation

Changes in logistics and goods transportation are information technology driven

It is not possible to manage flows of materials in a logistics system or flows of goods in a transportation system without the possibility of exchanging messages between the agents involved. Thus managing the necessary information flows has always been important, and as a result both logistics

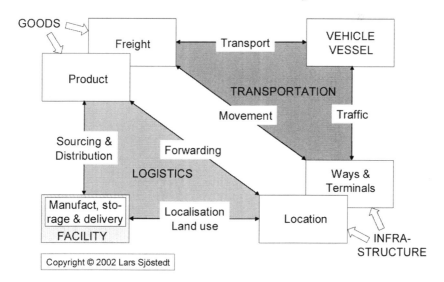

Figure 13.8 The complementary character and emerging integration of logistics and goods transportation.

and goods transportation are deeply impacted by changes in information technology.

The post World War II development of information technology can be split into three phases. The first is characterized by the introduction of the mainframe computer, closely watched by men in white coats behind glass walls. These computers were stand-alone machines used almost entirely for data processing. They were fed data on punched cards and delivered processed data back on paper. Although of limited use for most operational tasks in logistics, this was of considerable help in warehouse management and led to a strong focus on reducing costs by improved management of stock levels.

Phase 2 began with the arrival of the PC in the beginning of the 1980s. This allowed logistics managers to carry out their planning online, which paved the way for the JIT revolution and the control of supply chains. The modern fax, which was developed at the same time, complemented telephone voice communication, and together they enabled logistics managers to maintain the necessary level of contact with their suppliers and customers. It was suddenly possible concurrently to plan and synchronize logistics activities in production plants and storage facilities at different locations. This made it necessary to include the external transport between these facilities among the jointly planned operations instead of buying transport on an *ad hoc* basis in the open market. This internalizing of transport into production plans required long-term contracts with just a few forwarders or transportation companies. Instead of dealing with the bill of lading for single shipments, such contracts cover material flows that are split into a large number of repetitive shipments. Each shipment typically contains several components that are already sequenced for further manufacturing or assembly operations, which requires that the shipment is delivered at its destination within a prescribed narrow time window.

Over time, this led to the acceptance of the transportation manager or the forwarder representing him as a partner, supplementing the partnership between the consignor and consignee at both ends of the material flow. Companies with transport departments in-house were stimulated to outsource transport and the new partners in the transportation industry slowly gained the trust to carry out other logistics tasks than pure transport. Early examples are storage and transport of hanging clothes and postponed fitting of coloured doors to refrigerators and freezers for private homes. The concept third party logistics was borne.

Parallel to this development in transport a conversion from functional to flow-oriented production took place on the factory floor. This was also made possible through the use of the new computer technology. These two changes together completed the logistics revolution in production facilities.

The third phase is driven by the ability to connect great numbers of computers into networks, like the Internet, and the availability of browsers that serve as an easily managed interface between the user of such networks and the network itself. Another important factor is that information technology is now sufficiently cheap, robust, and miniaturized to be spread far beyond the permanent work place desk with a PC and a telephone. The next generation of mobile phone technology bandwidths will be large enough to tie portable computers into the large networks efficiently. This will put an important building block in place for provision of efficient information logistics.

The ability to perform information logistics efficiently will have a dramatic impact on society. It will likely produce a paradigm shift in the way intellectual work is organized, which parallels the paradigm shift 30 years earlier from functional to flow orientation of physical work. Information logistics and work flow management will allow efficient co-ordination of human intellectual work at a scale and scope beyond what has been previously possible. This will also allow the refinement of the extremely complex supply nets that will underlie the ever fast growing global trade.

Figure 13.9 summarizes the development trends discussed above. A more detailed discussion of various development phases in logistics and transportation is contained in Sjöstedt (1995) and OECD (1996).

The new role of information and communication systems

A classic industrial production system can be seen as an interaction between a technical system and a social system, where logistics helps to structure the contacts between the two systems. The formation of information logistics as briefly described above now motivates to identify an information and communications system (ICS) that bridges the technical and social systems as shown in Figure 13.10.

The ICS in the centre of the picture serves several purposes. It has of course the traditional role of providing the continuous horizontal information

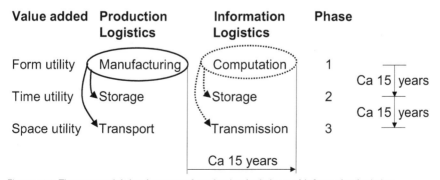

Figure 13.9 The sequential development of production logistics and information logistics.

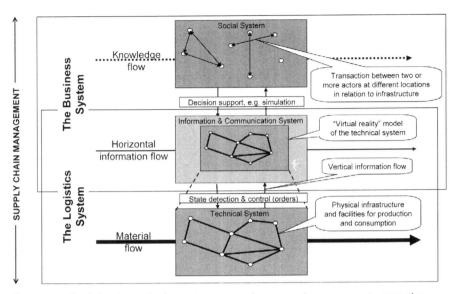

Figure 13.10 The industrial production system as seen from a supply management perspective.

exchange between all the actors at different locations who perform different roles in the value-added network. Another traditional role is to maintain the relational databases that keep the records of all transactions taking place in the business system. But in addition this system plays a new important role.

Natural and applied sciences as well as industrial development have long relied on a trial and error mechanism, involving on one hand an inductive, creative element resulting in hypotheses, theories and ideas, and on the other hand a deductive, validating element, based on empirical observations. New knowledge is created by alternating between these elements in an iterative, cumulative procedure, which adds new knowledge at each step. The communication between these two elements is mainly based on the use of symbolic languages. Computer modelling of technical systems has an increasing role in providing a better understanding of the behaviour of the system, but until now it has normally been required to perform the ultimate validation of a new or modified system in a real world environment.

Thanks to ICS, modelling has now reached a degree of sophistication, where it must be seen as a third leg in this iterative process. Thus the ICS in Figure 13.10 can be seen as an abstract or modelling level often referred to as a virtual world, inferring that it communicates with humans directly by means of their senses and not only by the use of symbolic language. Validation by the use of models is increasingly used as a substitute for observations in the real world. This trend is symbolized by the vertical information flow arrows in the upper part of the picture. An early example is crash tests of automobiles. In the mid-1980s the technical director of one of the large automobile producers in Germany stated in a key note address, that he believed that it would never be possible to simulate a car crash in enough detail in a computer to substitute these for real car crash experiments. However, less than 10 years later this was exactly what had taken place. As a result, the number of crashed cars needed when developing a new car model was drastically reduced.

Such modelling has another great advantage. It allows manipulations with the time dimension. Provided sufficient historical data have been previously recorded, going backwards in time gives an account of experience generated in the past, while going into the future gives forecasts.

In business, the use of sophisticated models is quickly replacing the simple use of raw empirical data as a basis for decisions. Business is organized around transactions, which essentially are timeless changes of system state. The buzzword 'business process' originated in the information industry. It indicates that business is no longer restricted to independent transactions, but increasingly involves studying the processes between large numbers of coupled transactions. This also widens the traditional meaning of the term transaction, which now seems to come close to the concept of the change of a state of a system. It also implies that business transactions increasingly rely on complex modelling at the abstract level as a complement to the combination of existing knowledge and raw data on the actual state of the real world.

Thus, the new and increasingly important role of ICS is to provide a 'virtual reality' type of model, an abstract copy of the real world that compensates for the lacking possibilities of the actors to inspect more than a diminishing part of the technical system by means of their own senses. This model provides the transparency of the system needed to create sufficient trust among the actors in and cohesion of the complex industrial system. One example of a company with this approach is Volvo that managed to cut the development time for their successful city jeep from 44 to 27 months by carrying out all design work including the production planning and its supply network by exclusive reliance on computer modelling (Chew, 2003).

The ability to use a virtual reality model as a substitute for the real world is dependent on continuous updating in real time of the virtual reality model to assure that it matches sufficiently closely the state of the technical system. In Supply Chain Management (SCM), this is provided by the vertical information flows at the bottom of the picture. Track and trace functions, i.e. the ability to indicate the exact position of any moving object in the system at any given time, is critically dependent on these vertical information flows and can be seen as a basic element in any virtual reality model.

Now it can be claimed that the development sketched above is only a vision and that industry is far from accepting such an abstract operating paradigm. The real situation seems to be that there is a spectrum from a few of the large global manufacturing companies, where these ideas are already exploited, to the very large number of companies where such ideas have not been heard of. This is in line with current research, for example, Patterson *et al.*, (2003), that concludes that new ICS are more likely to be adopted by large companies than small but also by decentralized companies than hierarchies. It is then logical that the adaptation of ICS in the transportation sector is lead by the large forwarders and mega-carriers and not the mode-specific transport operators like railways and hauliers.

Because of their closeness to production, these trends are very strong in logistics and goods transportation. In Figure 13.11, the four subsystems in the conceptual model have been classified according to the level in Figure 13.10 to which they primarily belong. Traffic belongs to the technical system at the bottom level, since it is a continuous process in the real world. Transport has only three system states; it has not started, it is underway, or it is completed. Land use involves earmarking specific land for specific purposes and changing ownership of land. Thus, transport and land use both seem to be predominantly transactional and therefore belong to the social system at the top level Accession, finally, deals with allocation of resources. Due to the increasing complexity of capacity allocation of resources in logistics and transportation, it is heavily dependent on modelling, which explains why development of models for use in accession processes is currently intense. This means that the accession process belongs to the middle abstract level and

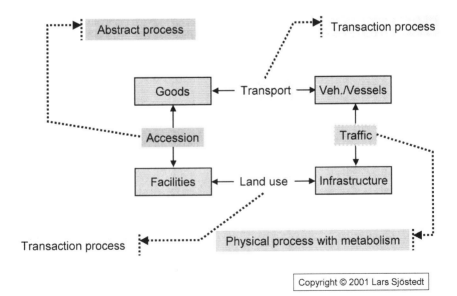

Figure 13.11 The different character of the processes in the conceptual model.

the ICS. This also explains why it has been necessary to coin a new term for this type of process.

The shift from an industrial society to a business process oriented knowledge society, as illustrated in Figure 13.10, is equivalent to a shift from the right side of Figure 13.11 to the left. Thus, interest is shifting from traffic both clockwise and counter-clockwise in the direction of accession. The trend may be illustrated by the rapid spread of modern yield management principles, where typically the price for an intended trip varies both with the time between the booking and the trip, and with the number of seats that have already been booked.

The need for collaboration and cooperation

The emergence of a negotiation and collaboration based economy

In the classic theory of markets it is assumed that all actors share the same information, that products are standardized, that each seller of a specific product offers the same price to all buyers, and that there is competition between several producers of each standardized product, which ensures a downward pressure on prices and incentives to rationalize production processes.

While this to some extent is still true in consumer markets, it is no longer true for the long supply chains in which the product, stepwise, reaches its final shape. It is a basic assumption in modern industrial marketing, that business no longer takes place in the form of stand-alone transactions in open markets. As mentioned above business is now seen as comprising more or less continuous process that involve closed or semi-closed networks of actors. In such networks, all the assumptions of an ideal market are violated. Most important of all is that information is not shared equally. Those actors who do not belong to the networks have poor access to all relevant information including prices, while actors inside the networks exchange information in a highly structured and selective manner. This means that also inside the networks information is not freely accessible to every actor. Instead, information is disseminated according to strict rules agreed upon by the members of the networks.

This has given rise to a new form of standardization. The old type of standardization is directed towards components and products. It is technically oriented and performed by public or industry-wide organizations such as ISO. The resulting standards are widely circulated, and their application often mandatory. The new standards are soft standards. They focus on business processes instead of on hardware, and they are based on the principle of voluntary collaboration. In the US, the Voluntary Interindustry Commerce

Standards (VICS) Association has, together with a number of consumer goods manufacturers, software producers and others, developed a business model called CPFR, which means Collaborative Planning, Forecasting and Replenishment, aimed at increasing the visibility downstream in a supply chain. This initiative is about 5 years old, has attracted considerable interest, and is rapidly spreading outside the US. A more recent initiative called CTM (Collaborative Transport Management) aims at achieving the same kind of visibility in intermodal transport chains. An overview may be found in Seifert (2003).

While so far these initiatives mainly involve the private sector and cover very limited portions of the total field of logistics and transportation the principle of a joint process approach based on structured voluntary collaboration needs to be extended as indicated in Figure 13.12.

Four professional perspectives on logistics and transportation

In order to move the idea of voluntary collaboration from a specific supply chain to the transport policy field and apply it successfully, actors from all disciplines need to become involved. In Figure 13.13, four professional perspectives have been identified, each focused on one of the four components of the conceptual model. These are logistics, supply chain management, classic single mode transportation, and physical planning including traffic planning.

It is important to stress the use of the word perspective, because obviously each of the four professions to varying degrees deals with the whole system. On the other hand, there must also be a reasonably clear separation of roles in order to make collaboration efficient.

The four professions singled out are only some of the increasing number of professions involved in logistics and transportation. This may be seen as

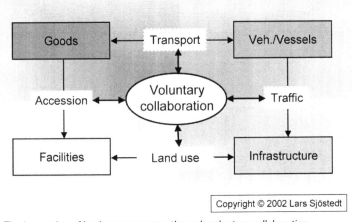

Copyright © 2002 Lars Sjöstedt

Figure 13.12 The integration of business processes through voluntary collaboration.

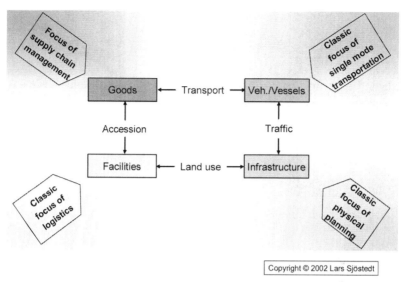

Figure 13.13 The different focus of the four major professional perspectives on logistics and transportation.

a further difficulty, but may in fact strengthen the arguments for using a voluntary collaboration approach, since this avoids the need to agree on the use of universal standards and procedures, which seems increasingly difficult to achieve.

Links between logistics, goods transportation, and environmental sciences

A similar gap as the one between traffic planners and logisticians has existed between environmentalists on one side and the logistics and transportation profession on the other. However, the Life Cycle Analysis (LCA) concept, which has become central to environmental work, bears strong resemblance to the value-added or supply chain concept in logistics. The only thing required to see the parallel is to replace turnover in facilities measured in monetary terms to turnover measured in energy terms, and to replace flow of materials and goods by flows of energy and emissions.

Figure 13.14 shows how the conceptual model can be transformed into a model for environmental analysis adapted to the four processes of the model. The traffic process is where the physical action is and thus where most of the system metabolism resides. A detailed analysis of the traffic process is therefore fundamental to all environmental analysis in logistics and transportation.

In Sweden, the leading companies in the transportation sector and some of the large manufacturing companies have formed the Network for Freight Transport and the Environment. Their work is based on voluntary collaboration

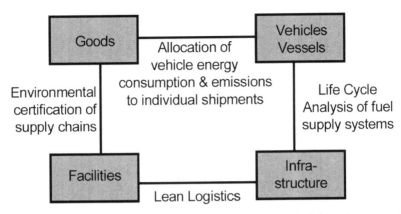

Figure 13.14 Techniques for evaluating the environmental dimension of logistics and transportation.

concerning LCA calculation methods and joint databases. Thus, it bears some resemblance with the VICS, although the motive for collaboration and the information content is quite different. Among the results of the work of NTM is a Freight Transport Data Base, which can be accessed online (NTM, 2003). Similar initiatives exist in other European countries.

Much can be done by improving fuel and vehicle technologies. But since traffic demand is derived, energy consumption and emissions must be traced back to transport, and from there back to the demand for access, and finally back to the activities causing this demand, in order to understand what can be done to improve sustainability in the society at large.

Allocation of vehicle energy consumption and emissions to individual products that pass through long transport chains have already been studied in depth, see for example, Bäckström (1999). But there is not yet an approved methodology for environmental certification of supply chains. Similarly, several researchers have studied how alternative locations of, for example, a shopping centre affect total energy consumption and emissions of both delivery vehicles and vehicles used by customers travelling to and from the shopping centre, see Hagson and Mossfeldt (1998). But there is a long way to truly Lean Logistics, where the full potential of environmentally sound thinking in all production and logistics processes is combined with the full potential for sustainability in the transportation processes.

Conclusions regarding sustainability of goods transportation and possible ways ahead

The various approaches used in this chapter have confirmed that sustainability of transport is a very complicated issue, especially for goods transportation.

While an informed and motivated passenger can judge, to some extent, whether her or his mobility meets expectations for sustainability or not, and has the power to do something about the situation by modifying her or his own travel habits, it is very difficult to judge whether goods, which have been shipped from a specific origin to a specific destination in a specific way, have met requirements for sustainability or not. Who is the problem owner, i.e. who should be blamed if a careful analysis shows that this transport should have been carried out in a different way? Or as the example with bottled mineral water shows: Who should ring the alarm bell, if the truth is that the goods contain products that should have been produced closer to this specific destination?

The answer is that the questions are put in a wrong way. Sustainability is not an absolute measure. Working with sustainability resembles the Japanese concept 'kaizen' used in production facilities, i.e. to find ways of making small improvements every day. Such improvements can only be achieved by a bottom-up approach. But since the work takes place in an unploughed field, it must lead to the establishment of formal and informal institutions, which to some extent requires top-down approaches with involvement of public policy-makers.

A first conclusion, therefore, is that work on sustainability of goods transportation must start with many parallel initiatives; each with the goal to improve some part of today's endlessly intertwined logistics and transportation systems. The TRILOG study showed that countries differ in their use of logistics because they are in different stages of development with diversified cultural backgrounds. This means that these initiatives must be adapted to regional and national conditions. Since there is a large difference between logistics practices in different industrial sectors, it seems rational to spread the initiatives across sectors and allow emerging institutions to be adapted to differences among the sectors. Finally, initiatives at the global intercontinental level are likely to differ from those needed at the intra-continental and national levels, and since both of these are primarily associated with business to business shipments (B2B), they are likely to be radically different from initiatives primarily aimed at improving distribution of food and other products to households in urban areas (B2C).

To succeed each initiative must engage a wide range of stakeholders, representatives of industry groups purchasing transport, forwarding and transportation industries supplying transport, physical planners, professional policy-makers, unions etc.

Although different initiatives must be allowed to find their own *modus operandi*, it is obviously essential to develop a multilingual terminology and exchange experience of the problems arising when trying to harmonize this with well established national and traffic mode specific terminologies. This is largely a task for researchers, who must act proactively to help initiatives get underway. The conceptual model used in this chapter may be seen as an attempt in this direction, but much more research is required to form some kind of joint platform for creating the institutional structure and the modelling tools that are needed to obtain the necessary joint force and impact of the various initiatives. There is also a need for universities to engage in educational programmes, such as international masters programmes, which bridge the transport diagonal and simultaneously offer a thorough understanding of how to tackle sustainability issues.

Although all companies involved in supply chains need to appoint a supply chain or logistics manager, it is normally one company that acts as a supply chain driver. This is either the original equipment manufacturer (OEM) that assembles the product, the owner of the trademark, or a specially contracted fourth party logistics provider. The supply chain manager working for this company naturally obtains a stronger position than his partners in the supply chain. This trend is reinforced as special software to support such supply chain leadership is increasingly used. A similar although slower trend towards identifying an intermodal transport chain manager or leader is evident in cases where the demand for transport becomes complex. Since developing and running a supply chain appears similar to establishing and running an initiative on goods transportation sustainability, it seems natural to give supply managers an increased responsibility for sustainability of goods transportation. In this way responsibility would be shared between transport buying and transport selling parties. Another reason for close cooperation with supply chain managers is that there is a severe lack of suitable performance indicators and data for supply chains in general and not only for sustainability. This makes it rational to design and agree on procedures for capturing data for both purposes in the same round.

It is important that initiatives in different parts of the world learn from each other. The impression from working with the OECD projects is that there is, for example, a lot to be learnt from the differences between Europe on one side of the Atlantic and the US and Canada on the other.

The shift from physical processes to focus on business processes has progressed further in the United States than in Europe. Accordingly, the role of the public sector changes from that of a provider of special systems components to that of a facilitator of business processes and a participant in an integration process with specific responsibilities for safety, security, and other specific aspects of the total system.

The United States have identified the need for, and its Department of Transportation (DOT) has initiated and supported, the development of new forms of public statistics on logistics and transportation, as suggested by its Bureau of Transportation Statistics a few years ago. This indicates that the

US has taken a lead in developing the databases needed to understand better the new meso-level economy where supply chains and supply networks are established. The integration trend at the meso-level seems to be confirmed by the rapidly increasing interest in the US for initiatives under VICS such as CPFR and CTM.

To some extent, it seems to be the other way around in the environmental field. Here Europe is ahead of the United States. This is illustrated by the Swedish NTM initiative briefly described on pages 217–218. The reason for this trend in Europe and its absence in the US may have the simple explanation, that cultural and other differences in the US have created less interest or commitment to addressing environmental issues. But another explanation may be that the clearer separation of roles has led to a situation where no single actor is willing to take responsibility. In Europe, in contrast, it has been natural for actors to treat responsibility for the environment as a shared responsibility.

Bibliography

Bäckström, S. (1999) Environmental Performance Calculations in Transport LCIA: Allocation Method Design Issues. Report 45, Department of Transportation and Logistics, Chalmers University of Technology, Gothenburg.

Chew, E. (2003) Volvo blends 'car elements' into 90 – Large-car platform allows Volvo to develop a car-like sports-utility – and get it to the market in only 27 months. *Automotive News Europe*. Online. Available HTTP: <www.automotivenews.com> (accessed 11 May 2003).

Demkes, R., ter Brugge, R. and Verduin, T. (1999) TRILOG European Summary Report. TNO-Inro, 99/NL/364, Delft.

EuroCASE (1996) *Mobility, Transport and Traffic in the Perspective of Growth, Competitiveness, Employment*. Paris: European Council of Applied Sciences and Engineering.

Franzén, S. (1999) Public Transportation in a Systems Perspective – a Conceptual Model and an Analytical Framework for Design and Evaluation. Report 45, PhD thesis, Department of Transportation and Logistics, Chalmers University of Technology, Gothenburg.

Hagson, A. and Mossfeldt, L. (1998) Varutransporter till externa köpcentra och innerstadshande: En jämförande studie av effekter på trafikarbete och miljö (Freight transport to external shopping centres and inner city shops – A comparative study of effects on traffic work and the environment). Report 1998:3, City and Traffic Planning, Architecture, Chalmers University of Technology, Gothenburg.

Manheim, M.L. (1979) *Fundamentals of Transportation Systems Analysis – Volume 1: Basic Concepts*. Cambridge, MA: MIT Press.

NTM (2003) *Environment Data for Freight Transport*. NTM Nätverket för Transporter och Miljön (The Network for Freight Transport and the Environment). Online. Available HTTP: <www.ntm.a.se/eng-index.asp>.

OECD (1992) *Advanced Logistics and Road Freight Transport*. Paris: OECD Transport.

OECD (1996) *Integrated Advanced Logistics for Freight Transport*. Paris: OECD Transport.

OECD (2002) *Transport Logistics: Shared Solutions to Common Challenges*. Paris: OECD Transport.

Patterson, K.J., Grimm, C.M. and Corsi, T.M. (2003) Adopting technologies for supply chain management. *Transport Research, Part E, Logistics and Transportation Review*, **2**, pp. 95–121.

SATW (1994) *Sustainable Engineering: The Challenge of Developing Transportation for Society*.

Proceedings of the 10th CAETS Convocation in Zürich 1993, P-277, Swiss Academy of Engineering Sciences SATW, Zürich, and Society of Automotive Engineers SAE, Warrendale, PA.

Seifert, D. (2003) *Collaborative Planning, Forecasting and Replenishment: How to create a Supply Chain Advantage.* New York: Amacom Books.

Sjöstedt, L. (1994) Sustainable mobility: a systems perspective on policy issues. Paper presented at the 10th CAETS Convocation in Zürich 1993, E, Swiss Academy of Engineering Sciences SATW, Zürich, and Society of Automotive Engineers SAE, Warrendale, PA.

Sjöstedt, L. (1995) Transportation and logistics: towards a unifying theoretical base, in *Yearbook of the School of Technology Management & Economics 1994/95.* Gothenburg: Chalmers University of Technology, pp. 35–48.

Sjöstedt, L. (1997) Managing sustainable mobility: a conceptual framework, in Tilanus, B. (ed.) *Information Systems in Logistics and Transportation.* Oxford: Pergamon.

Chapter 14

Intermodal transport markets and sustainability in Europe

Dimitrios A. Tsamboulas

An efficient transport system is an essential prerequisite for the European Union's (EU) competitiveness. With the projected growth of international trade, the extension of the EU to the Central and Eastern European countries and the enhanced cooperation with the Mediterranean countries, the role of transport will become even more important.

Between 1970 and 1998 European freight transport increased by about 116% (approximately 4% annually), a trend that might continue in the future. Road now makes up 44% of the goods transport market compared with 41% for short sea shipping, 8% for rail, and 4% for inland waterways. Delays due to congestion result in consumption of an extra 1.9 billion litres of fuel (6% of annual consumption). The external costs of road traffic congestion alone amount to 0.5% of Community GDP; traffic forecasts show that, if nothing is done, road congestion will increase significantly by 2010 (European Commission, 2001). The costs attributable to congestion will also increase by 142% to reach 80 billion euros a year, which is approximately 1% of Community GDP, with accidents, air pollution, and noise amounting to a further 2%. These costs may undermine European competitiveness.

Emerging policies

In order to achieve socio-economic and environmental sustainability, efficient and more balanced use of existing capacities throughout the European transport system have become key challenges (European Commission, 1992). The policy instruments used for a 'business as usual' approach cannot solve the future problems associated with transport and a systems approach should be used (European Commission, 1997b).

When intermodal transport services are provided, they are offered as mode-independent door-to-door connections based on a range of modal transport alternatives, considered by the shipper (or forwarder) as the most beneficial for his or her needs. Thus, no consideration is given to an efficient use of the existing transport system, reducing transport costs, and allowing the generation of added value.

The development of intermodal transport services today is hindered by the fragmentation of the modal and national systems in the EU, as well as by the lack of interoperability between systems. One of the consequences of this fragmentation is that much of the currently available data are provided on a national or modal basis with no consideration of the integrated transport logistical chain, although some attempts have been made by the European Commission (INFREDAT, 2001).

Consequently, intermodal freight transport in Europe seems unable to meet the increasingly complex logistics requirements of an economy which operates in a competitive and global market. Transfers between modes generally create too many additional costs. The absence of interoperability and interconnectivity between transport systems and services means that the integration of the existing and planned transport systems (infrastructure, services, technologies, pricing, legislation, etc.) is not carried out efficiently. However, this global integration cannot be achieved by each shipper/forwarder acting individually, and it requires a top-down approach provided in Europe by the European Commission.

The objective is to develop a framework for an optimal integration of different modes so as to enable an efficient and cost-effective use of the transport system through seamless, customer-oriented door-to-door services whilst favouring competition between transport operators (European Commission, 1997*a*).

By improving the potential of rail and waterborne transport and by offering, where appropriate, effective alternatives to unimodal road journeys, intermodality will help to overcome congested road networks. Performance improvements in railways, the full internalization of external costs, and the promotion of intermodality are part of an overall strategy for sustainable mobility.

Purpose of this chapter

This chapter analyses the policies of the EU related to Intermodal transport and sustainability of the transport system and how the former affects the latter. Whereas sustainability is an overall policy, intermodality is a specific policy measure for specific market segments. Consequently, the chapter sets the definitions and contents of these policies and identifies the freight market segments to which the intermodality policy measures will have an impact (intermodal market segments). The impacts of the policies are disaggregated for each intermodal market segment and the intensity of their impact is presented.

The EU is considered as the most relevant institution that influences the transport sector in member states. It has the power to introduce legislation as well as regulations that are followed for the national freight transport in member states. Such legislative measures also have far-reaching impacts on international transport, which is as important as domestic transport for the twenty-five European member states.

Intermodality

The European Commission uses two terms: intermodal transport and combined transport. *Intermodal transport* is the combination of at least two transport modes in a customer-tailored door-to-door haul. *Combined transport* is a specific market niche of intermodal transport. It excludes air transport and aims to shift cargoes away from road to rail, short sea shipping, and barge. The drayage (pre- and end-haulage by truck) has to be as short as possible. The main aim of combined transport is therefore modal shift.

Intermodality is about the synergy and coordination of a transport system that enables two or more different modes to be used in an integrated manner in a door-to-door transport chain. Intermodality may be viewed as a quality indicator of the level of integration between different modes. More intermodality means more integration and complementarity between and among modes, thus contributing to a more efficient transport system. The economic basis for intermodality is that transport modes which display favourable intrinsic economic and operational characteristics individually, can be integrated into a door-to-door transport chain in order to improve the overall efficiency of the transport system (European Commission, 1997a).

The aim of intermodality measures is to shift freight transport to other transport modes than road. Table 14.1 presents the total volume (in billion

Table 14.1 EU freight transport statistics

	1998	1997	1996	1995	1994	1993	1992	1991	1990
Sea	178.5	164.5	140.7	120.2	107.0	97.9	90.3	85.7	80.8
Combined as % of total sea traffic	15.6	14.6	13.1	11.2	10.5	10.3	9.3	9.0	8.8
Rail	62.0	61.1	53.7	46.5	42.2	37.2	34.8	33.2	33.4
Combined as % of total rail traffic	25.8	25.8	24.6	21.1	19.2	18.1	15.7	14.1	13.1
Inland waterway	5.1	5.0	4.7	4.0	3.8	3.3	2.7	2.9	2.7
Combined as % of total inland waterway traffic	4.2	4.2	4.2	3.5	3.4	3.2	2.6	2.7	2.5
Total of combined transport	245.6	230.6	199.1	170.7	153.0	138.4	127.8	121.8	116.9
Total traffic (all modes)	2852.2	2768.2	2641.2	2627.0	2525.6	2374.4	2411.4	2381.9	2329.0
Combined as a % of total traffic	8.6	8.3	7.5	6.5	6.1	5.8	5.3	5.1	5.0

Note: combined transport by mode, in 1000 million t-km.
Source: Vanel (2001).

tonne-km) of freight, disaggregated by transport mode. In the same table the share of intermodal/combined transport is provided. It is evident that the share is low (from 5% in 1990 to 8.6% in 1998). Hence, there is much to be done in order to increase this share. On the other hand, the observed increase of the share between 1990 and 1998 of 72% could be attributed to the persistent and systematic policies of the EU to promote intermodality.

Intermodal freight market

Introduction

A new approach is needed when issues related to intermodal transport are addressed. Furthermore, it is evident that the crucial 'base' for any analysis, is the generic freight market segments relevant to intermodal transport, that capture dimensions additional to transport related ones – these are the dimensions.

Another issue that arises from the analysis is related to the categorization of commodity types. They are usually categorized following classifications/ nomenclatures introduced by international statistical bodies, for example, EUROSTAT. However, intermodality analysis requires a new approach to commodity classification that is related to market segments. A new classification system is proposed, which is more appropriate for the intermodal transport and more specifically for policy measures analysis.

Dimensions

The dimensions identified as significant for intermodal freight market segmentation are (IQ, 1997; LOGIQ, 2000):

- user type, which includes shippers, forwarders, large or small transport companies and sea carriers;
- distance travelled and the origin-destination class that is related to intercontinental or continental chain, long or short distance and international or domestic transport;
- commodity type, which is classified as hazardous, perishable, high-value general cargo or low-value general cargo.

Of all the above dimensions, only the one related to commodity type is presented in detail below, since it is the most important one determining the requirements for transport, which are reflecting the user's requirements as well.

Commodity types

It is evident that the most important dimension for market segmentation is the type of commodity, and especially the identification of those suitable for intermodal transport. However the importance of commodity type for the economies of European countries has changed. As an example, the following commodities groups have gained in importance and as such may be called 'emerging commodities': vehicles, machines, manufactured and semi-manufactured goods; food and animal feed; and chemical goods.

Other commodity groups show only moderate growth, although coal and fertilizers have experienced reduced transport volumes. As a result, bulk goods, such as coal, iron, steel, non-ferrous metals, metal ores and metal scrap have lost relative importance in the European transport market.

Consequently, the change in the commodity structure has affected the modal split for freight transport (Rothengatter and Szimba, 2001). The reduction in volume of bulk goods has resulted in a decrease of rail and inland waterway mode shares, which were (and are) the main transport modes for these commodities.

Road and air transport shares increased, because the 'emerging commodities' are high value products (machines, electronics, vehicles etc.) that incur considerable time-related costs, due to the high capital costs associated with them. This results in high values for travel time, which compensates for high transport costs. Thus, they have different transport requirements from bulk goods, that is: quick, reliable, punctual, and flexible transport; special handling during transport (for example, protection against shocks or transportation at a pre-defined temperature); direct transport; and transport in small consignments.

The requirements of 'emerging commodities' determine the modal shares and which freight market segments are suitable for intermodal transport. For intermodal transport analysis these market segments are worth considering in combination with the other two dimensions (user type and distance).

Principles for market segmentation

The first comprehensive approach for market segmentation is carried out by the IQ research project (IQ, 1997). According to the IQ approach[1] the supply (service providers) and demand (transport services users) produce the following three key factors that will determine the market segmentation: (*a*) flow typology, (*b*) commodity groups, (*c*) customers typology.

Basically, the IQ approach is different from earlier practices, which looked at the supply side only, assuming that this is the critical factor. As an example, the European Conference of Ministers of Transport (ECMT) is looking at the dimensions of loading units, as a supply measure to promote intermodal transport (ECMT, 2002).

With IQ, the demand side requirements were introduced and considered as being of primary importance. Needless to say that the IQ approach does not neglect the supply side, which is considered with regard to logistic supply chains. To cope with the in-depth analysis of intermodal transport, twenty-three generic market segments were introduced They are: (1) carrier haulage; (2) merchant haulage, LCL or FCL,[2] export; (3) merchant haulage, LCL, import; (4) merchant haulage, FCL, import; (5) maritime transport, hazardous goods; (6) maritime transport, perishable goods (all pertinent for maritime transport); (7) hazardous goods, medium-distance; (8) hazardous goods, long-distance; (9) perishable goods, medium-distance; (10) perishable goods, long-distance (all pertinent for Continental transport); (11) medium-distance, high-value goods, long-distance, high-value goods; (13) low-value goods (all pertinent for Continental transport of general cargo for shippers); (14) medium-distance, high-value or consolidated goods – regular user; (15) long-distance, high-value or consolidated goods – regular user; (16) medium-distance, high-value or consolidated goods – occasional user; (17) long-distance, high-value or consolidated goods – occasional user; (18) low-value goods (all pertinent for Continental transport of general cargo for forwarder or road transport company); (19) captive short-sea transport (e.g. Ireland, Greece, Scandinavia); (20) captive rail transport (truck-restriction areas such as the Alps); (21) inter-plant transport for large shippers; (22) waste transport; (23) transport of empty container boxes. Their relationship with the three key factors is depicted in Figure 14.1 (Vanel, 2001).

The IQ approach to market segmentation, although a quite comprehensive one, is too complicated and requires a lot of data. Its main purpose is more at the micro-level and for the assessment of intermodal impact at the company level or at specific corridors. A more simplified policy oriented approach is required for the purposes of the present chapter, i.e. to determine the impacts of policy measures.

The proposed categorization is based on the principle of the three dimensions of intermodal market segmentation identified above (commodity, user type and distance), with some simplifications. The user types were substituted by users' quality requirements (for example, regularity, flow density, time factor); the commodity types were substituted by shipment size; distance is kept but is segmented into three categories; and the time factor is introduced as the most important user quality requirement. Hence, the resulting variables are:

1   shipment size and regularity;
2   distance and flow intensity;
3   time.

The suggested three distance categories are:

Short distance ($\leq$ 150 km): corresponding to the local distribution of the goods for which road transport is competitive because of the time and costs.

Medium distance (150–500 km): corresponding to the market in which there is strong competition with road haulage. Indeed, 80% of road haulage runs on a distance of 200 km. This is an intensive, generally domestic, and extremely remunerative market. However, the environmental stakes are the strongest in this case and could favour the use of intermodal transport.

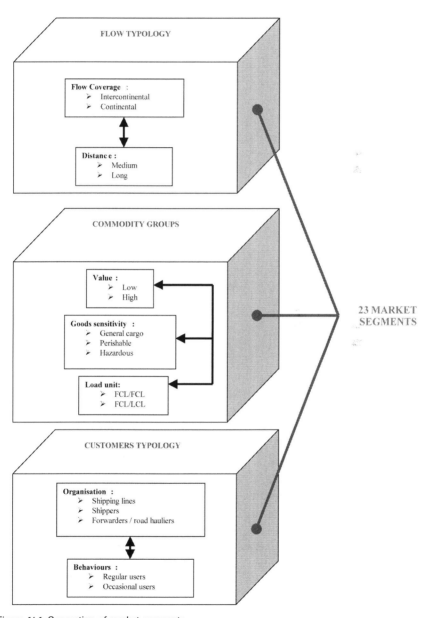

Figure 14.1 Generation of market segments

Long distance (≥ 500 km): corresponding to the market in which intermodal transport (including rail, short sea shipping and inland waterways) could become the principal mode. This is because over this distance the different modes intervening in the intermodal transport chain can be fully optimized. Also for such distances, the time and cost factors favour intermodal competitiveness, because of constraints imposed on road transport due to regulations (working hours, speed limits, second driver etc.).

The time variable is a decisive factor in the modal choice by users. Hence, it is becoming more and more integrated in the market analysis of any operator, and especially for intermodal transport decisions, since it is negatively valued. For the time variable four groups of times are proposed, representing the most commonly encountered door-to-door transit times in Europe:

12 hours corresponds to *express* delivery on medium and long distances. This market is unsuited to intermodal transportation (except postal services) because of the shipment characteristics (often less than FCL/LCL) and traffic diffusion.

24 hours corresponds to the transit time for most transport operators serving Origins and Destinations (ODs) within Central Europe (the so-called 'Blue Banana' zone) and using the European high volume traffic corridors.

48 hours corresponds to the servicing of European regions adjacent to the central 'Blue Banana' zone (Spain, southern Italy, northern United Kingdom).

>48 hours is accepted for the servicing of EU extremities (southern Spain, Portugal, Scandinavia, Greece, and to the new member states) and international routes (outside the EU).

Consequently, when the freight market segments are generated the above sub-categories for distance and time are represented with descriptions related to the origins of cargo, for example, urban, regional, interregional, intercontinental. Urban is related to short distances up to 150 km and short travel times (less than 12 hours); regional to distances up to 150–500 km and travel times less than 24 hours; and the interregional to distances more than 500 km and travel times less than 48 hours (except for EU extremities). In addition, a special case intercontinental sub-category is recognized that is related to distances of more than 500 km (and consequently times more than 48 hours) and concerns areas outside the EU.

Proposed freight market segments

Fourteen market segments are proposed as being suitable for intermodal transport, and as such they should be the target of European policies favouring intermodality:

1   bulk products suitable to be unitized (e.g. fertilizers, cereals);
2   bulk products unsuitable to be unitized with no special handling requirements (e.g. paper pulp, wood);
3   bulk products unsuitable to be unitized with special handling requirements (e.g. petroleum products, coal, iron ores, minerals);
4   perishable goods for regional markets;
5   perishable goods for interregional markets;
6   dangerous goods;
7   urban logistics;
8   regional flows of general cargo (regional consolidation and distribution, as well as regional exchanges);
9   regional flows of general cargo (regional exchanges);
10   interregional flows of general cargo suitable to be unitized, with high transport quality requirements (e.g. just-in-time, within 24 hours delivery);
11   interregional flows of general cargo unsuitable to be unitized, with high transport quality requirements (e.g. just-in-time, within 24 hours delivery);
12   interregional flows of general cargo suitable to be unitized, with no specific transport quality requirements;
13   interregional flows of general cargo unsuitable to be unitized, with no specific transport quality requirements;
14   intercontinental flows of general cargo (most of the trans-maritime containers).

The combinations of the above dimensions and corresponding variables have generated the freight market segments listed that have the potential to be transported with a combination of modes within an intermodal transport chain. Needless to say these segments are related to Europe, although the procedure for identifying them can be applied in other parts of the world, and possibly different segments will be generated. In the following section, the segments will be the basis on which the European policies related to intermodality will be analyzed.

Sustainability and intermodal transport

The demand for transport continues to increase, and to cope with this the EU is seeking alternatives to the construction of new infrastructure. The aim of such alternatives is to avoid jeopardizing economic development and welfare goals, and to achieve sustainable transport. The transport system needs to be optimized to meet the demands of sustainable development, as set out in the conclusions of the Gothenburg European Council (European Commission, 2001). A modern transport system must be sustainable from an economic and social as well as an environmental viewpoint.

Integration of transport and sustainable development

Sustainable development as introduced by the Treaty of Amsterdam, has to be achieved by integrating environmental considerations into Community policies (European Commission, 2001). Hence it will trigger the adoption of common transport policies by the member states, aiming at sustainable transport. Among these, the Gothenburg European Council identified the objective of shifting the modal balance of transport at the core of its sustainable development strategy. Achieving this objective will be a relatively long-term process of between 10 and 20 years (European Commission, 2001). The measures put forward so far are an initial step towards a sustainable transport system that will ideally be in place in the long run (more than 30 years).

The most important transport policies (although some of them in abstract form) introduced so far to accomplish this objective are: revitalizing the railways; promoting transport by sea and inland waterways; striking a balance between growth in air transport and the environment; turning intermodality into reality; building the Trans-European Network; improving road safety; adopting a policy of effective charging for transport; recognizing the rights and obligations of users; developing high-quality urban transport; managing the effects of globalization; developing medium- and long-term objectives

However, to achieve the goal of sustainable transport, other conditions have to be fulfilled at the same time, the most critical of which are:

- To safeguard economic growth that is expected to generate greater needs for mobility; this is due to anticipated demand increases of 38% for goods and 24% for people movements.

- To accommodate the growth in transport flows generated by the enlargement of the EU.

- To deal with the proposed significant investments in transport infra-structure, which are necessitated by the saturation of the major arteries, the low level of accessibility to remote areas and those in the periphery of the EU, especially in new member states.

This is the framework where sustainable transport policies have to be

Table 14.2 A typology of link breaking

Area of link-breaking	Economic activity	Transport system	Environmental impact
Indicators	GDP (passenger- and tonne-kilometres	Vehicle-kilometres	Polluting emissions
Link-breaking measures (examples)	Town planning	Charging	Less polluting vehicles and fuels
	Work organization (e.g. teleworking)	Intelligent transport systems	Speed control
		Modal transfer	Energy-efficient engines
	Industrial production system	Better rates of vehicle loading and occupancy	
	Land-use planning		

Source: SPRITE, 2001

formulated, so that gradually the link between economic growth and transport growth will break (de-coupling). It is within this framework that intermodal transport is considered as a viable and promising alternative to achieve the above objective. Table 14.2 clearly shows that the policies have a positive impact by increasing the intermodal share. There is a lack of such practices, although some attempts were made (Schmidt and Giorgi, 2000).

Available implementation options

Three possible options for implementing transport sustainability emerge from an economic viewpoint. The first could focus on road transport volume decreases through pricing, with no complementary measures to other transport modes. Pricing refers to the introduction of road charges, following the 'user pays' principle and by internalizing the external costs of transport. In the short term, the approach would curb growth in road transport through the better loading ratio of goods vehicles and occupancy rates of passenger vehicles, as a result of the increase in the cost of transport through pricing. However, failure to revitalize and enhance the quality of other modes, especially the low productivity in the rail sector and the insufficiency of infrastructure capacity, would make it impossible for the other modes to cope with the anticipated modal shift.

The second approach also includes road transport pricing, but at the same time is accompanied by measures to increase the efficiency of other modes, for example, through better quality of services, logistics, and technology. However, this approach does not include investments in physical infrastructure and does not address the implementation of other specific measures designed to shift traffic away from road transport. Although it might contribute somehow to the achievement of the objective, road transport will continue to be the dominant mode, as recent statistics show (European Commission, 2001). Therefore, this approach is not enough to guarantee a significant modal shift and does not contribute to the objective of sustainable development, as called for by the Gothenburg European Council.

The third approach, which is more linked to intermodal transport, comprises a coordinated series of measures ranging from pricing to revitalization of other than road transport modes and includes targeted investments in the Trans-European Network (TEN for railways, inland waterways, ports, short sea shipping and intermodal operations). This integrated approach would allow the market shares of the other modes to return to their 1998 or higher levels and thus produce a real shift of modal balance from 2010 onwards. This is an ambitious approach, bearing in mind that the road share has been constantly higher for the last 50 years. However, the rate of growth of road haulage modal share (i.e. the percentage of road traffic volumes to the total of all modes) will be slower in the long run, due to better use of the other means of transport (anticipated increase between 1998 and 2010 of 38%, compared with the accepted 50%, if no action is taken) (European Commission, 2001). This will be attributed to the introduction of faster, less expensive and reliable intermodal services, which will emerge at the transport corridors with high volumes, since the high traffic volumes will render such services viable and competitive.

Policies and intermodal transport

The focus of the 1957 Treaty of Rome establishing the European Economic Community was the economic development of the original signatory states through the establishment of a single market. The creation of a single market for intra-Community transport was judged to be one of the necessary conditions for achieving the 'four freedoms' (free movement of goods, services, capital, and labour).

The 1992 *White Paper on the Future Development of the Common Transport Policy*, followed by the CTP Action Programme 1995–2000 (European Commission, 1992 and 1995), constitutes a milestone in the history of the European Transport Policy.[3] What is significant about the White Paper is that it enlarged the set of objectives to be achieved by the Common Transport Policy to include sustainability and social cohesion. Most of these are presented above, being the basis for the proposed action plans by the European Commission. They are mainly calling for the continued reinforcement and proper functioning of the *internal market*; the development of *integrated transport systems*; strengthening of *economic and social cohesion*; ensuring the development of transport systems that contribute to a *sustainable pattern of development* by respecting the environment; promotion of *safety and social integration*; and finally development of appropriate *relations with third countries*.

These policies are mainly related to transport and as such they affect the modal share. In addition, they are introduced with the goal to contribute (at least) to sustainable transport. Consequently, they will be used as a basis (together with the policy actions presented previously) to promote intermodal transport, being identified as the more effective alternative option for sustainability.

Assessment of intermodal policy instruments

There have been no proper assessments for the impacts generated from the introduction and implementation of policies for the promotion of intermodal transport.

To promote intermodal transport, the European Commission has introduced, besides relevant legislation, some financing instruments in the form of pilot actions: PACT (Pilot Action for combined Transport) concluded in 2001 and the more recent Marco-Polo programme, started in 2003. The main objective of the PACT programme was to assist organizations (public and private) to increase the use of combined transport by using for the transport of loading units non-road modes. The PACT programme has focused on specific European corridors.

The main goal of the Marco Polo programme is the same, although it is wider in scope: it aims to reduce road congestion and improve the environmental performance of the whole transport system by shifting freight from road transport to short sea, rail and inland waterway transport. The Marco Polo programme supports commercial actions in the market for freight transport services. It is therefore different from the support given through research and development programmes and the Trans-European Network programme. Further, the programme will foster modal shift projects in all segments of the freight market, not only in combined transport.

The impacts of the PACT programme on the promotion of intermodal transport (its main objective) are positive, according to the conclusions of the study for the evaluation of the PACT Programme (AEA, 2000). Furthermore, the study has found that PACT projects may be innovative in terms of the combined transport (CT) route, the technology employed, the way the CT service is delivered, or some combination of these options. Furthermore, it is estimated that the traffic shift for 34 of the 63 PACT operational actions (i.e. excluding feasibility studies) between 1997 and 1999 is a total of at least 3.5

billion tonne-km. If those 34 projects are representative of the total in terms of traffic shift per project then the total traffic shift from the PACT programme 1996–1998 was about 6.5 billion tonne-km, or 2.2 billion tonne-km per year of funding. This is a conservative estimate based on available data and some assumptions on distance travelled and container loading. The traffic shift estimates above suggest that PACT directly contributed to about 1% of combined transport in 1996, excluding the effects of replication. This is a significant impact considering the relatively small budget of the programme.

The Marco-Polo programme is designed to help the transport and logistics industry to achieve sustained modal shifts of road freight to short sea shipping, rail and inland waterways. The Commission originally proposed a budget of €115 million (2003–2007) to achieve its ambitious goal of shifting the expected yearly increase of road freight to the other modes mentioned above. The main goal of Marco-Polo is to reduce road congestion and improve the environmental performance of the whole transport system by shifting freight from road transport to short sea, rail, and inland waterway transport. The programme thus aims to support one essential transport policy direction outlined in the Commission White Paper (European Commission, 2001).

The analysis above has demonstrated the continuous efforts of the European Commission to achieve the promotion of intermodal transport, and the positive results (even on a preliminary basis) that such efforts have achieved.

Transport policy objectives

Transport policies. From the more general policy objectives, as presented above, those referring to intermodal transport as a factor to achieve sustainability can be grouped into four categories. The first concerns the development and improvement of an integrated transport system. The various transport modes must be used more efficiently and in a more environmentally friendly way, enabling energy to be saved and providing more modal interconnections and greater interoperability. Thus, this is directly addressing the intermodality option.

As for the second, the promotion of efficiency in transport services objective, it clearly remains an important priority to monitor the application of the rules for creating a single market. Furthermore, in a liberalized market, the strict application of competition rules and State rules is of particular importance. The experience gained until now shows that new legislation is necessary in certain areas, in particular the increased liberalization of rail transport, the allocation of slots at airports, the gradual abolition of the queuing system for certain inland waterway markets and improved application of the responsibility rules and arrangements in the road haulage sector.

The third is about the provision of transport services that take into consideration the needs of the user that complement the second. As for the fourth, the improvement of trade links, this requires sufficient infrastructure links and transport services and interoperable transport systems.

Transport sustainability objectives. Several measures and policy instruments are needed to initiate the process leading to a sustainable transport system. It will take time to achieve this ultimate objective, and the measures set out here amount only to an early mapping of a strategy.

A sustainable transport system needs to be defined in operational terms in order to provide policy-makers substantive information. Where possible, objectives need to be quantified that can be used to assess impacts. A monitoring tool has already been put in place by way of the TERM mechanism (transport and environment reporting mechanism) by the EU. This is produced by the TERM project, which offers a series of annually calculated indicators to follow the evolution of transport related environmental pressure in European countries (European Environmental Agency, 2000). Although these indicators are well constructed, they only tackle the environment and do not consider other aspects.

Additional parameters refer to the risk of congestion on the major arteries and the possibility of creating regional imbalances. The conditions for shifting the balance between modes also need to be clarified, as well as users' needs and the globalization of trade.

Classification of transport policy elements

Here the broad objectives are addressed, but not the specific measures, which come under the more detailed action plans. To assess the policies, it is appropriate to identify the elements that are associated with them, so that the assessment can be more focused on the specific measures.

For assessment purposes, the elements of the transport policies are identified (Berquin *et al.*, 2000) and those related to the promotion of intermodal transport are grouped into four categories. These elements are a sub-set of the transport policy elements and are based on the preferred third option for the implementation of intermodality.

The most important policy element is the *development of transport infrastructure*. This refers to the upgrading of existing highways or rail freight corridors, constructing new infrastructure to abolish missing links and congested sections, improving the efficiency of existing infrastructures using new communication technologies, creating multimodal nodes for freight and passenger transport, improving short sea shipping connections, and achieving technical interoperability and interconnectivity for the transport systems. This is mainly the responsibility of the national governments of member states, as well as the EU through its financial instruments and co-financed large projects like the TEN network.

The second element concerns the *administrative or regulative policies*. This refers to the harmonization of technical standards or national regulations, the achievement of interoperable systems (from a regulatory/legal point of view), the reduction of administrative procedures for international freight transport, and the harmonization of social related legislation within EU (for example, working hours for drivers, wages). It is mainly the responsibility of the EU to impose these policies, since national governments might have conflicting objectives or different priorities.

The third element is closely related to the second but it is more specific, and as such it deserves to be considered alone. It concerns *pricing policies*. They refer to road pricing/user charges, to the introduction of congestion pricing, to the internalization (through special taxes) of external costs, to the harmonization of the tax schemes, to the introduction of subsidies for intermodal operators to cover the difference of costs due to the absence of a fully competitive transport market, where all costs are recorded and paid. Here it is also the responsibility of the EU to impose pricing schemes, since national governments might have conflicting objectives or different priorities.

Finally, the fourth element is about *land-use policies*. This is not equally important for all intermodal transport types. It concerns the establishment of a link between land-use strategies and transport planning. This is important for the location of intermodal terminals and maritime/inland waterways ports, as well as the distribution centres necessary for urban logistics. This is the responsibility mainly of the member states, and in particular of the regional/local authorities. The EU could assist in providing general guidelines.

These policy elements are directly associated with the transport policy measures for the promotion of intermodal transport. Hence, the expected impacts on the identified freight market segments from the implementation of the transport policies are presented according to each of these four policy elements.

Impacts of transport policies on intermodal market segments

Having identified the policy elements and the freight market segments, the impacts of transport policies (represented by the groups of policy elements) on market segments can be estimated. The impacts refer to the attainment of the objective of intermodal transport promotion, which according to the analysis presented before is critical for sustainable transport. Due to the nature of the policy elements and the absence of detailed data for each market segment, the assessment is made only on a qualitative basis.

The assessment comprises two layers: the first layer records whether it is worth pursuing the specific policy for the specific market segment. It assesses the potential for the specific market segment to choose intermodal transport. The second layer focuses only on those market segments that have a potential, and for these the degree of the impact is assessed qualitatively. The impact intensity is based on experts' opinion and additional sources (LOGIQ, 2000; Tsamboulas and Kapros, 2000).

Table 14.3 presents the results of these qualitative assessments. The cells correspond to the combinations of the transport policy elements and the identified freight market segments. In each cell with a symbol, the results of the assessment are represented, as described below.

For the first layer assessment, the potential of the specific market segment is identified and thus intermodal transport could produce a competitive advantage regarding the other transport modes. Consequently, three alternative situations are identified: competitive markets, potential markets, and non-competitive markets. Regarding the *competitive markets,* these comprise those freight market segments where intermodal transport appears to be as competitive as other modes, especially road. Consequently, the introduction of policy elements might have a strong positive impact on these markets regarding modal shift, without any major improvements in services and techniques of intermodal transport. Regarding the *potential markets*, these are defined as the markets for which the intermodal transport could become competitive after technical-operational, commercial, and regulatory adjustments are introduced. Finally, regarding the *non-competitive markets*, these concern those markets that no matter what is done for the improvement of intermodal transport, this will have no effect for modal shift.

Thus, policies are worth pursuing for intermodal transport (regardless how significant the impact is), if they are related to competitive and potential markets. The non-competitive markets are not considered, and so are not presented in Table 14.3.

Three market segments fall within the competitive market classification: (1) bulk products suitable to be unitized; (8) regional flows of general cargo (regional consolidation and distribution as well as regional exchanges); (14) intercontinental flows of general cargo (most of the trans-maritime containers).

Four market segments fall within the potential market classification: (5) perishable goods for interregional markets; (6) dangerous goods; (7) urban logistics; (12) interregional flows of general cargo suitable to be unitized, with no specific transport quality requirements). These constitute the first layer. The remaining seven market segments are non-competitive.

The second layer assesses qualitatively the degree of the impact.

In Table 14.3 the groups of policy elements are provided as headers, while

Table 14.3 Impacts on intermodal freight transport from EU policies elements

Policy elements/ measures	Freight Market Segments						
	Bulk products suitable to be unitized	Perishable goods for interregional markets	Dangerous goods	Urban logistics	Regional flows of general cargo (regional consolidation and distribution) regional exchanges	General cargo interregional flows suitable to be unitized, no specific transport quality requirements	Intercontinental flows of general cargo (most of the trans-maritime containers)
Transport Infrastructure Development							
Development TEN-T		→	→	→→	→	→	
Intermodal terminals/ports	++	++	++	+	++	++	++
Transport networks							
Interconnectivity		+					+
Information-communication technologies	++	++	++	++	++	+	+
Rail freeways	++	++	+		++	++	++
Short Sea Shipping connections						++	→ (rail)
Rail interoperability	++		+				
Administrative / Regulative Policies							
Technical standard / regulation harmonization			++→				
Market liberalization	→	→	→	+→	+→	→→	+→
Border effect with non-EU countries			→	→			
Harmonization of social regulations in transport sector within the EU	++	++	++		++	+	++

Table 14.3 *continued*

Policy elements/measures	Freight Market Segments						
	Bulk products suitable to be unitized	Perishable goods for interregional markets	Dangerous goods	Urban logistics	Regional flows of general cargo (regional consolidation and distribution) regional exchanges	General cargo interregional flows suitable to be unitized, no specific transport quality requirements	Intercontinental flows of general cargo (most of the trans-maritime containers)
Pricing Policies							
Road charges and tax harmonization	+			+	+	+	+
Introduction of "eco-points"	++	++	++		++	+	++
Internalization of external costs				+	+		
Congestion pricing				+			
Introduction of subsidies to intermodal operators	++		+	+	+	+	+

Note: ++: significant impact; +: some impact; 0 or blank: no impact; ↓: slightly negative impact; ↓↓: significantly negative impact.

some examples of detailed policy elements/measures are presented for each group.

Conclusions

Intermodality lies at the core of the EU's policies for a sustainable transport development. The EU has to deal with a steadily increasing demand for transport services, at a speed that cannot be accomplished simply by infrastructure expansion. What is more, the demand for freight mobility concentrates on one particular mode, road transport, which does not contribute to sustainable development, due to its negative impacts on the environment and traffic congestion. To help remedy this situation the EU is willing to provide the policy tool for a systems approach to transport in order to integrate the different modes into one coherent transport system which caters for the needs of Europe's citizens and industry.

To accomplish this objective, an action programme for the promotion of intermodal freight transport in Europe has been established. However, its implementation requires the co-operation of transport operators and users, the relevant supply industries, the national governments of the Member States, and regional and local authorities.

It is noted that the main challenge lies with the market response, which could be positive, if seamless and customer-oriented door-to-door transport services are offered with the intermodal transport. The role of the European Commission and the member states is to define the framework in which the market can operate and be sustainable. The rules and conditions must be such that they create a level playing field for all operators and foster innovation.

This chapter has provided all relevant dimensions affecting the promotion of intermodal transport. In addition, it has identified those market segments that are more suitable for intermodal transport, and for these a further analysis is introduced, by estimating qualitatively the intensity of the policies' impact on the promotion of intermodal transport. Consequently, with this *ex-ante* evaluation of the proposed policies, it could be advantageous to identify those measures that will produce the greater impact and pursue them on a priority basis.

It was found that three market segments: bulk products suitable to be unitized; regional flows of general cargo (regional consolidation and distribution as well as regional exchanges); intercontinental flows of general cargo (most of the trans-maritime containers) are the most suitable ones to change mode and adopt intermodal transport, while four others (perishable goods for interregional markets; dangerous goods; urban logistics; interregional flows of general cargo suitable to be unitized with no specific transport quality requirements) have the potential of changing to intermodal transport.

As for the proposed measures, the ones with the highest impact are: the intermodal terminals/maritime ports; the adoption of advanced information/communication technologies; rail freeways (for rail) and short sea shipping (for maritime); rail interoperability (*from the elements related to infrastructure development*); harmonization of social regulations in the transport sector within the EU (*from the elements related to administrative/regulative policies*); the introduction of 'eco-points'; the introduction of subsidies to intermodal operators; and to a lesser extent the internalization of external costs (*from the elements related to pricing policies*).

Priorities for policies can be facilitated through the approach presented here, so that the expected impacts and the effectiveness of measures can be estimated. A large number of political measures and instruments will be needed over a long period so that a sustainable transport system can be achieved.

Notes

1   IQ was a research project of the European Commission that looked at the quality characteristics of intermodal transport and produced scenarios for intermodal transport growth.
2   FCL: full container load, LCL: less than (full) container load
3   Although the European Commission has published in 2001 the new White Book, no specific measures and legislation ahs being implemented yet. Hence the analysis that follows is based on the introduced policies as the follow-up of the 1992 White Paper.

Bibliography

AEA Technology Environment (2000) Evaluation of the implementation of Council regulation 2196/98(PACT). Final report for the European Commission, DG Energy, and Transport. Online. Available HTTP://europa.eu.it/comm/transport/marcopolo/pact/doc/pact-evaluation_pdf.

Berquin, P., Gayda, S., de Jong, G. and Gunn, H. (2000) Discussion of Reference Scenario and Policies for EXPEDITE. THINK-UP workshop on Setting the Policy Context. Vienna, 4–5 December 2000. Online. Available HTTP:www.netr.fr/think-up/uk/reports/policycontext.

Ehmer, H.-J., Ortmann, C., Stader, A., Wilken, D., Berri, A., Madre, J.-L., Potier, F., Bristow, A., Clark, S., Tavasszy, L.A., Martinez, O., Sirio, A. H. and Frondaroli, A, (1999) *Descriptors and Determinants of Passenger and Freight Transport Demand*. Deliverable C2, SCENARIOS Research project. Brussels: European Commission.

European Commission (1992) The Future Development of the Common Transport Policy: A Global Approach to the Construction of a Community Framework for Sustainable Mobility, White Paper, COM(92)0494.

European Commission (1995) The Common Transport Policy: Action Programme 1995–2000. Communication to the Council, the European Parliament, the Economic and Social Committee and the Committee of Regions, COM/95/302 final.

European Commission (1997*a*) Intermodality and Intermodal Freight Transport in the EU: A Systems Approach to Freight Transport, Strategies and Actions to Enhance Efficiency, Services and Sustainability. Communication from the Commission to the European Parliament and the Council, COM/97/243 final.

European Commission (1997*b*) Communication on intermodality and intermodal freight transport in the EU. COM(97)243.

European Commission (1998) Economic and Social Committee and Committee of the Regions.

The Common Transport Policy Sustainable Mobility: Perspectives for the Future. Commission Communication to the Council, European Parliament.

European Commission (2001) European Transport Policy for 2010: Time to Decide. White Paper, COM (2001)370.

ECMT (2001) *Sustainable Transport Policies*. European Conference of Ministers of Transport. Paris: OECD.

ECMT (2002) *Dimensions of Loading Units*. CEMT/CS/COMB(2002)4, European Conference of Ministers of Transport. Paris: OECD.

European Environmental Agency (2000) *Are We Moving in the Right Direction – Indicators on Transport and Environment Integration in the EU*. Online. Available HTTP: <www.eea.eu.int>.

Harker, P.T. (1985) The state of the art in the predictive analysis of freight transport systems. *Transport Reviews*, 5, pp. 143–164.

Holmberg, J., Robert, K.-H. and Eriksson, K.-E. (1996) Socio-ecological principles for sustainability, in Costanza, R., Olman, S. and Martinez-Alier, J. (eds.) *Getting down to Earth – Practical Applications of Ecological Economics*, Washington, DC: Island Press.

IQ (1997) *Intermodal Quality*. Final Report, Research Project of the 4th Framework Programme on Research and Development of the European Commission. Brussels: European Commission.

INFREDAT (2001) *Intermodal Freight Data Requirements*. Final report. Research Project of the 4th Framework Programme on Research and Development of the European Commission. Brussels: European Commission.

LOGIQ (2000) *The Decision-Making Process in Intermodal Transport*. Final report. Research Project of the 4th Framework Programme on Research and Development of the European Commission. Brussels: European Commission.

Rothengatter, W. and Szimba, E. (2001) Trends on the Demand and the Supply Side of Freight Transport Markets. THINK-UP Workshop on Cross-segmentation and trends in the freight transport market, Naples. Online. Available HTTP:www.netr.fr/think-up/uk/reports.

Schmidt, M. and Giorgi, L. (2000) Successes, Failures and Prospects for the Common Transport Policy: A Preliminary Assessment. THINK-UP workshop on Setting the Policy Context, Vienna, 4–5 December 2000. Available HTTP:www.netr.fr/think-up/uk/reports.

SPRITE (2001) SePaRating the Intensity of Transport from Economic Growth. Research Project of the 5th Framework Programme on Research and Development of the European Commission, Brussels.

Tsamboulas, D.A. and Kapros, S. (2000) Decision making process in intermodal transport. *Transportation Research Record*, No. 1777, Transport Research Board, Washington DC.

Vanel, S. (2001) Cross-Segmentation of Intermodal Transportation as Considered as One Mode, Taking as a Basis the IQ Project Research. THINK-UP Workshop on Cross-segmentation and trends in the freight transport market, Naples. Available HTTP:www.netr.fr/think-up/uk/reports.

Zaccai, E. (2002) From conceptions of sustainability to indicators, in Kopp, U., Martinuzzi, A. and Schubert, U. (eds.) *Conference Proceedings EASY-ECO* (Evaluation of Sustainability European Conferences), Vienna. Online. Available HTTP: www.sustainability.at/easy/easy_eco1/pdf/easy1_proceedings.pdf.